Teaching Harry Potter To Creative Writers

An Educator's Guide

S.P. Sipal

Dalton Perkinson

Deep River Press, Inc.
Sanford, North Carolina

Teaching Harry Potter to Creative Writers

ISBN 978-1945561054

Library of Congress Control Number 2016959345

Published by Deep River Press, Inc. November 2016

Copyright S.P. Sipal

ILLUSTRATIONS by Kayla Laine Perkinson

COVER DESIGN by Greg Schultz

Dedication

To David Perkinson,
who taught us well the magic of love.

Contents

Introduction

Since the first edition of *A Writer's Guide to Harry Potter* was published five years ago, the wizarding world has suddenly come back to life, expanding at the seams like Perkins' tent or Hermione's handbag.

As of this writing, almost nine years have passed since *Deathly Hallows* was published, five since the last film was released. *Harry Potter and the Cursed Child* has opened in London and the script book published. In November, all Harry Potter fandom will be treated to the first of a new trilogy of films, all set in the wizarding world, but with fresh new characters and storyline.

Rowling and her wizarding world appear completely poised to capture a whole new generation of fans as well as young writers. Therefore, it seemed the time was ripe to update this guide and provide an edition specifically geared for use in the classroom. Through the analyses, lesson plans, handouts and activities provided within, we will dip beneath the pages of Rowling's magical books to seek insight and examples to inspire your students to release their own creativity. So please join me as we weave our way through the halls of Hogwarts and nip into a classroom to learn before the Headmistress of Magic herself, JK Rowling.

Private Lessons with the Headmistress

Harry Potter. The very name conjures up images of magic and books, movies and fans, and the extraordinary midnight release parties that looked more like mega rock concerts than a mere book release.

JK Rowling. For writers, this name brings visions of wealth and prestige. Of an author so high in the publishing stratosphere that she could eschew review copies and demand security so tight for her pre-release books that stores had to sign secrecy oaths in order to stock her latest release on their shelves.

The popularity of J.K. Rowling's Harry Potter series reached monumental heights, which were never before considered possible for a novel, let alone a children's story. With the release of the final book *Harry Potter and the Deathly Hallows* in the summer of 2007, 8.3 million copies were sold in the first 24 hours in the US alone[1]. The series as a whole, throughout the world, has sold over 450 million copies and been translated into 73 languages[2]. Think of where just a small smidgen of this magic "Floo Powder" could carry many of your students as they learn the basics of creative writing.

But, it's all hype, isn't it? Though many an envious writer would like to think Ms. Rowling's secret to success is just a bunch of magical mayhem, we do ourselves a disservice by focusing on her writing imperfections and not appreciating—and more importantly learning from—the skills which have made her Harry Potter series more than beloved, but truly an obsession among millions.

While I understand the desire to criticize a popular-selling work, and indeed there is much to learn from understanding the mistakes of others, I think that the greater learning experience is to understand the techniques that made a NYT bestselling author what she is today. After all, millions of people on various continents and across many cultures do not plunk down their hard-earned cash solely because of hype. *Something* must ring emotionally true to a wide band of readers to create this hype in the first place. I believe that this something can, to some extent, be learned. In the pages of Harry Potter, Rowling has gifted the creative writing classroom with seven books of magical examples from a series that most will be familiar with, and many will love.

Writers learn first through imitation before practice and experience develops an author's own unique voice. Since

---

[1] http://www.usatoday.com/life/books/news/2007-07-24-potter-sales_N.htm
[2] http://en.wikipedia.org/wiki/Harry_Potter

antiquity, apprentices have studied by the side of their mentors. Just as Harry Potter learns the power behind the magic from the greatest wizard in a hundred years, Headmaster Albus Dumbledore, so too can your students learn the power behind their words, to tell their own stories, by studying the craft of the headmistress of bestselling fiction, JK Rowling.

The evidence is all there, in black and white, on the pages of the books so dog-eared and well read by millions. And yet, the first Bloomsbury print-run, back in 1997 for *Harry Potter and the Philosopher's Stone* was only 500[3]. Yes, 500 copies. Obviously the now beloved Harry Potter series did not burst through the opening gate by way of a high-level marketing campaign and push from the publisher. JK Rowling earned her success the old-fashioned way—*word of mouth*.

Word of mouth comes from crafting a story so engaging that satisfied readers hurry to tell everyone they know to immediately go out and purchase the book for themselves to share the same wonderful, emotional rush they just enjoyed. Word of mouth is born of the words on the page. With Harry Potter, I believe that there are three fundamental aspects that drove these fans to share with their friends from the very beginning—characterization, worldbuilding, and mystery.

First, Rowling breathes to life a motley assortment of quirky people with varied emotions and viewpoints—such as a half-giant gamekeeper who drinks too much, and a greasy-haired, nasty old professor who hangs out in dungeons and antagonizes Harry. She sets these fun and engaging witches and wizards into motion against the backdrop of an extremely large, delightfully depicted world, so rich with details that we want to eat their cockroach clusters and visit their Leaky Cauldron. And then, to tie the whole series together, and keep the reader forever looking forward, she envelopes each story in an ongoing mystery, one that takes place both on the superficial level and as a giant squid below text. She enticed her fans, engaging their minds as well as their imaginations, to scour old myths and legends in search for clues that would guide them to who was the next to die, or what had really happened in Godric's Hollow. In all ways, she gave the reader more than they were expecting.

Indeed, the greatest asset that Rowling had as an author was her reader involvement. From online searches for clues, to sharing their latest theories on forums, to fan fiction, wizard rock, and fansites, her fans were (and still are) completely immersed in her world. They felt compelled to continue living the wizard experience even after they'd put the books down. This engagement of the reader by giving them more is the ultimate secret to Rowling's success.

Rowling not only engaged a generation of readers, however, but young writers as well. Read the bios of many emerging voices in fiction today, and you will find Harry Potter often cited as the story that inspired them to create their own. Through this guide, as we dissect Rowling's series, we hope to engage your students in the ancient art of storytelling. From cave wall to papyrus scroll to book to screen, storytelling has always been, and will always be, an inherently human endeavor that draws us together to understand both who we have been as we question where we are headed. Your student can participate in bringing this magical art to its new form.

Through twelve overarching lessons, we'll give you the tools you need to engage your students as you awaken their sleeping dragon of creativity. We'll first guide you through our framework that aligns our activities with your already full curriculum and our three scenarios on how to pace our assignments.

Common Sense in the Classroom with Engaging Activities...*Why this book is worth the investment.*

Students grow fond of familiarity when they return to your classroom each day. They have expectations of you as an educator just as you do of them as students. They expect your activities to require hard work that they must complete or deal with the consequence of incomplete grades. It is a never-ending mission to elevate these expectations to a higher level by offering an enjoyable plan of study that your students can fully engage with.

Our guide is designed to teach specific techniques to improve their creative writing while creating a story of their own imagination. In the next section, we layout three pacing options to meet the flexibility of various classroom structures and needs. The activities are practical, proven, and require minimal work for teachers. We aim to engage students, to challenge their imaginations, and to provide them the tools to communicate their ideas to others more effectively. Students will be exposed to a wide range of activities that incorporate group collaboration, interdisciplinary skills, cultural awareness, and career skills. As such, we hope to create life-long learners who are respectful of others, accepting of diverse opinions, and better equipped to harness their imaginations to improve their world.

If Only We Had Time-Turners

Time in the classroom is a precious commodity that seems to continually slip through our hands as educators.

---

[3] http://www.tomfolio.com/PublisherInfo/HarryPotter.asp

Caught between the demands of local, state, and federal standards, we teachers find ourselves scrambling to honor the requirements tossed at us, which often restrict our own autonomy. The search for resources that not only engage but entertain our students is an ongoing pursuit, especially considering we must justify time spent in the classroom as an effective means to prepare productive citizens who are college or career-ready when they walk across the stage at graduation.

As if the search couldn't be more challenging, with every new superintendent or Secretary of Education hoping to stamp their name on education reform, the standards which have yet to be accepted as common practice are replaced, reshaped, or abandoned for the next trend promising inclusive redesign of the education system around the country. However, as most have realized, the standards have consistently agreed on core ideas that in some form are present in each reiteration and revision—a group of which I call common-sense approaches to teaching.

Sorting Through the Standards

We often become lost in a cloud of ambiguity when addressing standards. Sometime we even doubt the effectiveness or practicality of their criterion. Regardless of their intention or longevity, however, most educators naturally cover most of these requirements through their every-day instruction as professionals in their field. Painting with a broad stroke, most teachers, without consulting governing guidelines, will incorporate the following skills in their lessons:

1. Preparatory Skills for Future Employment
2. Independence in Life-long Learning
3. Awareness of Diverse Cultures and Peoples
4. Collaboration and Reflection
5. Interdisciplinary Creativity

Most skills taught through any standards can be justified through these five common-sense approaches to teaching. Your work as an educator is to decide where your standards align with these skills. We won't leave you high and dry, however. Consult the following explanations as you align our approaches with your local standards.

Preparatory Skills for Future Employment

Often referred to as College and Career Readiness, 21st Century, Workforce, or Employability Skills, Preparatory Skills for Future Employment is not restricted to students who plan to begin working straight out of high school. Employment, in this regard, refers to the broader sense of employing their skills to aid in societal improvements. These skills are practical and typically can be deployed immediately in student lives. They are contingent on the demands of society and its evolution.

In the past, students were taught to format letters, address envelopes, write checks, use print media sources, and other necessary life skills. Now we are encouraging students to create profiles online to connect with potential employers, how to address emails, navigate the cluster of information on the Internet, and use technology as a means to create content as opposed to solely consuming what they see. In the ever-changing world in which we live, these skills are often overlooked and most regard them as common sense. We are teaching common-sense skills that aren't so common among our students. In many respects these skills target students destined for higher education where these preparatory skills will aid the acquisition of new ones. This theme of continuing education aligns closely with our second common-sense skill: Independence in Life-long Learning.

Independence in Life-Long Learning

In former years, it was not uncommon for a student to go to college, acquire a brand of skills, and use them throughout an entire career until they retired with a healthy pension to live out their days. The popular networking tool LinkedIn estimates recent graduates from college will change companies an average of three times within the first five years in the workforce. With job hopping becoming more common, students should prepare to compete for jobs throughout their entire career. Maintaining a competitive edge requires students to stay up-to-date on common practices and developments in their respective fields. Our mission as educators is to inspire students to engage with the complex world around them while remaining curious of the unknown and seeking enrichment through acquiring knowledge constantly. Asking *why* is a powerful undertaking, but not as powerful as searching for the answer.

Awareness of Diverse Cultures and People

Our students live in an era of media culture plastered with conflict and feud among nations. Stemming from barriers in beliefs, language, and cultural practices, how are students expected to handle and react to these streams of conflict? Even domestic fights between communities and government, or political parties, fill our students' timelines, storyboards, and newsfeeds. Many educators steer away from confronting these problems as they can lead to unruly debates and undesired tension within the classroom. Unfortunately, neglecting these issues is a disservice to students. Without proper guidance, they may not be prepared to evaluate and understand critical issues that will affect them throughout life. Crafting a lesson that addresses these situations without students offending their classmates or causing a disruption is a tricky task.

Fortunately, many of our activities provide a fictitious world to shroud current events. For example, students may debate the injustice among the various bloodlines and the cultural beliefs which stem from them in the wizarding world of Harry Potter. You can have students defend a stance or social concern from the point-of-view of a Muggle, Mudblood, Halfblood, or Pureblood wizard. Have them consider the social norms that revolve around each heritage and respond to prompts that tie in a current or historical event, but in a setting from the wizarding world. Maybe the Ministry of Magic has mandated the arrest of all Mudbloods following the events of a single wizard who happened to disobey their decree. How could students discuss these scenarios in light of the Holocaust or a recent, local event? The possibilities to address contemporary issues are endless when you have a fictitious world to both cloak and enhance the direct relevance to your students.

Collaboration and Reflection

Collaboration and reflection are many writers' wheelhouses. Any well-developed story is the product of careful planning, collaboration, and revision, revision, revision. Effective communication is an essential skill coveted by employers and co-workers throughout any industry. Businesses thrive when the gritty determined project manager meets the ingenuity of the process analyst, or when the copy editor finally understands the columnist's angle and mood. The power of collaboration is no secret, and students of middle and high school are pioneering their first group assignments where they discover quickly other peoples' mistakes—and in the end, hopefully, their own faults, too.

Our activities are either targeted directly at collaboration among students or easily adapted to include a discussion component. A method we have found to be most beneficial is the process of reapplication. Reapplication is taking a skill or process learned and simply reapplying it to a new context. Reapplication is a great tool to drill material without downing your students with boredom. Paired with reflection, students can evaluate an activity they have just completed by how easily they complete another, similar practice.

Having student write a reflection may suit certain activities, but our activities teach students to use their previously learned skills to apply them in a new situation. Through reapplication, they discover the facets that make their work more manageable as they apply them in a more challenging way. We are not condemning the use of written reflections; in fact, we recommend having students log weekly journals as they navigate our guide's activities for later view. At the end of all the lessons, when students read prior entries, they are often surprised at their progress. Along with their completed activities or short story, the final reflection ends up being a delightful treat.

Interdisciplinary Creativity

Perhaps a cliché catch-all, interdisciplinary creativity is simply an avenue where we can expand the classroom to other subject areas to engage interests and bind standards together. Often separated in published standards, interdisciplinary connections and creativity are more similar than we typically think of them. A great definition of creativity is the brain's ability to put together two unrelated items or ideas to create a curious or fascinating product: what more could define interdisciplinary skills?

If you would like a challenge in interdisciplinary skills, try selecting a random Internet article and a random standard within your curriculum and devise an activity linking the two. If you can achieve a justifiable connection, then you can connect many helpful resources to your lesson plans. Some connections are more difficult than others, but by seeking out such connections, you will gain more flexibility in your classroom.

A Few Additional Notes

Technology is an expanding requirement in today's standards and are often given their own focus in the classroom. Nevertheless, technology is nothing more than a medium to view and create content. It should exist throughout the classroom in a fluid or serendipitous form, but never distract from the content of the lesson. It should also not be the only way to realize objectives. The technological era is expanding rapidly, but not so quickly that we should denounce all other forms of delivering content, because they are still common place in the workforce and universities across the world.

Practice the delivery of content with new technologies ahead of time and have a seamless plan B if the technology doesn't want to cooperate that day. Wasting time dealing with audio and video problems distracts from the lesson, and downtime is the quickest way to dissolve all motivation from your students. For one important electronic asset, be sure to check our living documents option for all handouts, as mentioned below.

Navigating Our Guide

The common-sense approaches mentioned above are layered throughout all our activities. In the standards section of each activity you will find which of the five skills it is designed to address. You may also find alternative activities that are designed to practice skills through reapplication or just as another method to deliver the same content.

These lessons are not about how to write fantasy exclusively. Most of the techniques we will discuss apply to any form of writing. It is also not our intention to teach students to clone Rowling's story, but rather to learn the specific techniques which she employed to create their own story in their own voice.

Bolding, *italics*, and ALL CAPS have been added to certain passages within cited examples to point out specific technique examples.

We hope you enjoy our guide and that you visit our Writer's Resource page on www.DeepRiver.press. Here we have downloadable PDFs of some of the charts in the book as well as electronic, expandable versions of many of the handouts. This will allow students to create assignments digitally through powerful tools such as Google Classroom and Blackboard. We will continuously add more activities to complement the ones in this book, so be sure to check back frequently.

Pacing for Your Class' Needs

Our guide is intended to give students and teachers as much flexibility as they might need to use our activities as an entire unit or as complements to a larger semester of tasks. In recognition that classroom makeup, curriculum, and standards vary widely, we will discuss three options designed to meet varying needs. These three pacing scenarios take into account the vast amount of work traditional English classrooms are charged with. We hope that one of these will provide the activities you need to supplement your curriculum and engage your students.

Choose a modest scenario that you can easily accomplish where your students do not feel rushed. Some students may not have been exposed to such an extensive draw on their creativity, and they may struggle with these exercises at first. Also, while many exercises are geared to working in collaboration, we also understand that writing may be an intensely personal activity for many students. Therefore, feel free to allow individuals to work solo if they prefer.

As mentioned in the Introduction, students will periodically write reflections on their progress through journal entries. We recommend students keep all their reflections in the same place to refer back to later in the unit. When you reach a milestone in our pacing guide, you will be prompted for students to complete a reflection. Allow your students the freedom to write what they choose in reference to their progress, but make sure they keep the following questions of orientation in mind.

What skills have I worked on to improve my creative writing skills?
What activities were most helpful in developing my written work?
How do I plan to incorporate these writing techniques in future assignments?
What elements of my story am I most excited to develop next?
What have been the most challenging tasks while writing my story?
Since my last reflection, how have my ideas or opinions changed regarding my work?

Reflections are not required to complete our activities, but they can have meaningful influence on student growth. Students can better appreciate the improvements they accomplish if they have points of reference showing where their writing or even confidence has become more developed. Moreover, the use of these notebook entries address a movement among educators to inspire individual growth through the process of reflection. When students understand the tasks at hand well enough to describe their sentiments toward completing them, they are exercising higher-level brain function—being aware of one's own thought process—referred to as metacognition.

Below are the teacher plans and activities needed for each scenario in chronological order. Our pacing schedules are assuming teachers will be supplementing with other activities throughout the semester. A committed group who only focuses on the content in our guide would most likely finish the materials before the time mentioned.

SCENARIO ONE – A COMPLETE COURSE

If you are gifted with the flexibility to focus on building creative writers for an entire quarter or even an entire semester, scenario one will be the most enriching sequence for you and your students. Through this complete tour of our guide, you will dive into all our chapters' themes and pick apart each activity where each task aids in the culmination of a well-developed short story for each student. This is the most effective use of our activities and leaves no page unturned.

Lesson One: Characterization	Mapping Out Your Cast: Activity & Living Document
	Mapping Out Your Cast: Student Handout & Living Document
	Character Hooks: Activity & Living Document
	Character Hooks: Student Handout & Living Document
	Point of View (POV): Mini Activity
	Character Relevance: Student Handout
	Obstacles and Pain: Mini Activity
	What's at Stake?: Student Handout
Lesson Two: Voice	Finding Your Voice & Style: Activity
	Strong Verbs and Pinpointed Nouns: Student Handout
	Improving Style: Mini Activity
	Finding Your Voice: Student Handout
	Finding Your Voice: Group Reflection
Lesson Three: Worldbuilding	Worldbuilding: Activity
	Worldbuilding: Student Handout
	Worldbuilding: Continuing with Real World Skills
Lesson Four: Mystery Plotting	Sleight of Hand: Mini Activity
	Hiding Your Clues: Activity
	Techniques for Hiding Clues: Student Handout
Lesson Five: Backstory	Postponing Backstory: Activity
	Postponing Backstory: Student Handout
Lesson Six: Myth & Archetypes	Plotting A Hero's Journey: Activity
	Your Hero's Journey Chart
	Storyline Archetypes: Mini Activity
	The Filk Challenge: Mini Activity
	Personality Archetypes: Activity
	Character Archetypes, a Netflix Study: Student Handout Part 1 & 2
	Understanding Personality & Storyline Archetypes
Lesson Seven: Antiheroes and Ambiguity	Creating Your Snape: Student Handout
	Creating Your Snape: Mini Activity
Lesson Eight: Real World Relevance	Real World Integration: Activity
Lesson Nine: Writing with Humor	Writing with Humor: Activity
	Adding Humor to Your Story: Student Handout
Lesson Ten: Writing with Pleasure	Pep Talk (Continue with a classroom discussion.)
Lesson Eleven: Fan Fiction	Fan Fiction: Activity
	Fan Fiction: Student Handout
Lesson Twelve: Words of Inspiration	No Activities

SCENARIO TWO – PAVING THE WAY FOR AN INDEPENDENT JOURNEY

Maybe you don't have the time to complete all our activities, but you would like an in-depth tour of the most important pieces of creative writing—the most bang for the shortened time you have. Ideally you would have four to six weeks for this option. The pacing scenario below includes the most important chapters and essential activities to get students started on their own work. Alternatively, teachers could use this plan to introduce a year-long competition to be completed in the students' free time due at the end of the period—maybe in lieu of taking the final exam.

Lesson One: Characterization	Mapping Out Your Cast: Activity & Living Document
	Mapping Out Your Cast: Student Handout & Living Document
	Character Hooks: Student Handout & Living Document
	Point of View (POV): Mini Activity
	Character Relevance: Student Handout
Lesson Two: Voice	Finding Your Voice & Style: Activity
	Finding Your Voice: Student Handout
	Strong Verbs and Pinpointed Nouns: Student Handout
Lesson Three: Worldbuilding	Worldbuilding: Activity
	Worldbuilding: Student Handout
Lesson Four: Mystery Plotting	Sleight of Hand: Mini Activity
Lesson Five: Backstory	Postponing Backstory: Activity
	Postponing Backstory: Student Handout
Lesson Six: Myth & Archetypes	Plotting A Hero's Journey: Activity
	Your Hero's Journey Chart
	Character Archetypes, a Netflix Study: Student Handout Part 1 & 2
	Understanding Personality & Storyline Archetypes
Lesson Seven: Antiheros and Ambiguity	Creating Your Snape: Student Handout
	Creating Your Snape: Mini Activity
Lesson Eleven: Fan Fiction	Fan Fiction: Activity
	Fan Fiction: Student Handout

SCENARIO THREE – THE HIGHLIGHTS OF CREATIVE WRITING

Lastly, we offer a plan that includes fewer activities to introduce students to creative writing. Intended for teachers with heavy time restrictions, these activities can be completed between one and two weeks of focused instruction. We understand teachers focus on more than one topic at a time—giving students a break from continuous instruction and making the most out of the time they have. Thus, scenario one and two are designed to work in-line with other activities. Scenario three, however, is intended to be the central focus of the entire one or two-week period.

Lesson One: Characterization	Point of View (POV): Mini Activity
	Character Relevance: Student Handout
Lesson Two: Voice	Strong Verbs and Pinpointed Nouns: Student Handout
Lesson Three: Worldbuilding	Worldbuilding: Activity
	Worldbuilding: Student Handout
Lesson Six: Myth & Archetypes	Plotting A Hero's Journey: Activity
	Your Hero's Journey Chart
Lesson Eleven: Fan Fiction	Fan Fiction: Activity
	Fan Fiction: Student Handout

ADAPTATION FOR A YOUNGER AUDIENCE

While our exercises are created with high school students in mind, there are several that have practical application to younger, advanced groups in middle and perhaps upper primary classrooms. Younger students could tackle scenario three above where they explore the highlights of creative writing. Also, we include adaptations for several activities geared to a younger or less experienced class. For further activities suited to a middle grade audience, be sure to check the Writer's Resource page at DeepRiver.press.

FINAL COMMENTS

While we recommend the prescribed pathways above, we never want educators to feel their autonomy dissolving. Feel free to use the activities and handouts in any form you choose. We understand you are a professional educator capable of making decisions considering your unique classroom. Therefore, if there is content within a chapter that is not explicitly labeled as a student handout or activity and you feel your students would benefit from having the information, feel free to make copies to share with your class.

Also, if you find a topic that you enjoy, but the included activities do not dig as deeply as you would like, visit our Writer's Resource page on www.DeepRiver.press and browse our additional resources. Our resource page will feature complementary files for you and your students, including editable digital documents to give your students greater flexibility in expanding the tables and sharing their work with their classmates. Be sure to check our site often as we will continuously add a wider range of affordable activities to offer more options for engaging your students in creative writing.

Lesson One

More Emotional Range than a Teaspoon

(Characterization)

The secret to JK Rowling's success lies in open view on the well-read pages of her much-loved books. For almost two decades, readers from across generations, cultures, and continents have been drawn in to Harry Potter by her delightfully detailed world, her intricately woven mysteries, and her wide range of quirky people with varied backstories and viewpoints. Of these three primary elements, however, Rowling's vivid and diverse characters breathe life into the first two. A fantastic world and a compelling mystery are empty without engrossing and emotionally charged characters to pull the reader in and make the story beat inside their heart.

Rowling employs many techniques that successfully craft her characters into people her fans want to spend time with...constantly. In fact, she fashions her imaginary friends so well that many a fan fiction story has been written because her readers insist on spending more time with them than her mammoth books allow.

How does Rowling do this? More to the point, how can *your students* create a cast as deliciously and disgustingly flavored as a magical pouch of Bertie Bott's Every Flavor Beans? Perhaps, if we study the details of how Rowling shapes her characters, you can better help your students breathe life into the figments of their own imagination.

Overview:

Challenge your students with these character development techniques:

1)   Employ a varied cast of characters.
2)   Plant a hook on every character.
3)   Choose POV wisely.
4)   Firm up each character with a fully realized and carefully revealed backstory.
5)   Challenge them with obstacles to overcome that force growth.
6)   Probe into the heart of your hero and make him go where it is scary.
7)   Know your character's internal logic: the rules, beliefs, and assumptions that guide their every move.
8)   Pitch your stakes high enough to show your characters at their best and worst.
9)   Give them loyal friends and dastardly enemies to increase the emotional tension.
10) Embolden your characters with the power of touch, used to show strong emotions rather than to tell.

1) A Cast of Thousands, almost

Rowling's cast of characters, including animals, ghosts, other magical beings, and even portraits, stands at well over 400! That's a lot of people (or creatures) to develop.

Of course, not all these 400 are fully fleshed and crucial characters, but a surprising number of them are. It helps that she had seven books to develop them.

Each character is carefully crafted to show a different aspect of the magical world, to highlight certain emotions or beliefs, or to hide or reveal important clues to the ongoing mystery. Every character has a purpose, and each one adds to the emotional depth and resonance for the reader. With such a large cast, over time a wide spectrum of complex emotions can be revealed and studied.

While your students may not develop a cast of 400, especially in a short story, it's important that they learn to create a cast that is varied and diverse. What's most important is that they and their reader find themselves in the emotional ranges of the characters they create Each created person should count for something in the fulfillment of their storyline.

Challenge your students to envision a complement of characters to portray all sides of their themes. To reflect all the nuances of emotions and beliefs that their story deserves. Rowling created both brave and righteous Order members and greedy and power-hungry Death Eaters. Within the Order existed both a loyal but thieving Mundungus and a bumbling but good-hearted Tonks. The ranks of the Death Eaters included a cruel, crazed Bellatrix *and* a Regulus with a core of decency. Help your students reflect on the themes and beliefs that are important to their story to ensure that all the various viewpoints in their magnificent shades of gray are covered.

Aside from the personal development aspects, also consider the world building. Have your students placed characters in sufficient places to fully flesh-out the world they have built? Even if they are dealing with the real world rather than fantasy, they still must shape-up their vision of that world for the reader. Characters are the elements that breathe that world to life. In Rowling's Diagon Alley, Fortescue's shopkeeper imparted wizarding history while serving up Harry's favorite ice cream. While inside St. Mungo's Janus Thickey Ward, with her tender care of Frank and Alice Longbottom, the Healer helps the reader understand the loss Neville has been hiding from his friends all these years.

Mundungus and Tonks, Bellatrix and Regulus, Florean Fortescue and the Healer—these characters not only serve to fill out a world, but to flesh out the primary characters as well. They are not throw-aways and should be crafted with great care and respect.

Finally, if your students are plotting a story that contains secrets and mysteries, have they scattered crucial clues among this forest of characters, so that one or two don't hold all the critical answers? Rowling scattered her clues widely, from Caractacus Burke, who buys the mysterious locket off the starving and pregnant Merope. To the fiercely loyal house-elf Winky, who guards Barty Crouch's hidden secret. If clues are widely scattered, and hidden well within many characters, it will make it that much more difficult for the protagonist to seek out and uncover each hidden gem, thus stringing the reader along for a far more interesting ride.

A high character count like Rowling's is not the secret of a well-crafted story. What *is* necessary is to craft the number of characters needed to ensure the author's vision is fully portrayed—its themes, its emotions, and its plot. Challenge your student to create a story as robust and full-flavored as their imagination. To employ sufficient characters and give them each an important role. Use the activity **Mapping Out Your Cast: Activity & Living Document** on the next page to illustrate this.

You may be surprised at how well HP fans know all Rowling's multitude of characters, even the minor ones. She has cast them in such a strong way, carefully distinguishing one from the others, that each is identifiable and memorable.

How does she do this? One way is through the power of character hooks.

2) A Hook for Every Character

In the section above, we looked at the overview—the forest of character variety and development. Through the rest of this lesson we will analyze each tree to see what your students can do to make each individual character they create come across stronger.

One technique Rowling utilizes to make each character stand out unique from the others is to give them a hook; a description, personality trait, or association which defines him or her and distinguishes them from everyone else. A hook is one of the earliest and simplest tools a writer can utilize to familiarize their reader with their people. Simply put, a hook is something the reader can hang their memory on, that helps them, especially in the early stages of a story, remember who that character is and what their place is in the new world.

The hook may be **another character**: Fred and George are twins and are always together (which makes the ending of *Hallows* so sad). The same holds true with Padma and Parvati. However, each twin does have a distinguishing characteristic. Fred tends to be the one who takes greater risks, whereas George is the more serious and sensitive of the two (just slightly!). Padma is in Ravenclaw and had to go with the poorly dressed Ron to the Yule Ball, whereas Parvati is in Gryffindor and got to be escorted by Champion Harry.

Then there are the **animal counterparts** that act like hooks. Within Rowling's feline kingdom, Mrs. Norris represents Filch's stalking and spying through the castle for miscreants, while Crookshanks, who no one else wanted, represents Hermione's care and concern for the undercat. McGonagall transforms as an uptight cat sitting stiffly on a brick wall for hours—all the while watching protectively for the arrival of baby Harry. Indeed, we see this constant transformation between sternness and nurturing with the transfiguration professor.

Mapping Out Your Cast: Activity & Living Document

DURATION:
Ongoing with an initial 45-minute introduction.

SYNOPSIS:
Students will be engaged through an essential question: How many characters will you have, and what will their importance be in your protagonist's journey? There is an optional adaptation to this activity where students will develop their characters through a mock interview process. Details below.

CONTEXT:
Students often begin with this activity. Use the worksheet on the next page (or the electronic version available on the www.DeepRiver.press/pages/educationresources, to create a living document; we recommend using Google Docs). As characters become more in-depth or obsolete, students should update and remove then as needed.

COMMON-SENSE APPROACH TO TEACHING: Interdisciplinary Creativity

STANDARDS:
This activity will have students deploying their creativity to develop characters for the beginnings of a short story. They will record clear thoughts on paper that will serve as a cornerstone to build a story upon. We are focusing on creativity, but also students are exercising clear writing skills—a sought-after skill for future employment. If their classmates can easily understand each character profile without asking many questions, then they are writing clearly.

BEFORE YOU BEGIN:
The first of our activities are the most challenging. Many students suffer in the area of creativity; they are too focused on a grade and may be unwilling to take a stab at something new. You may struggle to engage your students, but through our activities we hope to alleviate their apprehension. Deploy all your tools to get them started. Have groups work together to create a unique character. Some students will shine through, and hopefully they can lead their classmates to their own creations.

QUESTIONS TO ASK YOUR STUDENTS:
1. Have you got a complement of personalities to portray all sides of your themes and diverse beliefs and emotions? Have you envisioned brave and righteous Order members as well as power-hungry Death Eaters? Within the Order, have you got a loyal but thieving Mundungus and a bumbling but good-hearted Tonks? Do your Death Eaters include a cruel, crazed Bellatrix *and* a Regulus with a core of decency?
2. Have you placed characters in sufficient places to fully flesh-out the world you have built? Have you got your Fortescue's shopkeeper who happens to impart wizarding world history while serving up Harry's favorite ice cream?
3. Finally, if you are plotting secrets and mysteries, have you scattered crucial clues among this forest of characters, so that one or two don't hold all the critical answers?

OPTIONAL INTERVIEW ACTIVITY:
In part, this is an option for younger students, but also super useful for older writers as well. Sometime it's difficult to write down the aspects of each character without seeing them in action. Consider framing the activity as if the students are interviewing or even *interrogating* (the antagonist, perhaps) each character. One useful way to do this is by pairing up students with one interviewing the other, who assumes the role of the character they wish to create. Have the pair openly brainstorm questions to ask each character. This can be a discussion activity that precedes the interview activity.

Mapping Out Your Cast: Student Handout & Living Document

Your first task is to dive in by creating unique characters for your story. Even though you may not have a complete vision of what will happen in your story, you can still begin developing intriguing characters and backgrounds. Every character will have a unique purpose to the story, and as those purposes become more evident, you will return to this document and update your changes.

Using the chart below, take time to analyze the wider world view of your cast. Have you created people to fully expand your theme, to inhabit every corner of your world, to enact every aspect of your plot, to hide all the secrets your mysteries will require? (Note: *Theme and Mystery may not need to be completed for each character.)

Character	*Theme Point	Part of World	Plot	*Mystery
Dumbledore	Trust is important, but not easy	Hogwarts	Acts as mentor and guides Harry to his destiny.	Holds secret of the Deathly Hallows.

Hooks can lurk in **physical description** as well. Who can forget that Nearly Headless Nick has only a thin ghostly sinew holding his head, almost, in place? And Mundungus, well, his name suits him as he's most often described like a dung heap. You'll never displace Olympe Maxime. After all, how could you overlook an elegant half-giant with a French accent?

In fact, that leads to another hook—**accent or manner of talking**. You'd know Hagrid's speech with his dropped "g"s and West-country expressions anywhere in Potterverse, even without a dialogue tag. Fleur got the nickname Phlegm for a reason. Even if we don't hear the late, great Alan Rickman delivering the lines, Snape's method of slithering words together is far silkier and shiftier than McGonagall's clipped, direct speech.

Character traits also present a plethora of hook possibilities. Mrs. Figg is the lovable, batty old cat lady. Uncle Vernon is always angry—at least when he's talking with Harry. Aunt Petunia is a clean freak. Narcissa Malfoy, like her namesake, is quite narcissistic. And Dumbledore, of course, is the wizened wizard and mentor.

Dumbledore's function as mentor leads us to the next hook—**roles**. Traditional roles help us know a character more intimately from the moment we meet them and understand their role in the story. Sirius is the substitute father figure, Ron the loyal friend, and Hermione the know-it-all who helps Rowling insert necessary information into the story. Mrs. Weasley portrays the ultimate loving mother. In fact, the whole Weasley clan functions as Harry's adopted family. Finally, everyone knew Dumbledore's number was up long before Harry did—after all, what else do you do with an aging, gray-haired mentor?

Another highly effective character hook Rowling uses is that of **concealing a mystery clue**. No one will forget that it was Pettigrew who hid as a rat for twelve years and thus concealed vital information through the course of three books. Mad-Eye's frequent swig from his flask hinted for a full school year at a character who had more to hide than a drinking problem. And Snape...well Snape stands alone as the master of concealment. Before *Deathly Hallows* was published, discussion boards overflowed with arguments as to whether Snape was good or evil—or the question more to the point—loyal to Voldemort or Dumbledore's man through and through. Snape's hook (besides his nose) *is* his very mystery, his delightful ambiguity.

Here are a few more ways your students can hook their characters:

1) jobs—Perkins is the old warlock who works with Mr. Weasley. Stan Shunpike worked as a conductor on the Knight Bus until he was wrongly arrested.

2) family connections—The red-haired, large family Weasley clan stands juxtaposed against the pale, single-child Malfoy snobs. Don't forget the mercurial Blacks. Family connections helps the reader place certain characters in context.

3) physical abnormality or impairment—This is related to appearance, but slightly different because in Rowling's world the impairment plays a greater role in the plot and is probably concealing a key clue or embodying an important theme. Mad-Eye Moody's mad eye, Rufus Scrimgeour's limp, and Lupin's furry little condition are prime examples. Not only does Mad-Eye's magical eye help us remember who he is next time we see him, but it also hides the clue that Mad-Eye is watching over Harry for a specific reason. Likewise, Lupin's monthly transformation into a werewolf not only distinguishes him from other professors, or hides a key clue for the *Azkaban* story, but also contributes to the theme of caring for the marginalized and oppressed that Rowling is very fond of. I expect that Scrimgeour's limp, like Dumbledore's blackened hand, marked him as a doomed man, a lame duck politician.

How can your students incorporate these hooks into their own writing? They may not have werewolves and giants and merpeople to help give the wild range of characterization that's possible in a fantasy world, but they can work with what they have. Diversity is real. We live it; we breathe it on a daily basis. Encourage them to utilize the rainbow of humanity fully in developing their characters so that no two can be confused for each other. If a writer could take the dialogue from one character and transpose it onto another without changing a word, the writer hasn't properly developed either.

Your students can use all these types of hooks to help distinguish one character from another and to aid in developing that each one's role in the story. They should make sure their hooks are mentioned in creative ways often enough to help the reader remember, but not so frequently as to become annoying. Lastly, challenge them to always make sure that their hooks and their characters add a relevant nuance to the overall story. The activity **Character Hooks: Activity & Living Document** illustrates this.

Character Hooks: Activity & Living Document

DURATION:
Ongoing with an initial 45-minute introduction.

SYNOPSIS:
Character hooks are key to engaging the reader. If characters are not intriguing to the audience in the beginning, or if the reader gets too confused as to which character is which, they will not continue. We have a list of techniques that students can use to hook their audience with each new character that appears.

COMMON-SENSE APPROACH TO TEACHING: Interdisciplinary Creativity

STANDARDS:
Students will use intentional cues to achieve a specific outcome. Using a hook, they will create a character to entice the reader and help them remember that character when they reappear. Writing with intention is powerful writing.

BEFORE YOU BEGIN:
Keep in mind the essential question for your student: How can I make characters intriguing and memorable to the reader? Use a variety of hooks to involve the reader in various ways.

TYPES OF CHARACTER HOOKS:

Physical Description – the character's physical appearance or clothing helps characterize their background or personality.
Occupation – their job or role in society shows their interests and experience.
Relationship – they have a familial or meaningful connection with other characters.
Mannerism – their unconscious gestures or movements give a hint to their personality.
Speech Pattern – they may talk with accents, favor certain words, or articulate their thoughts in a unique way.
Role/Archetype – they serve a specific and critical role to the protagonist or plot.

Character Hooks: Students Handout & Living Document

At this point you should have an idea of a few characters—what their role will be in the story and how they will aid your protagonist on her journey. Now we need to sell these characters to the reader with the use of character hooks. Hooks intrigue the reader and draw their attention. Simply put, a hook is something the reader can hang their memory on, that helps them, especially in the early stages of the story, remember who that character is the next time they appear.
Keep in mind our essential question:

How can I make characters intriguing and memorable to the reader?

Some common hooks:

Physical Description – the character's physical appearance or clothing helps characterize their background or personality.
Occupation – their job or role in society shows their interests and experience.
Relationship – they have a familial or meaningful connection with other characters.
Mannerism – their unconscious gestures or movements give a hint to their personality.
Speech Pattern – they may talk with accents, favor certain words, or articulate their thoughts in a unique way.
Role/Archetype – they serve a specific and critical role to the protagonist or plot.

Use this chart to plot your hooks. Return to this document as you introduce new characters and be sure to use a variety of different hooks—don't overwhelm your readers with a ton of characters with weird physical ailments.

Character	Role	Hook	Hook Type
Fred & George	Allies, friends	Always together, twins	Relationship
Hagrid	Mentor	Huge size	Physical description

16

3) Inside Harry's Head.

In storytelling, Point of View (POV) is everything.

Think about it. Where else in life can you get into somebody else's head?

You can't do it in real life. No matter how close you are to your husband or wife, no matter that you've loved and watched your child's every development since the moment of conception...you still cannot get inside their head to hear their thoughts and feel their emotions as if they were your own.

Even TV and film do not offer the deep POV which we can find inside the pages of a book. Aside from a few voice-overs, most of what you see on the screen is watching characters from the outside...just like in real life...though the story may be so focused that we may come away with greater insights.

It is the unique opportunity presented by reading fiction that allows the reader to fully enter into another's point of view—to feel their emotions, understand their beliefs, experience their fears—which makes novels forever appealing to readers. If we as writers can truly immerse ourselves in the thoughts, beliefs, and fears of someone who is not "me," we can expand not only our own world view, but that of our readers as well.

There is much to say on helping your students develop the POV of their characters, but I'd like to offer them two pieces of advice: Choose a compelling POV(s) and then dive as deeply into that head as they possibly can.

Basic point of view choices are usually considered to be first person, omniscient, or third person. Whereas first person gives the reader the most intimate view of a story, it limits the scenes the author can show to only one character's location. Omniscient allows for the widest range of scene possibilities, but is considered out of fashion because of its lack of intimacy with the reader (unless written from a strong narrator's voice). For this reason, third person that allows for multiple POVs while remaining intimate to the current POV character has been one of the most popular choices. It also has recently taken a turn to even greater intimacy.

Many teachers may be familiar with the term **deep POV**, but your students may not. Deep POV is the technique for getting the reader as deeply into the POV character's head as possible, aside from writing in first person. In fact, it is likened to first person in that one exercise for constructing a scene in deep POV is to write it initially in first person, and then go back and simply switch each *I* to *he* or *she* (or *they*, if non-binary).

With deep POV, every word should reflect the character's voice. Every turn of phrase, whether in dialogue or exposition, should sound like it is coming out of their mouth and from their brain, not filtered through a narrator.

Rowling does not write deep POV, at least not consistently, and especially not in the first few books, though she does approach it in her latter ones. Her POV is mostly a traditional third person, but sometimes early on borders on omniscient. This is not a criticism. Deep POV is a tool, it is one tool, it is not the only POV available to a writer. However, it is one tool that, when done well, creates a powerful voice.

Personally, I prefer to use deep POV as much as possible, but that's just my choice. I have scenes, however, which are deliberately constructed outside deep POV because of the needs of that scene.

What Rowling gains by not writing in deep POV is a lack of long introspective passages. Most of her emotional scenes are revealed through action and dialogue.

Here's a passage with bold and italics to give you a visual example of her ratio of action and dialogue to introspection in a high-crisis scene (also available on DeepRiver.press Writer's Resource as one-page handout):

Harry turned to look where Neville was staring. Directly above them, framed in the doorway from the Brain Room, stood Albus Dumbledore, his wand aloft, his face white and furious. Harry felt a kind of electric charge surge through every particle of his body—*they were saved.*

Dumbledore sped down the steps past Neville and Harry, who had no more thoughts of leaving. **Dumbledore was already at the foot of the steps when the Death Eaters nearest realized he was there. There were yells; one of the Death Eaters ran for it, scrabbling like a monkey up the stone steps opposite. Dumbledore's spell pulled him back as easily and effortlessly as though he had hooked him with an invisible line—**

Only one couple was still battling, apparently unaware of the new arrival. **Harry saw Sirius duck Bellatrix's jet of red light: He was laughing at her.**

"Come on, you can do better than that!" he yelled, **his voice echoing around the cavernous room.**

The second jet of light hit him squarely on the chest.

The laughter had not quite died from his face, but his eyes widened in shock.

Harry released Neville, though he was unaware of doing so. He was jumping down the steps again, pulling out his wand, as Dumbledore turned towards the dais too.

It seemed to take Sirius an age to fall. His body curved in a graceful arc as he sank backwards through the ragged veil hanging from the arch....

And Harry saw the look of mingled fear and surprise on his godfather's wasted, once-handsome face as he fell through the ancient doorway and disappeared behind the veil, which fluttered for a moment as though in a high wind and then fell back into place.

Harry heard Bellatrix Lestrange's triumphant scream, but knew it meant nothing—Sirius had only just fallen through the archway, he would reappear from the other side any second....

But Sirius did not reappear.

"SIRIUS!" Harry yelled. "SIRIUS!"

He had reached the floor, his breath coming in searing gasps. Sirius must be just behind the curtain, he, Harry, would pull him back out again....

But as he reached the ground and sprinted towards the dais, Lupin grabbed Harry around the chest, holding him back.

"There's nothing you can do, Harry—"

"Get him, save him, he's only just gone through!"

"It's too late, Harry—"

"We can still reach him—"

Harry struggled hard and viciously, but Lupin would not let go....

"There's nothing you can do, Harry...nothing....He's gone."

(p. 805-806, *Phoenix*)

Key: **Bolded** = action

      Italicized = dialogue

      Left normal = narration or introspection

Note: I marked "they were saved" as dialogue because even though it is technically not voiced, by the fact that it's in italics and written as Harry's thoughts, it has the impact of voiced words. My analysis isn't perfect as not everything can be labeled only action, dialogue, or introspection, but this visual shows how little introspection Rowling uses.

Sirius' death is a hugely important and emotional scene for Harry, the reader, and a critical turning point in the series. Yet, only one and a half sentences and a couple of fragments could be considered introspection. This from a book which I consider to have the highest amount of introspection Rowling had used to that point. Sirius falling behind the Veil delivers an active, visceral punch.

I love deep POV, but one aspect we can learn from Rowling is to let dialogue and action show the emotion. Introspection is good and has its place, but too often writers overuse it and depend on it to carry the full load. That is abusing the tool as well as the reader.

Help your students choose which style of POV they will utilize. If choosing deep POV, challenge them to dive deeply into that head. They should try, as much as possible, to get out of their own world view and into the perception of how their character would experience the plot. Filter everything through their character's perception—the setting, the other characters, the dialogue, and especially the conflict. Make this POV so real and so compelling that the reader will feel as if he or she is truly inside someone else's head experiencing the world through their eyes.

Choosing to use deep POV does not limit your student to only one character's perception. A writer may employ multiple POVs and make each of them deep. However, working with multiple POVs, whether in first, third, or deep, requires a higher level of writing skill and may not be suited to a short story.

Should your student decide to use more than one POV, they must determine which is the best for each scene.

Switching POV within a scene can be confusing to readers. Therefore, have your students choose carefully which POV they use and for what reasons. The intimacy established by limiting themselves to one POV, or the wider locations and perceptions shown by utilizing multiple, will directly affect the readers' involvement and understanding of their story.

Encourage them to choose the POV(s) that is the most compelling, the one sure to engage both themselves and their reader. Where appropriate, they should write as deeply from that perspective as possible. Get their reader into the head of their character and let them feel from the inside what can never be experienced from the outside in real life: the intimacy of complete empathy with another human being.

For more activities on reader engagement visit our Writer's Resource page on www.DeepRiver.press. The mini activity **Point of View (POV)** is on the next page.

4) Fully Realized Backstory

Rowling knows way more about her characters than she reveals on the page. She developed and collected stacks and boxes of notebooks and sketches over years before she ever published *Philosopher's Stone*. However, she does not spill her guts at the first opportunity. All this carefully crafted backstory is greedily hoarded and doled out in crumbs to be fully revealed at the most opportune moment, when the reader is beyond dying to know. Some backstory will never be revealed (through the course of the seven-book series at least) as it is not necessary to the plot. But Rowling knows it, of that the reader is assured.

In this section, we'll focus on helping your student develop their characters' excess baggage. When and how to reveal this carefully planned backstory will be covered in lesson five.

All characters need to be as fully fleshed and realistically portrayed as time and space for their role in the story permit. Each character needs his own GMC—goal, motivation, and conflict. (See the next two points in this list, as well as Debra Dixon's book *Goal, Motivation and Conflict* for more detailed information). With each character, a writer needs to be clear regarding what their character wants, *why* they want it, and who or what else in the story is standing in their way of obtaining their goals. Each character's GMC relates to their backstory in that their motivation, the *why* they want what they want, is usually determined by what has happened to them in their past.

This type of careful character development takes time. Some of it will come from preliminary work before a scene is ever crafted, though much of it will come through the actual writing and especially through the endless rounds of revisions. Pen-to-paper is the lightning-to-neck-bolts which spark to life the heart and soul of our characters.

Crafting backstory takes work, pure and simple. It also takes a lot of time. Rowling had six years between the inspired moment she first "met" Harry on that famous train trip to the time *Harry Potter and the Philosopher's Stone* was bought in Great Britain. She had five years to get fully acquainted with Harry and his friends—to develop his enemies, to plot their interactions, and to ground them with enough luggage to ensure the reader an endless amount of surprises and a lengthy exciting journey into Harry's world.

Even Rowling herself has been quite amazed to see how seriously her fans have taken her backstory. Who knew that the exact years of their history would be counted up and an elaborately detailed timeline constructed? I doubt even she plotted her backstory in that minute detail. Thus, she acknowledged that she'd nip into *The Harry Potter Lexicon* when she was away from home and needed to look up a fact or a date (http://www.hp-lexicon.org).

Still, she's the headmistress of her backstory. She filled notebooks with rosters of classes at Hogwarts, including which student had Muggle parents, which House each was in, and meanings behind their names.

She knew enough of her backstory that she was able to drop Sirius Black into the first chapter of *Philosopher's Stone*, even though he didn't make an appearance as a character until two books later. Then she withheld enough of her backstory that fandom is still clamoring, nearly a decade after the publication of the last book, to know exactly what happened at Godric's Hollow and those elusive missing twenty-four hours between Voldemort's back-fired curse and Harry's arrival at Privet Drive.

Point of View (POV): Mini Activity

For this activity, you will reflect on which style of POV best fits your story. You will then experiment with writing scene snippets based on deep POV.

POV STYLES:
Omniscient: Written in the voice of the author or narrator who knows and sees all. Allows for greatest flexibility of scenes that can be presented, but is distant from the characters.
First Person: Written from only one character in their voice. Limits scenes to what that character experiences, but builds great intimacy between the reader and that character.
Third Person: Can be written from the perspective of one or more characters. Limits what can be shown to the number of POV characters chosen.
Deep (or Limited) Third Person: Combines the intimacy of first with the flexibility of third. While it can be written from more than one character's POV, must remain deeply inside the head of the POV character of the moment.

Deciding which POV style to use is a personal choice of the writer based on the needs of their story. Each style offers its own strengths and challenges. If you're writing an epic story that will highlight the actions of many characters who may not always be connected, you may want to choose a POV that allows for greater flexibility of scenes, such as omniscient or third. If you're writing a story deeply based on the emotional journey of the protagonist, you may want to consider the more intimate first or deep POVs.

These are guidelines, not rules. An epic story can be deeply personal, written from multiple deep POVs, while a personal drama could be presented from a strong omniscient narrator whose voice puts a twist on the story. Take a few minutes to reflect upon your story, and write in the box below which style of POV suits your story the best and why.

POV Choice:

Experiment with deep POV. As deep POV is such a popular and powerful choice in fiction, try your hand at it. With the prompts below, write a paragraph initially from your character's perspective in first person. Then rewrite it in deep POV by only switching out the first-person pronouns to third. See how personal to that character you can make each sentence.

Show your character reading the text of someone breaking up with them, whether a friend or romantic partner. What are their emotions? Memories?

Show your character exiting the airport in a foreign country for the first time. What are they seeing, smelling, hearing, maybe even tasting and touching? Show how it makes them feel.

Show your character witnessing a child playing with a ball and about to run into the street in front of an oncoming car. How do they react? How do they feel?

Some writers love to immerse themselves in developing their characters…to the point that they never write a word. Some writers just plunge right in, without introducing themselves properly to the people whose lives they plan to wreak havoc upon…and then must go back and revise. Every writer has to suit his or her own style, but by the end of the first draft, your student should have a fairly comprehensive backstory for every major and secondary character. Backstory that makes it into the final draft must be relevant to the overall plot of the novel.

Backstory that goes nowhere and has no meaning is a dead-end and will only weigh the story down.

STUDENT CHALLENGE

Take the time to fill your journals with detailed backstory regarding your characters. Plot out their personal histories. Some people like to do this by way of an interview, having their character answer questions in their own voice and role. Or you could fill out character charts covering aspects such as physical description, favorite foods, or astrological sign that then help to shape their life experience. Others get into real-world character analysis, such as the Myers Briggs personality types.

Remember that every choice your character makes is dictated by their past, by who they are at the core of their being. Every decision they make or every event that happens to them affects their next step in the course of your story.

To make sure that your character's backstory as well as actions throughout the plot are properly motivated and cohesive, you must consider their **GMC**: Goal, Motivation, and Conflict.

- **Goal** = The primary driving need or desire of the character in the story.
- **Motivation** = Why they want what they want.
- **Conflict** = Who, or what is standing in their way of obtaining this goal.

Plot out your main character's GMC well. And, if you wish to deepen your story, develop the GMC not only for your protagonist, but for the antagonist and as many secondary characters as possible.

Character Relevance: Student Handout

For this activity, you will begin creating the goals, motivations, and conflicts that surround each of your main and secondary characters.

Each character needs their own **GMC**—goal, motivation, and conflict. And each GMC should contribute to the overall storyline. With each character, you need to be clear regarding:

Goal: what they want
Motivation: why they want it
Conflict: who or what else is standing in their way of obtaining their goals.

Each character's GMC relates to their backstory. The *why* they want what they want is usually determined by what has happened in their past, thus we will also develop a bit of backstory in this activity.

Using the chart below, plot out your characters' goals, motivations, and conflicts. Use these details to consider the backstory of the character and why they are acting in such a manner.

Character	Goal	Motivation	Conflict	Backstory
Hermione	*Read all the books. Be the brightest in her class.*	*To prove she fits in.*	*Other students don't like her.*	*First witch in her family. Her parents are dentists.*

5) Obstacles to Overcome

A specific technique of character development related to plotting is to give the character an important obstacle to overcome. This obstacle can be either external or internal. The antagonist blocking their way is external. Overcoming their low self-esteem in order to believe in their own powers is internal.

Many times obstacles are both. The example of the maze in the Triwizard Tournament is a good example. The maze was a physical impediment to the goal of winning the cup. Harry overcoming his jealousy was an internal accomplishment.

As in real life, when characters overcome obstacles, they grow. This is the crux of character development. Character development is not what the author writes out as descriptions of their character. Character development occurs when the character, through the plot of the story, makes choices—right or wrong—and changes because of it. When you look at a character from the beginning to the end of a story and see this change, it should be dramatic and noticeable. That is the character arc or growth arc.

We're all familiar with Harry's overall series growth arc. He goes from being an unloved orphan stuffed away in a closet to the celebrated savior of the magical world. Along the way, he must overcome many obstacles to obtain the maturity, skill, and wisdom to defeat the darkest wizard of all time.

Each book presents its own set of obstacles and challenges that Harry must face. Some of these obstacles are external—such as Snape's hatred, Dumbledore's slowness to reveal crucial information, and Voldemort's increasing shenanigans to kill Harry off. Other obstacles are internal—Harry's lack of belief in his own powers coupled with his lack of knowledge of the wizarding world. Internal conflicts also include his inability to trust in the manner of Dumbledore and his disbelief that love is more powerful than hatred.

Most writers understand the importance of carefully plotting their protagonist's growth arc. They'll spend much time and energy charting their hero's GMC, torturing their heroine, and assuring that the turning points are strong and powerful. However, the strength of a truly good novel often rests in how much energy the author puts into developing their secondaries as well.

Let's look at some secondary characters and their obstacles that take place in the Potter world.

Character	Beginning Situation	Obstacle to Overcome	Ending Triumph
Dobby	Enslaved to the Malfoys.	Cannot act on his own against Malfoys without punishing self.	Due to his loyalty to Harry, wins his freedom.
Ginny	Crush on Harry.	Tongue-tied around Harry.	Increases strength and self-confidence. Dates and marries Harry.
Ron	Youngest son with five older brothers.	In shadows of brothers. In shadows of Harry.	Overcomes his fears of living in shadows and returns to his best friends. Achieves greater fame than any of his brothers.
Neville	Living with grandmother, who belittles him. Unpopular at school.	Poor memory, inept, lack of confidence.	Shows the power of his magic in killing the last Horcrux, the one closest to Voldemort.
Snape	Hates Harry. Unlikable professor.	Death Eater background. Distrusted.	Helps to save the life of Lily's son and restore the Wizarding World.

Help your students to throw obstacles into the path of their characters. Challenge them to new heights with the problems they must overcome. Don't ever let their way be too easy. Otherwise, who does the reader have to cheer for?

Remember the power of the underdog. Everyone cheers when the underdog wins out against tremendous odds. But when an underdog is not challenged, or fails, he remains an underdog that no one cares about or remembers.

6) Torturing the Heart of the Hero (and Secondaries!)

What obstacles your student chooses to throw at their hero and how he goes about overcoming them, will all point to and flow from the nature of the character's personality at his very core.

To stroke a reader's heart, the writer must strike at their character's worst fears. Characters must battle their inner demons, go where it's painful to achieve their pleasurable reward. This is the rationale behind the oft-given advice to "torture your characters." Only someone who has been forced to triumph over his base nature, to probe his own wounds, to fly into the face of pain, and away from self-serving pleasure—only this hero deserves the elusive, final reward of "all was well."

At heart, Lupin, a werewolf, is betrayed by society, an outcast, unwanted and unloved. Readers who feel the same really latched onto Remus. He is forced to move into painful territory, living among the unsavory of his kind—those truly deserving of the fear they arouse—until finally, Lupin is able to accept that he himself is deserving of love and acceptance.

Hermione, the only witch in her family, is thrust into an unfamiliar world where she is left out and unpopular. Knowledge is her only power. Thus she seeks initially to possess it above everyone else. Any child who has felt like a newcomer among a closed group of old friends will surely understand why Hermione acts the way she does—until she learns that friendship and bravery trumps books and cleverness. Hermione uses this hard-earned knowledge to help others who are left-out and powerless.

Any adult who has ever destroyed their life through a major mistake will understand (even if they disparage) the bitterness that seeps through Snape's hate-filled words cast at Harry. His anger at himself is projected onto the one he hurt the most.

In the end, Lupin finds a home, first in his Defense Against the Dark Arts class, then the Order of the Phoenix, and, finally, with Tonks...even unto death. Hermione becomes the brightest witch of her age, who bravely and loyally helps to prepare her dear friend for his final battle. And Snape redeems himself by saving the child of the woman he hurt, and lost, but *always* loved.

Encourage your students to seek out and probe their character's innermost wounds and fears, not only for the hero, but the secondaries as well. The layers of characters that the writer weaves this concept into will greatly enrich the depth and emotional impact of their story.

The chart below shows many HP characters and what tortures them through the series.

*This chart looks similar to the obstacle chart because the best laid obstacles will relate to the heart of the character and what he must do to probe his pain.

Character	Heart	Probing the Pain	Reward
*Harry	Seeking what was lost.	Accepts death, and then chooses life.	Finds his family, both old and new.
Ron	Always second best.	Returns to friends he betrayed.	Wins Hermione's heart.
Neville	Doesn't measure up.	Becomes leader of a resistance movement.	Kills the final Horcrux. Outshines his father.
Hagrid	Unfairly maligned and misunderstood.	Must visit the giants who first abandoned him and bring one home to nurture.	Creates a new, loyal family for self, both in Grawp and friends.
Voldemort	Unloved and unable to love.	Fails to do this. Always self-serving.	Loses himself to his inability to love.

One thing I'd like to point out through this analysis—Rowling seems to have a thing for insecure characters. Hermione, Ron, Neville, Hagrid—all of them share a sense of not fitting in, not measuring up. Perhaps this points to Rowling's own inner heart, her author's theme, so to speak.

Most writers will discover as their number of completed stories pile up, that they pursue certain character types and themes above all others. This central issue is considered by many to hint at the author's theme, the heart of the writer that she is trying to heal through her work. (We'll explore this more in the next chapter.)

Ask your students: What is your inner core? What character hearts appeal to you the most? What wounds do you feel compelled to probe?

Then challenge them to stick it to their characters. Find their childhood fears, their gaping sores. Then, make their characters go where it is scary. Make them confront their worst fears and challenge their pain. Only then can the author grant them their greatest reward.

The **Obstacles and Pain Mini Activity** on the next page will help your students through the process.

7) Knowing Your Character's Internal Logic

To effectively torture their characters and then grant them their reward, your student is going to have to know each character's internal logic—the rules, beliefs, and assumptions that guide their every move.

A young girl who has been abused by the people who are supposed to love and cherish her the most won't think and act like the beloved daughter of a couple deeply in love with each other and at peace with their world. Likewise, a man who always received validation growing up for his impressive academic achievements won't choose the same profession and lifestyle as the football superstar.

Characters, like people, come from different families, cultures, religions, and socio-economic conditions. All these elements, plus more, will greatly affect each character's basic way of understanding themselves and their place in the world. Humans are creatures of habit, both in the way we think and in the manner we act. Rarely do we stray outside our comfort zones. What those comfort zones are, however, can vary widely from person to person. A serial killer, for example, while committing an act that is horrific and atrocious to most of society, still performs these acts in a fairly reliable *modus operandi*.

What this tells us about characterization is that to portray a person honestly on the page, a writer must determine that character's internal logic. To make their created world come fully alive, the writer must draw from a wide range of characters with a rich diversity of internal logic.

In Harry Potter, it is Hermione, with her logical mind and her need to categorize and understand her world, who embarks on the most dangerous quest of her life toting a "mobile library," as Ron puts it. While it was the twins, with their humorous and outside-the-box outlook on life, who dropped out of school, established a joke shop, and sold bottles of U-No-Poo with advertising that made fun of You-Know-Who. Even Voldemort, though coldly comfortable with murder when it suited his purpose of gaining power and eternal life, spared the lives of two young trick-or-treaters on his way to the Potters' home in Godric's Hollow because that would have been an emotional killing that served no greater purpose.

Remember, the more exotic a character, the more foreign their internal logic needs to be. An alien who thinks and acts just like a human would be incredibly boring and unrealistic. A writer should not let their own internal logic get in the way of creating a character who sees the world drastically different than they do. To imagine a view outside their own POV is the writer's job.

To determine a character's internal logic, ask your students some questions: What is the primary force which drives your character? Is it his need to fit in? Her need to stand out? His desire to seek justice for a past transgression? Her determination to heal old wounds? His inability to act because of fears? Her continual push to new adventures and exciting locations? How does all this shape the core of their being?

Your student must know this internal logic for each character if they're going to properly motivate their people to act honestly in their story rather than simply following the orders of the author-puppeteer.

*(I owe a thank-you to former workshop attendee Shelley Souza for inspiring this section. It was her determination to see and understand Rowling's internal logic of the story which made me contemplate character internal logic as well.)

Obstacles and Pain: Mini Activity

As part of the *Conflict* of **GMC**, characters must face and overcome obstacles, whether external or internal. The antagonist blocking their way is external. Overcoming their low self-esteem in order to believe in their own power is internal.

Many obstacles are both. The example of the maze in the Triwizard Tournament is a good example. The maze was a physical impediment to the goal of winning the cup. Harry overcoming his jealousy was an internal accomplishment.

The best obstacles are those that force the character into the heart of their inner pain, what they most fear.

Using the chart below, analyze what obstacles your character is facing, how it relates to what hurts him or he fears the most—*Heart*, how he acts to face those fears—*Probing the Pain*, and what he gains in triumph for doing so.

Character	Beginning Situation	Obstacle to Overcome	Heart	Probing the Pain	Ending Triumph
Dobby	Enslaved to the Malfoys.	Cannot act on his own against Malfoys without punishing self.	Longs for freedom.	Goes back to the home where he was enslaved to save his friends.	Due to his loyalty to Harry, wins his freedom.
Neville	Living with grandmother, who belittles him. Not popular at school.	Poor memory, inept, lack of confidence.	Doesn't measure up.	Becomes leader of a resistance movement.	Shows the power of his magic in killing the last Horcrux, the one closest to Voldy.

8) Staking Your Characters

Strong character actions require strong emotions, and strong emotions result from high stakes. Challenge your students to have their character emotions hit the highest pitch possible. Their goal: force the reader to experience fully the passions of their characters, whether love or hate, trust or betrayal, laughter or sorrow. To escalate their reader's experience in such a manner, your student must raise the bar for what's at risk.

This doesn't mean that your student has to write a story about a poor, unloved, defenseless orphan who must save the entire wizarding world, indeed the Muggle world as well, from the darkest and most powerful wizard who ever lived. Not all stories can be set with stakes at such high world-effect levels.

However, the stakes that are most important are uniquely emotional to their character. Whether writing a drama, a comedy, or a romance, the stakes need to be as high as is appropriately possible. Have them brainstorm—what is the worst thing that could happen to their hero or heroine, and then make it their plot. Perhaps their heroine is terrified that if she admits hacking into her best friend's Tinder account to manipulate her matches, she'll lose her friendship forever. Then this must be what the heroine faces. The higher the personal risk, the more rewarding that character's triumph will be.

One aspect of high stakes I feel is extremely important is that not just the hero or heroine benefit from triumphing over the antagonist. The good of a community, no matter how large or small, must also be at risk. It's the carrying the elixir back to the tribe of the "Hero's Journey" (which we'll cover in lesson six). Triumph over the antagonist is so much richer when there is a community of people who benefit from it.

With Harry Potter, we have the large end of the spectrum when it comes to a community benefit. Wizards and Muggles alike will enjoy a more peaceful world when Voldemort is no more. However, even a story that is focused tightly on the burgeoning romance between two people can include the return of the elixir. A family can be reunited, a school returned to order, or a city relieved of a crime spree. The possibilities are as endless as the writer's imagination.

High stakes should also show characters not only at their best, but also at their worst. Many readers had trouble with Harry in *Order of the Phoenix*. This was Harry's fifth year of school, and at age fifteen, he was every bit the angry, angsty teenager that no one but his friends want to be around. I got tired of Harry's outbursts in that book as well.

But it was real. After all, here was a teenager who had a lot of weight on his shoulders, so much that Dumbledore did not make him a prefect. Harry had been tested and tried since the beginning. He'd been pushed into developing skills, such as producing a Patronus, that other witches and wizards his age would never consider. He must be pushed in this manner because he had an enormous task ahead of him.

No one will believe that a seventeen-year-old boy could defeat the darkest wizard in 100 years, unless he'd been properly prepared and thoroughly tested. Nor will anyone feel your student's heroine deserves her triumphant ending unless she's proved to herself, along with the reader, that she can survive and triumph over any obstacle her mean-hearted author has thrown at her.

Help your students understand that their protagonist doesn't have to "save the world." Stakes are emotional, not physical. What their protagonist does have to do, however, is face his or her worst possible fears, probe that inner wound we talked about earlier, pass through the fires of refining conflict, and emerge a better, stronger person on the other side.

Tell your students: Have no mercy! Raise your stakes to bring out the full emotional depth your hero must face and rise above. Torture and torment your characters to make them prove their worth. Use the chart on the next page to help.

Don't let compassion hold you back! After all, you won't have to meet him in real life.

9) Loyal Friends and Dastardly Enemies

You student won't have to physically meet their hero or heroine, but their supporting cast of characters will. Each character needs to connect with the hero in a way that is unique to that particular relationship and builds emotional depth.

On one hand, Harry meets the wildly enthusiastic Colin Creevey who follows him around like a puppy, while on the other he must suffer under *Professor* Severus Snape who absolutely loathes him. Harry's inner circle is composed of friends he can always rely on—Ron, Hermione, Neville, Luna, and Ginny (each with their own unique relationship to Harry) — and thus the reader experiences this comfortable base of support as well. Outside his circle, however, Harry must face the opposition of Draco Malfoy, Severus Snape, and He-Who-Must-Not-Be-Named, along with his legions of Death Eaters and Dementors. If readers are going to be driven into dark and scary places, even if comically presented, they shouldn't have to go it alone. Your students can give them the security of friendship, through their supporting cast of characters, to see them through.

What's at Stake?: Student Handout

Strong character actions require strong emotions, and strong emotions result from high stakes—what your character is in danger of losing should they fail. You want your emotions to hit the highest pitch possible. You must have the reader experience fully the passions of your characters, whether love or hate, trust or betrayal, laughter or sorrow. Escalate your reader's experience by raising the bar for what's at risk.

However, the stakes that are most important are uniquely emotional to your character. Brainstorm—what is the worst thing that could happen to your hero or heroine, and then make it your plot. The higher the risk, the more rewarding that character's triumph will be.

Using the chart below, plot what is at stake for each of your characters and how you can make it more intense. Who is their ally for this particular stake? And who is opposed?

Character	Stakes	Antagonist	Allies
Draco	Saving his own life and that of his father.	Voldemort, Harry, Snape	Snape, Crabbe, Goyle, Harry

On the opposite pole, the hero's triumph will only be as powerful as his antagonist is strong. That's not to say that every antagonist needs to be the quintessential evil villain. However, every antagonist must be the strongest force pushing against the hero as is possible. Your student's villain needs to prove every flaw, in their hero to force him to develop into the fullest person he can be, and ultimately, by defeating his antagonist, prove himself worthy of the reader's full support.

Perhaps the primary antagonist to Harry was actually Snape. After all, Snape was on hand, each and every day, to torment Harry, to act as sandpaper rubbing abrasively against Harry's skin, putting on display his imperfections and taunting his beliefs about himself and his parents. Harry did not have to defeat this antagonist, but instead learned to see him anew through Dumbledore's eyes of trust. Snape was designed to push against Harry and mold him in ways that a loving influence could not have done. Everyone needs a bit of vitriol in their life, no matter how unwelcome.

One nuance we see that works effectively in Rowling's protagonist/antagonist relation is how Harry and Voldemort grow apace of each other. There's only one way Rowling could effectively portray this immensely powerful dark wizard not killing off an eleven-year-old boy, and that was to strip Voldemort of his power. As Harry grows in his knowledge and magical skills, so too Voldemort transforms from Vapormort to parasite, to grotesque embryonic baby, to regaining his human form. Thus Harry did not have to face a fully powerful Dark Lord until he was a more powerful opponent.

Voldemort is in fact the shadow of Harry. He reflects the darkened nature of Harry himself, the imperfections Harry must overcome in his own transformation. Harry was forced to deal with anger, trust, and his own prejudices (primarily against Slytherins) before he emerged fully equipped to combat his Shadow.

When he did, he did not face his demons alone. Harry's loyal friends were there by his side, because his friendships were the ultimate show of Harry's true nature. This was the part of Harry that completely distinguished him from the Dark Lord. Harry loves and is loved. He has friends. While Voldemort was busy destroying lives, Harry saved them. Voldemort tried to capture eternal life through the murder of innocents; Harry willingly threw himself in harm's way to save those he loved, and those he didn't even know.

A heroine won't look very smart if she triumphs over an idiot. Challenge your students to spend as much time crafting their villain and his goals, motivation, and conflict as they do their heroine. Maybe even more. Make their antagonist strong enough to force the ultimate growth within their protagonist, as Voldemort and Snape forced Harry to explore the darkest recesses of his own soul.

Help them carefully construct their hero's base of support whether that is one loyal friend or several. Whereas some thriller stories give their protagonist no friends or trusted allies, I think the reader experiences an innate need to know that there's at least one true safe base the hero, and they, can rely on. After all, a large lesson in life is recognizing and appreciating those we hold most dear. How to go about showing this depth of friendship and loyalty? One good way is through touch.

10) The Power of Human Touch

One technique Rowling uses excessively well is to employ the power of human touch to *show* emotion rather than to *tell*. Throughout her stories, she utilizes words conveying touch between her characters to express the heights and depths of what her people are feeling. You can guarantee, in a high-intensity scene, there will be a lot more touching going on.

Have your students study these examples, noting the bolded action, to see how in crucial, emotionally charged scenes, the physical act of touch is used to great effect.

Take Away

I hope that studying these techniques from Rowling has given you some ideas for how to help your students better craft their own pen-and-paper people. Characters must be real for the reader to invest time with them. If a writer's characters fall flat, no matter how intricate the plotting or fast the pacing, the story will be set down not to be picked back up.

Challenge your students to:

- Get to know their people fully in their own mind before they finalize them on paper.
- Make sure they delve deeply into their character's hearts and know their darkest fears and highest aspirations.
- Go where it's scary in their writing. For themselves as well as their created people.
- Portrays their world accurately and vibrantly through the diversity and strength of their characters.
- Bond their loyal friendships as deeply as they alienate their adversaries.
- Then show all this emotion through the power of human touch.

Using Touch to Show Character Emotions: Student Handout

Note the bolded action. See how in crucial, emotionally charged scenes, the physical act of touch is used to great effect.

"Where are we?" he [Harry] said.

Cedric shook his head. He got up, **pulled Harry to his feet**, and they looked around....

And then, before Harry's mind had accepted what he was seeing, before he could feel anything but numb disbelief, he felt himself **being pulled to his feet**.

(p. 636 & 638, *Goblet*)

This example above works double duty: not only does the paralleled wording show the touch of loyalty between Harry and his former competitor seconds before Cedric is killed, but Rowling also uses the same words to emphasize and contrast Harry's relation to Wormtail just two pages later. Harry has gone from being the loyal friend to being betrayed by his father's friend and betrayer, and must now fight for his life.

Then a pair of hands seized him roughly and turned him over.

"Harry! Harry!"...

Harry let go of the cup, but he **clutched Cedric to him even more tightly**. He **raised his free hand** and **seized Dumbledore's wrist**, while Dumbledore's face swam in and out of focus.

(p. 671, *Goblet*)

With touching words such as "seized" and "clutched," the power of Dumbledore's fear and Harry's mounting anxiety are powerfully conveyed. The reader can feel the emotions, rather than being simply told that Dumbledore was afraid.

"RUN!" Harry yelled, and as the shelves swayed precariously and more glass spheres began to pour from above, he **seized a handful of Hermione's robes** and **dragged her forward**..."

(p. 787, *Phoenix*)

It touches the reader's heart, the force with which Harry protects Hermione. It also fueled a lot of Harry/Hermione shippers, but we won't go there.

...Harry **seized** him and **helped** him back to his seat...

And **pulling Dumbledore's uninjured arm around his shoulders**, Harry **guided** his headmaster back around the lake, **bearing most of his weight**...

"I am not worried, Harry," said Dumbledore, his voice a little stronger despite the freezing water. "I am with you."...

"When did it appear?" asked Dumbledore, and **his hand clenched painfully upon Harry's shoulder** as he struggled to his feet.

(p. 577-581, *Half-Blood*)

How satisfying is it for the reader to see, to feel, Harry taking care of his mentor. Here, Harry becomes the stronger one, actively conveyed through numerous "touching" verbs.

Just so we don't think that the power of touch resides only with our hero and his friends, notice this from *Half-Blood*:

...Snape had burst into the room, his face livid. **Pushing Harry roughly aside, he knelt over Malfoy**, drew his wand and **traced it over the deep wounds** Harry's curse had made, muttering an incantation that sounded almost like song. The flow of blood seemed to ease; Snape **wiped the residue from Malfoy's face** and repeated his spell. Now the wounds seemed to be knitting...

...When Snape had performed his counter-curse for the third time, **he half-lifted Malfoy into a standing position**...

... "There may be a certain amount of scarring, but if you take dittany immediately we might avoid even that...come..."

He supported Malfoy across the bathroom, turning at the door to say in a voice of cold fury, "And you, Potter...you wait here for me."

(*Half-Blood*, p. 489 Bloomsbury, p. 523 Scholastic)

"Pushing," "knelt," "traced," "wiped," "lifted," and "supported." The power of human touch, of healing...in Snape's hands. Look for places where you can weave more touch, in all its varied forms, into your story. Especially consider scenes of high intensity and action. Don't limit touch to your hero and his friends. After all, even villains can love their children, and not all touches are good.

Touch is elemental, archetypal even. It transcends centuries and cultures, and the sexes. It has the power to convey emotions as far ranging as love from hate and trust from betrayal. It is a powerful tool in your writing arsenal. Use it well.

Lesson Two

Freeing Your Prisoner of Azkaban
(Voice & Engagement)

One of the features fans love best about JK Rowling's Harry Potter series is the exciting new worlds to explore—city streets, castles, and whole villages that are fresh and intriguing, yet diagonally connected to our own. The magical world is the same as the one we inhabit, yet special and unique.

Doesn't that sound familiar? It's exactly what teachers often get accused of asking from students in their stories. *The same but different*. In other words, we ask that they meet the requirements of the particular writing assignment, but do so in such a way that incorporates their own fresh perspective.

To me, one of the greatest challenges we face in teaching creative writing, is in challenging our students to dig deep inside to seek this fresh perspective. To find their own voice, and then communicate it effectively for both themselves and their reader. Indeed, assisting our students to discover their own magical world that lies within, and learning that sharing it can make a difference in the world, is perhaps one of the greatest rewards of teaching. And it's all about what writers call *Voice*.

An important benefit to note is that once a student discovers their voice and learns to channel this into whatever they write, making each assignment more personal, it can totally change their perspective on writing. Making what they once saw a drudge work something exciting instead. Have them read **Discovering Your Author Voice** on the next page.

Engagement

The subtitle of this lesson is "Engagement." It may not be self-evident how these two subjects relate and why they are lumped together in one lesson. Put quite simply, the stronger the voice, the deeper the engagement, of both the student and their reader—as we will explore side-by-side through the rest of this lesson.

For your student, tuning into their own voice may sound so intangible or even ethereal. However, there are a few tricks for putting their voice down in black and white that will make it come across stronger on the page. To me, this is where voice and style join. While a writer's voice guides them in the big decisions they make, such as setting, characters, and conflict, it is the style in which they write, the way in which they choose words and string them together, that carries the weight of their voice onto the page and engages the reader.

Overview:

1) Challenge each scene's structure
2) Employ strong verbs and pinpointed nouns

Discovering Your Author Voice: Student Handout

As a young writer, one of the most important questions you can ask yourself is *what do you have to offer the reader that no other writer has offered before?* Yes, you do have something fresh to share. Everyone does, just not everyone will seek hard enough to unearth it within themselves.

Harry Potter did not spring out of nowhere. It burst forth out of someone's life—Joanne Rowling's life. The story of a young boy alone in his world, discovering talents he did not know he possessed, and struggling against deep-seated prejudices and hatred was born of a woman discovering her own place in the United Kingdom. A woman who during the course of writing her first book experienced marriage, childbirth, and divorce; poverty, single-parenting, and the British welfare system; and who had grown up amid a centuries-old culture that valued purity of blood.

Her parents had joined the British military at a young age, and she'd listened to stories of how they met on a train out of King's Cross Station. (I always knew Ginny was meant for Harry from this very fact—they met on Platform 9¾ at King's Cross. The romantic in me recognized that Rowling had inserted her parents' meeting into her story from the beginning). Rowling had also named her first child, a daughter, after a woman she'd admired since childhood—Jessica Mitford. Ms. Mitford was a woman who turned her back against her noble heritage during the turbulent, war-torn days of WWII and beyond to protest the systemic prejudice and ethnic genocide which was tearing her world apart.

That took guts. Jessica Mitford was probably the original Gryffindor in JK Rowling's eyes.

Harry Potter sprang from somewhere. He bubbled forth from a deep, flowing spring of a lifelong concern with equality and racial justice. Rowling, who once worked for Amnesty International, has since used her well-heard public voice to take stands against what she sees as the Death Eaters of our day—the orphan institutions throughout the world that maintain a system where children are locked in cribs or separated from their family due to poverty or disabilities; the social deprivation of women and children; and most recently, certain political campaigns which she considers oppressive, especially to minorities.

The messages in Rowling's work are always cloaked in fantasy forms, with many of her themes coming to the reader through subtext. Her writing shows that she understands clearly that the best way to reach a mind is to open it first through entertainment. Whether to write overtly about social or political causes is an individual choice. However, as Rowling's example clearly shows, messages can be woven into subtext through engaging storytelling.

Each writer must find their passion inside themselves. Let your passion flow from your perspective on life. This passion can shape your voice and make your story powerful, unique, and recognized and adored by readers.

Ask yourself a few questions—what is it in real life that gets you riled up the quickest and the angriest? Channel this energy and rage in some form into your antagonist. What in real life gives you so much pleasure and satisfaction that you're willing to devote many unpaid hours in its pursuit? Channel some of those emotions and ideals into your protagonist. Finally, what are some of your experiences in life, your school, your travels, your friends? Channel all these real-life details when creating your full, vibrant world.

As a professional writer, I hear a lot about *voice* in the business end of writing and how every editor is looking for fresh, new voices. It's easy to get confused and think this means, perhaps, a sarcastic way of delivering our words, something hip or flippant, as often found in young adult literature. Or maybe voice is dark and tortured as in romantic suspense, paranormal, or a gothic. I believe this explanation only scratches the surface of voice.

Voice goes much deeper than how words are strung together on paper. Voice reflects what you believe, what you know, what you understand, what you have experienced in life. It reflects where you choose to put enormous amounts of your time and energy.

You may be entertained by reading many divergent books that take up a few hours of your day. But when it comes to spending several months of your life writing **one**, it's going to reflect who *you* are deep inside. Your cares and concerns, your beliefs, and your passions. Your Voice is You. Voice reflects your writer's soul.

Please note here that the voice I am speaking of is the author's voice, not a particular character's voice. Once developed, you take your author voice with you from story to story, and it is quite distinct from the sound of the characters within those stories. Your author voice is what guides you to the type of story you choose to write, the conflicts between the people you write about, and the themes and resolutions you work toward in your climax. Your voice encapsulates your reason for writing.

Author voice is what prompted Rowling to write *The Casual Vacancy*, her first novel after the end of the Potter series, to the Cormoran Strike detective series, where she is once again pursuing her love of a good mystery. Even though her newest releases are a jump in format, with a stage production for *Harry Potter and the Cursed Child* (written by Jack Thorne), and a film script for *Fantastic Beasts and Where to Find Them*, she is taking her author voice into these new frontiers.

So, take some time and explore your own. As Snape would ask, where do your loyalties lie? What type of story do you want to spend significant time crafting and sharing with your world? What experience do you have, unique to you, that can touch the hearts of others?

Find your passion, recognize your voice, and clothe it in an interesting, entertaining garb. Just like JK Rowling did.

1) Challenge Each Scene's Structure

You've had your students take some time to reflect on their voice as a writer. Even though this is a life-long process of discovery that cannot be completed with one simple exercise, hopefully they have developed some basic understanding, a glimmer, as to who they are and what excites and motivates them the most. So far, this has all been about their author voice and not a particular story.

Now it is time to help them supercharge each scene of their WIP. To do this, we will examine each scene's setting, conflict, and characters.

First, ask them—where is each scene set? Is it somewhere the reader will find fresh or interesting, or a location they've already used many times before? I recently critiqued a mystery where the author had several scenes set in the office of the detective agency. That setting was good for a certain number of scenes, but not the best choice for all. Readers quickly get bored and want to explore new places. If the same location is necessary, it needs to change and deepen along with the story.

Have them beef up those scenes that must be set in the office. Make the office a bit quirky, unusual. Describe what sets it apart from the ordinary office environment. Re-envision it in a way that contributes to the mystery and themes of the story. Then, each time they revisit that setting, show a new aspect, a new vision, either from a different POV, or the changing POV of the protagonist. Show the reader, through the setting, the increasing conflict and mystery of the novel. Most importantly, whenever possible, choose a different setting.

For your students, the beginning of a new assignment is a crucial time in defining their world. If they're like me, once they get words down on paper, especially a significant number of words, they're much less likely to initiate dramatic change—such as stripping out a setting and substituting another. From the start, have them challenge their settings. Is this room, this town, this fantasy world the most interesting and unique they can show to engage their reader? And what are the details inside which will attract, engage, and distinguish it as fresh and original? Get that right first and they'll do a lot less revising later.

This same technique of questioning, challenging, and re-envisioning they should repeat with each scene in regard to conflict and character as well. Conflict and character go together because it is through conflict, and the characters' reaction to it, that they change and grow. Each scene absolutely must have conflict. The best conflict is not simple bickering or fighting. Conflict is the protagonist pushing against existing boundaries and the antagonist pushing back. Conflict involves something happening, something changing, something created anew.

One of the strongest tips for your emerging young writers is to have them look at each scene and examine where their conflict lies. Is it strong enough? Where is the urge for the reader to read on? Where is the tension, that need for the protagonist to push forward, the antagonist to push back? Where is your protagonist being forced to change?

I picked up my copy of *Half-Blood* and flipped it to wherever the book fell open to examine the conflict and setting in a random scene. The one revealed is Christmas Eve at the Weasleys in "A Very Frosty Christmas." It's a beautiful, homey scene. You have a large, loving family with friends gathered 'round, a Christmas feast, festive decorations—including the delightful detail of the garden gnome who gives the setting that extra bite.

> Stupefied, painted gold, stuffed into a miniature tutu and with small wings glued to its back, it glowered down at them all, the ugliest angel Harry had ever seen, with a large bald head like a potato ***and rather hairy feet***.

(p. 309, *Half-Blood*, Bloomsbury)

Note: This is a zoom lens worldbuilding detail which we will discuss in a later lesson, not conflict, but I include it here because it's such a delightful note in this scene we are discussing.

Even though this is a warm, loving, homespun Christmas scene, Rowling does not allow it to get maudlin. Conflict abounds. You've got the budding mother-in-law against soon-to-be daughter-in-law with Mrs. Weasley ruffling at Fleur's criticism of her favorite singer, Celestina Warbeck. As the others scurry to stay out of the fray, we have the hushed conversation between Harry and Mr. Weasley regarding the conflict within the Ministry, with Harry echoing Dumbledore's questioning of the Ministry's false arrests. However, all this preliminary conflict simply sets the stage and builds toward the main conflict of the scene, which is delivered in a one-two punch.

Harry repeats the overheard conversation between Draco and Snape the night of Slughorn's Christmas party, conveying his suspicion to Lupin that Snape is up to no good. In a brilliant laying down of one of the most disputed texts which kept readers speculating between the release of *Half-Blood* and *Hallows*, Lupin replies:

> "People have said it, many times. It comes down to whether or not you trust Dumbledore's judgment. I do; therefore, I trust Severus."
>
> (p. 311, *Half-Blood*, Bloomsbury)

At this point, Harry doesn't trust Snape, not for a moment. He's pushing against Lupin to agree and help him do something about it. Lupin pushes back with the trump card of Dumbledore's trust. Which is all fantastic foreshadowing as we know what happens at the end of *Half-Blood*....*Sob.*

Lupin's gratitude for Snape preparing the Wolfsbane potion faithfully each month during his tenure at Hogwarts is contrasted sharply by the image of Greyback positioning himself before the full moon so he can strike to maim or kill more powerfully. The Snape image we're left with is one of healing (an old enemy, even) contrasted against a true Death Eater who savagely kills indiscriminately.

But the conflict doesn't stop there. In the second punch Harry tells Lupin about his Half-Blood potions book and tries to find out if the Half-Blood Prince could have been one of the Marauders...his father even, which Lupin denies. Harry is searching, still, that connection to his lost family, to his father especially. How ironic is it that the author he thought might be his father is instead the man he distrusts most in this world—Snape?

Delightful detail in scene setting, conflict layered upon conflict, building to the most important at the end of the scene, with character growth emerging as Harry is forced to see Snape through Lupin's eyes, eyes that are a bit more tolerant than Harry's own. Lupin has lived among the vilest killers of his world, he has been shunned by his own society, he's a true "half-breed" in the sense of not belonging to either group, and yet he looks with compassion on a man whom he could hate, but instead sees him with more understanding than Harry is yet prepared to accept.

This is writing to the max. This is a supercharged scene. This is imagination carried into every detail, and yet there are no murders, no exotic locale, and no explosions (except for a bit of exploding Snap).

Oh, one more thing. There's subtext. Take a moment and look again at those unimportant lyrics Celestina warbles out that Fleur finds so distasteful.

> "You ***Charmed the Heart Right Out of Me***"...
> "Oh, my poor heart, where has it gone?
> It's ***left me for a spell***..."
> "and now ***you've torn it quite apart***
> I'll thank you to give back my heart!"
> (p. 311-312)

Who do all these torn and missing, charmed-out hearts remind you of? Voldemort and his Horcruxes. He's there, he's lurking, he's still at large causing disaster and heartbreak and could intrude on our merry Yuletide scene at any moment. Voldemort's heart, his soul, with the aid of the Horcrux spell, has been torn into pieces and removed from where it belongs. In the next book, Harry and friends will be forced to search and destroy those missing, torn pieces of Voldemort's "heart."

This is just a simple little scene, not a turning point, definitely not a climax or a dark moment, and yet it pays off. This is the kind of subtext that gives the reader that extra reward for paying attention, that gets reader buzz buzzing. And this is the kind of delightful exuberance in setting, conflict, and character which makes Harry Potter such a joy to read.

Challenge your students! Every scene they create must stand strong. Each scene must present something new and interesting to the reader. Every scene must have conflict that forces character development, that pushes their protagonist toward his fate. If they challenge themselves this deeply with their story, they will engage not only themselves, but their reader as well.

2) Employ Strong Verbs and Pinpointed Nouns

As educators, one of the strongest challenges we face with our students is getting them to go beyond the basic requirements of the assignment to embrace the spirit of it. Writing is all about communication. Communication with oneself and the outside world. Once a student is truly engaged with their writing, they can more effectively explore their own beliefs and imagination, and convey this in story to their reader.

If you want your students to truly excel; if you want their passion, their voice, to shine through, then help them to see that every single word must contribute to the overall sparkle and depth of their story. A reader cannot get inside a writer's head to see what they *meant* to say. Use this handout below to help your students understand the fine sculpting of their story through word choice. A writer's voice is only as strong as the words that convey it on paper (or screen).

Make Every Word Count: Student Handout

One of the primary lessons in writing is to make each word count. Every single word must carry its weight. It needs to get the job done with the strongest impact in the most compact package possible.

I like to think of a sculptor. A sculptor must first take their block of wood or their slab of marble and cut hunks away to give it general shape. This process is more rough than refining.

For the writer, this first crude step is like vomiting on your page. Get it all out. Dredge up all the passion, all the conflict, all the emotion, intertwined with your characters and your plot, and slap it on the page. Don't worry about making it neat and pretty. The refinement comes later. Then, once you've got your basic shape, look at your emerging sculpture and determine where to refine.

I read once that, when asked how he created his masterpiece David, Michelangelo said something like: "I see David inside the giant marble, and I simply chip away all that is not David."

Michelangelo worked from a philosophy of art called *disegno* (design in Italian), which, for Michelangelo, meant that the human form was there, captured within the marble, lurking in the heart of every slab he carved. His job was simply to find it and release it. *To chip away anything that was not David.*

I feel this in my writing. The story is there inside me. I may not know its form in detail when I start out, but by constantly chipping away and polishing all that is not *it*, the story is released. It comes alive, the soul of the work is freed. I'm merely the tool to release it. To do so, I must chip away all that is not true.

You, too, must find your inner story and release it to the world. You do this with your tools of word refinement: hammers and chisels to give initial shape, rasps for honing and detailing, and vast amounts of sandpaper to sharpen and smooth. Brainstorming, plotting, character analysis, and writing a rough draft are your hammers and chisels. They create the rough, basic shape from which your story will emerge. Next comes revising and editing, endlessly. With these rasps you add the details you couldn't see before, and chip away at anything that is not David. Finally, minute analysis of word choices, strong verbs, pinpointed nouns, overused words, and varied sentence structure will work sandpaper to your creation, polishing and shining it for readers to understand and enjoy.

Two tools that Rowling wields masterfully are strong verbs and pinpointed descriptions. Use the strongest verb to convey your action that doesn't sound unnatural or ludicrous. Why say, "He turned around and walked quickly to the door," if "He pivoted and raced for the door" conveys your meaning stronger and better?

Likewise use precise descriptive nouns or adjectives instead of a generic word that paints a bland picture. Why say, "Liz wiped the wetness off her hands on her new clothes," when you can say, "Liz rubbed sweaty palms against the rough tweed of her new suit."

Instead of general descriptive words, use detailed, pinpointed ones to create a fuller image. Of course, this can all be overdone and become purple prose, but judiciously used and interwoven with action and dialogue, strong, detailed description will allow your reader the feel of watching a vibrant movie on the wide screen.

Rowling does this so much better, so let me give you an example from *Chamber of Secrets*. Notice the bolded key words or phrases.

"Let me introduce my **assistant**, Professor Snape," said Lockhart, **flashing** a wide smile. "He tells me he knows a **tiny little bit** about dueling himself and has **sportingly** agreed to help me with a short demonstration before we begin. Now, I don't want any of you **youngsters** to worry—you'll still have your Potions master when I'm through with him, **never fear**!"

"Wouldn't it be good if they finished each other off?" Ron **muttered** in Harry's ear.

Is **sportingly** a word any of you would use in regard to Snape? Lockhart is clearly, as usual, all fluff and nonsense. He tries to pump himself up with words like **assistant** and **tiny little bit**, **youngsters** and **never fear**! But we know who the true master of dueling is.

Snape's **upper lip was curling**. Harry wondered why Lockhart was still smiling; if Snape had been looking at him like that he'd have been running as fast as he could in the opposite direction.

Lockhart and Snape turned to face each other and bowed; at least, Lockhart did, with much **twirling of his hands**, whereas Snape **jerked his head** irritably. Then they raised their wands like swords in front of them.

35

"As you see, we are holding our wands in the accepted combative position," Lockhart told the silent crowd. "On the count of three, we will **cast our first spells**. Neither of us will be aiming to kill, of course."

"I wouldn't bet on that," Harry **murmured**, watching Snape **baring his teeth**.

While Lockhart is posturing and **twirling**, Snape is **curling** his upper lip, **jerking** his head, and **baring his teeth**. Wonderful word choices that characterize each man delightfully and accurately.

"One—two—three—"

Both of them swung their wands above their heads and pointed them at their opponent; Snape cried: "Expelliarmus!" There was a **dazzling flash of scarlet light** and Lockhart was **blasted off his feet**: He **flew** backward off the stage, **smashed** into the wall, and **slid** down it to **sprawl** on the floor.

Malfoy and some of the other Slytherins **cheered**. Hermione was **dancing on tiptoes**. "Do you think he's all right?" she **squealed through her fingers**.

"Who cares?" said Harry and Ron together.

Lockhart was getting unsteadily to his feet. His hat had fallen off and his wavy hair was **standing on end**.

"Well, there you have it!" he said, **tottering** back onto the platform.

(p. 189-190, *Secrets*)

With a **dazzling flash of scarlet light**, Lockhart is "**blasted off his feet**: He **flew** backward off the stage, **smashed** into the wall, and **slid** down it to **sprawl** on the floor." Note the strong verbs. The action punches from **blasted**, **flew**, **smashed**, and **slid**, to **sprawl**. No wimpy **looking** or **turning** here.

Then, of course, we've got Ron and Harry **muttering** and **murmuring** while Hermione **danced** on tiptoes and "**squealed** through her fingers." Each character acts in a manner appropriate to their personality, but with interesting, strong verbs with punch.

You have to laugh as Lockhart **totters** back onto the platform. No staggering for him.

Indeed, certain words choices in and of themselves hint at a masculine or feminine character. It's interesting to highlight the words choices of Snape, Lockhart, and Hermione, because with Snape we're basically getting a strong, angry adult male, with Lockhart, a puffed-up, slightly effeminate male, and with Hermione, a young girl. Therefore, we should see some strong contrasts in the descriptive words used:

- *Snape*: upper lip curling, jerked his head irritably, baring his teeth
- *Lockhart*: flashing, tiny little bit, sportingly, youngsters, twirling of hands, getting unsteadily to his feet, wavy hair standing on end, tottering
- *Hermione*: dancing on tiptoes, squealed through her fingers.

The Snape word choices are very strong, almost animalistic with that **baring of teeth**. Traditionally speaking, you would not paint a flattering picture of a female by using any of those descriptions, but you can paint a strong angry male with them. Snape does not "almost" bare his teeth, nor does he "grimace." He doesn't "wince" or "twitch" his head irritably—none of those words choices are what is traditionally considered masculine.

With Lockhart, however, we've got **flashing, twirling, unsteadily**, and **tottering**—while all good strong verb choices, they paint an entirely different picture, also rather juvenile. The words he speaks, **sportingly** and **youngsters** are also more feminine than say something like "grudgingly" and "brats."

Then Hermione—we see her here, in the midst of her twelve-year-old infatuation, acting positively schoolgirl giddy—**dancing on tiptoes, squealing through her fingers**. Could you see Snape dancing or squealing? Word choice makes the man, and the young girl!

A bit of clarification on defining words as masculine or feminine—you'll notice that I characterized this concept as "traditional." As a writer, *you* decide which words fit your characters best, even if it is contrary to traditional understandings. However, the trick in playing with reader expectations is knowing what those expectations are in the first place.

For me, this kind of careful word choice takes place in the various revisions that follow a completed first draft. The

Word find function and the thesaurus are my greatest friends with fine-tuning each verb. Seek out the words that you know you overuse or fall back on, those that are easy to think of but don't add much in the way of action. Then use your thesaurus to pinpoint the exact verb to give your story needed punch.

Aside from strong verbs, Rowling also uses detailed and pinpointed nouns and adjectives to bring her fresh and vivid worldbuilding to life. For a great example, I turned to a section in *Deathly Hallows*, where Harry, Ron, and Hermione are approaching Luna Lovegood's home for the first time:

> ...Ron was pointing upward, toward the top of the hill on which they had appeared, where a most strange-looking house rose vertically against the sky, a **great black cylinder** with a **ghostly moon hanging** behind it in the afternoon sky. "That's got to be Luna's house, who else would live in a place like that? It looks like a giant **rook**!"...

> ...The gate creaked as they opened it. The **zigzagging path** leading to the front door was overgrown with a variety of odd plants, including a bush covered in the **orange radishlike fruit** Luna sometimes wore as earrings. Harry thought he recognized a **Snargaluff** and gave the **wizened stump** a wide berth. Two **aged crab apple trees, bent with the wind, stripped of leaves but still heavy** with **berry-sized red fruits** and **bushy crowns of white-beaded mistletoe**, stood **sentinel** on either side of the front door. A little owl with a slightly **flattened, hawklike head** peered down at them from one of the branches.

(p. 397-98, *Hallows*)

There's so much here to notice in such compact space! In the first paragraph, the use of the one noun **rook** carries more than one meaning. Not only is it specific in describing the tall cylindrical "castle" in which the Lovegoods live, but it also provides a link between them and their Ravenclaw (birdlike) heritage. Furthermore, and this is the coolest part, that **rook** along with the ominous moon **hanging** in the sky provide the reader a warning that something is about to go down. Rowling has used much chess imagery in her novels before, especially in *Philosopher's/Sorcerer's Stone*, and here she's using this **black** rook as an allusion to a chess "siege tower" to hint that the trio is going to be attacked once they enter.

In the second paragraph cited, the **zigzagging path**, **orange radishlike fruit**, and the other fruit images characterize the Lovegoods as nature-lovers, but a bit wacky. Notice that the specific, detailed descriptions help the reader to visualize clearly what Harry is seeing: "**aged crab apple trees**," "**berry-sized fruits**," "**bushy crowns of white-beaded mistletoe.**" No generic "they passed by trees and flowers" here. The **"bent with the wind, stripped of leaves"** provides more description in a slightly dark tone. And see how cleverly she uses the foreign word **Snargaluff**, but then provides us with the description **wizened stump** in a natural, non-instructional manner to help us remember what it is.

The last thing I wish to point out about this packed scene description is the undertone of warning carried through from the first paragraph. **Sentinels** stand by the door, and the owl with the **hawklike head** spies down on them. Not only is that "hawklike" another nod to their Ravenclaw heritage, the use of these guarding, spy-like words is a warning to the reader: be on the lookout. Something dangerous is afoot.

One distinction I'd like to note—Rowling utilizes many more *'ing* verbs (the progressive form) than we've been taught to use in our own writing. I've heard that the progressive form is more common in British literature in general. The *'ed* conjugation (the past tense) is stronger, but not meant as the sole diet by any means. Variety is the spice of life, especially when it comes to word choices in writing.

Every writer has words they overuse. Quite often, unfortunately, these are also weak words. Some of mine are just, quite, almost, there are, about, might, stepped, moved, turned, smiled, nodded, shrugged, and looked. These are perfectly good words that must be used upon occasion. Words like "just" and "quite" are often unnecessary and can *just* be eliminated. Cut them out.

As far as **turned**, **looked**, **stepped**, **smiled**, and **moved**—I liken these words to oatmeal or mashed potatoes. Good old comfort words. Easy to use, getting at necessary action, but not requiring much in the way of chopping, spices, or imagination.

These weak words are mine, plus many, many more. Define your own weak or overused wordlist, then conduct your own word hunt. *Word search* is a powerful tool. Use it well. Seek and destroy any weak, impassive, or overly used words that keep your prose from sparkling. Make your verbs, your descriptions, the absolute strongest they can be *without turning purple*—you **can** go too far. Keep your reader glued to your every single word until the end.

Take Away

Rowling has challenged us as writers to break free from the inhibiting bars of our own Azkaban prison. Imagine limitless possibilities. Ask yourself at the end of every scene, and especially at the end of every story, have you given your reader something extra, a touch they can only get from you? Have you included a piece of magic in everything you create? If not, go back and revise.

I find that this magic comes through most strongly in revisions. It seems to take me several edits of cleaning, paring down, beefing up, and fine sculpturing to finally polish that necessary gleam into my stories.

We can even take some advice from Barty/Mad-Eye—know your strengths, and play to them. Understand your writer's soul and release her into every story, every scene, every carefully constructed word you produce on the page.

STUDENT CHALLENGE
STRONG VERBS AND PINPOINTED NOUNS

One of the primary lessons in writing is to make each word count. Every single word must carry its weight.

Instead of general descriptive words, use detailed, pinpointed ones to create a fuller image. Of course, this can all be overdone and become purple prose, but judiciously used and interwoven with action and dialogue, strong, detailed description will allow your reader the feel of watching a vibrant movie on the wide screen.

Study the examples from the duel scene in the handout and note how each descriptive word matches the character it is attached to. Also note how it is specific and strong, creating a very vivid scene.

Choose your words wisely to make your scenes come as alive in your reader's head as they are in yours.

Finding Your Voice & Style: Activity

DURATION:
Approximately one (1) hour.

SYNOPSIS:
In this activity, students will think critically about how they react in different situations. They must identify an event in their lives where they were filled with anger, happiness, fear, love, or disbelief. Using these events as fuel, they will create short scenes that **show** their emotions in each situation and how they acted. Students will then share this experience with a partner and see if their partner would have reacted the same or differently. Through this activity, they will reflect on what events have shaped their personality and voice as well as the importance and impact a strong voice has on the reader and their engagement with the story.

COMMON-SENSE APPROACHES TO TEACHING
Collaboration and Reflection

STANDARDS:
This activity requires strong reflections on behalf of the students. They must be aware of their reactions in different environments and be willing to write honestly about their feelings.

TEACHER INSTRUCTIONS

UNCOVERING EMOTIONS FROM THE PAST
Have students use the accompanying student handout to pinpoint events from their past that have had an intense effect on shaping them as an individual.

MAKING SENSE OF THE EMOTIONS
Once students have completed their story handouts, they will think critically about the nouns, adjectives, and verbs they have used to describe each emotion. Using the examples and lessons learned in Employ Strong Verbs and Pinpointed Nouns, have them evaluate and edit their scene to make sure it's as strong and vivid as they can make it.

GROUP ELEMENT (OPTIONAL)
If students feel willing to let their classmates read their experiences, then this activity is a great tool to practice awareness of diverse points of view. On the following group activity page, students will rewrite the strongest event they described in the prior exercise. Their partner must write a brief description of how they would feel if the event happened to them. Afterwards, the students should compare the similarities and differences to their reactions to the same event.

Finding Your Voice: Students Handout

BEFORE YOU BEGIN

In this activity, you must think about events in your past that helped shape you into the individual you are today. Think critically about a specific situation where you felt angry or happy due to unfolding events or the actions of another. In each of the boxes below, prepare a short scene of what happened. Be sure to be as descriptive as possible. Use strong verbs and pinpointed descriptive nouns and adjectives to show through action the emotions you experienced. When you finish, read your descriptions and make sure they are free of errors.

Emotion of study	Event that caused your feelings	Description of your event in first person.
Anger		
Happiness		
Fear		
Love		
Disbelief		

Improving Style: Mini Activity:

Take the voice exercise you just completed showing how you reacted to various emotions and choose a few different color highlighters.

Highlight your descriptive words in one color. Highlight your verbs with a different color. To make it even more challenging, those that apply to a certain character should have its own color.

Examine your word choices. Are they specific to that character? Are they as strong and pinpointed as they can appropriately be? How could you make it stronger?

Finding Your Voice: Group Reflection

PARTNER 1 INSTRUCTIONS: Now that you have written short descriptions of five (5) events in the *Finding your Voice* activity, choose the one that had the most impact on your life. Rewrite the event in the space below, refining it to **show** (through action and dialogue) as much emotion as possible. Then, give it to your partner.

PARTNER 2 INSTRUCTIONS: Read the event that your partner has written below. Write a short description of how you would react to the same situation. Be sure to write in first person and be honest in how you would react if you were to go through the same event.

Partner 1: Event that shaped you:

Partner 2: Reaction:

REFLECTION:

Each partner will read the other's reaction. Consider any differences or similarities. What elements of your life and culture might affect the differences? In the space provided below, work together to write a SINGLE definition of the word CULTURE. Make sure to include the importance culture has in shaping our reactions and the people we become.

DEFINE: Culture

Lesson Three

The Dark Lord is in the Detail
(Worldbuilding)

Worldbuilding. It's a concept that drives terror into the heart of many a young writer. Others seem to thrive on it, but maybe to the extreme. Many writers associate worldbuilding exclusively with the Science Fiction or Fantasy genre. In reality, all writers must do it to one degree or another.

Helping your students create a world for their characters to inhabit in a coherent, enchanting manner will make their world come alive for them just as much as for their reader. As I noted in the first lesson—although there are many technical reasons for the HP phenomenon, there are three that top the list:

    1) engaging, quirky characters,

    2) the trail-of-clues mystery, and

    3) a fabulous world to play in.

Most readers cite the worldbuilding as the lure that drew them into the series to begin with. Rowling constructed her world as solidly as the Shrieking Shack to hold the magic together. She riddled the text with such delightful detail that readers fully believed that they were living among wizards and witches, goblins and house-elves, giants and ghosts, and basilisks and hippogriffs.

Rowling uses many layers to create her world. The details are rich, well-developed, and usually quite fun. They also have deeper layers of meaning. Many of the details are taken from mythology and/or hide clues to the series' ongoing mysteries. Most are used more than once, in different ways. The chocolate frogs are not just a kid's sweet treat that binds Harry and Ron, but also reveal an important clue about Nicolas Flamel. Likewise, the gillywater is not just a drink McGonagall favors in *Azkaban*, but produced from a weed Harry needs in *Goblet* to breathe under water. Fans went crazy over Drooble's Best Blowing Gum trying to find anagrams and meaning in the wrapper Neville's mom repeatedly gives him (until Rowling zapped that theory on her website).

Through this lesson your students will examine the techniques Rowling successfully employs for worldbuilding and practice applying it to their own work.

Overview:

    1) Use a wide-angle lens—the broad characteristics that create a sense of a complete, bustling world.

    2) Zoom in on the detail—adding depth, layers, and hiding places for clues.

    3) Give that extra zing in detail and interaction.

    4) Rule-build your world—how to ensure it all make sense together.

    5) The laws of magic—constructing a coherent system.

    6) Introduce your reader to your world.

Viewing Through a Wide-Angle Lens

When you look at the magical world Rowling has created through a wide-angle lens, you'll see a setting bursting at its seams. Although until *Hallows* Harry spends the bulk of his time in one location, the reader knows through references, Pensieve scenes, and "field trips" that Hogwarts is centered in a world as full and complex as the one we Muggles call home.

I find it highly significant that Harry's introduction to the wizarding world was not at Hogwarts but at Diagon Alley. Think about it—Rowling could have had Harry's books and supplies provided by the school once he arrived. However, she wanted the reader to experience from the start that the Special World Harry was entering was full and complete and only diagonally set apart from our own.

At Diagon Alley, in that first visit with Hagrid, Harry encounters the Leaky Cauldron, Tom the barman, all the customers who are thrilled to finally meet him, Doris Crockford several times, and hears about vampires from the stuttering Professor Quirrell. He passes shops and pedestrians on his way to the wizarding bank, Gringotts, where he meets goblins and hurtles hundreds of miles below London on a wild amusement park ride, past an underground lake and dragons, to his own vault of gold. He notices several boys his age with their noses pressed up against a shop window, all gazing longingly at the Nimbus 2000. And he meets a snotty rich kid trying on robes at Madam Malkin's who asks if his parents were "our kind." He visits Flourish and Blotts, the Apothecary, and Eeylops Owl Emporium as he acquires his books, quills, parchment, a cauldron, potion supplies, and a birthday gift from Hagrid—Hedwig. Finally, at Ollivanders, his wand chooses him, and he learns the special connection he has through his wand's phoenix core to He-Who-Must-Not-Be-Named.

All of that in one chapter.

As the book and the series progress, Harry's Special World, like Perkins' tent or the trunk of the Ford Anglia, magically enlarges even more. He hears about, experiences as visions through the Pensieve or dreams, or visits places that all play a major role in not only fleshing out his world, but properly casting and telling the story. There are vital clues and information that need to be conveyed to the reader in each of these settings, shown on the chart on the next page.

The chart is by no means an exhaustive list. I just hit the biggies. All these added dimensions gave a wide scope to Harry's world. Even the minor settings, however, contributed to the whole.

Azkaban is fully realized in most readers' minds, even though Harry never actually visited there. The witches from Salem Massachusetts are mentioned in the Quidditch World Cup scene as a nod to her American audience. And who would have loved to see Stubby Boardman get hit in the ear with a turnip at his concert in the Little Norton Church Hall, as mentioned by The Quibbler?

Through inexhaustible details supplied by the magical witch or wizard cards, history of magic classes, articles in the *Daily Prophet*, mentions in the schoolbooks *Fantastic Beasts and Where to Find Them* and *Quidditch Through the Ages*, and notes and updates to Rowling's website, various other locations are mentioned. As well as hiding clues, these secondary settings contribute to the build-up of a world that feels as if it's been around for a long time.

Rowling displays her series through a very wide lens. The reader experiences a vibrant world thriving and interacting on a daily basis. A world full of people who are going to be affected by Harry's choices. Some of these people live or die as a direct result of Harry's actions.

Harry is an epic hero. His actions and choices have wide-ranging consequences. In a story such as this, the world must be set extra-large in order for the reader to truly accept that Harry's fate affects so many.

Of course, Rowling had a seven-book series to work in these various scenes and elements. Your student, most likely, is working with a story of more limited word count. Plus, their story may be of a quieter nature. Their hero or heroine may not determine the fate of the world. However, their characters' actions will still affect others, and those others must be determined and portrayed before the end of the story.

To me, worldbuilding starts with three key questions:

1) Who will be affected by my protagonist's choices?
2) Who are the necessary support characters to aid my protagonist on his or her journey?
3) Where do these people live, work, socialize, shop, and otherwise interact with others?

The Wide Angle Lens of Harry's Magical World

Setting/Element	Muggle Parallel	Important Element(s)
Hogsmeade	An entirely magical village	Aberforth, Madam Rosmerta, secret passageways into Hogwarts, as well as places for dates, candies, and pranks for students.
St. Mungo's	Hospital	The condition of Neville's parents.
Ministry of Magic	Government	Fudge, the Department of Mysteries, the nature of power and corruption.
Department of Mysteries	Research facility	A prophecy, some brains, a veiled arch, and lots of mysteries.
Beauxbatons and Durmstrang	Foreign schools	Fleur, idea of international cooperation.
Azkaban	Prison	Sirius and Bellatrix, and political abuse/torture through the Dementors.
The Burrow	The Weasley home	The Weasleys, Harry's adopted family.
Grimmauld Place	Sirius Black's home and Order headquarters	Familial connections in the wizarding world. Oh, and a Horcrux.
Godric's Hollow	Lily and James' home village	Where it all started, Harry's parents' grave, and one very important symbol.
Quidditch World Cup	The World Soccer Cup	Krum and both Barty Crouches.
The Daily Prophet	Newspaper	Lots of propaganda and misinformation, and a few nuggets of truth.
The Quibbler	A tabloid	An alternative view of the world as well as a few nuggets of truth.
Little Hangleton	Riddle and Gaunt hometown	Tom Riddle's first murder and a Horcrux.
Tom Riddle's orphanage	Riddle's "home"	The nature of the orphaned Tom.
Tom Riddle's cave	Riddle's hiding place	A fake Horcrux and the transition from Dumbledore leading Harry to Harry supporting his mentor.
Slughorn's home	Muggle dwelling	A good Slytherin with a crucial memory.
Malfoy Manor	Rich "gated" mansion	The Malfoy's; Voldemort's "Council" meeting.

Encourage your students to build their world based on those who will affect their heroine and those who will be affected by her. Then spread out from there as needed. An epic quest will require a broader world than a short story. Each requires an interesting world, though, a world the reader believes in and wishes to spend some time in.

Focusing in Through a Zoom Lens

Before we get into this section, I'd like for you (and your students) to read chapter five, "Diagon Alley," in *Philosopher's/Sorcerer's Stone*. Pay attention to the extreme detail with which Rowling created this introduction to the magical world. Notice not only the meticulous listing of uniforms, books, and equipment Harry will need to purchase, but the "windows stacked with barrels of bat spleens and eels' eyes, tottering piles of spell books, quills, and rolls of parchment, potion bottles, globes of the moon." (p. 72) Remember the smell of the Apothecary, "a mixture of bad eggs and rotted cabbages. Barrels of slimy stuff stood on the floor; jars of herbs, dried roots, and bright powders lined the walls; bundles of feathers, strings of fangs, and snarled claws hung from the ceiling." (p. 80-81)

Go on, read. I've only noted a couple of items and you must read this chapter, focused on her minute worldbuilding, to truly appreciate the imagination she put into creating Harry's world.

Now that you've returned—Rowling filled her world with such exquisite details, and loads of them, that her critics claimed it was overdone. But consider her primary market—kids eat this stuff up, quite literally:

Check out the next page. I kept the Magical Flavors list short, just to give you the idea.

From the Department of International Magical Cooperation in *Goblet* to the Department of Mysteries in *Phoenix*, every single floor of the Ministry played a role in the series. With all of the hexes, Hagrid's creatures, and threatened poisonings passing through the halls of Hogwarts, Rowling could probably have filled every one of St. Mungo's floors as well.

She puts an incredible amount of thought behind each element she creates to not only meet the story's needs, but to contribute beyond mere window dressing. Whether emphasizing a theme, providing information, or hiding clues, the details pack a powerful whomp.

The purpose of creating the zoom-lens detail is similar to that for creating the wide-lens view: providing plaster and paint to the themes and tone of the novel. In Rowling's world, this all fleshes out a world of fun and magic. Later, the details contribute to the increasing dark tone, to the mysteries, and the sense of impending doom.

Your students should determine the parts of the world that greatly affect their story and spend their world building energy there. Encourage them to choose their descriptions judiciously, opting for those that set the item out of the ordinary. In other words, don't describe a closet as dark and cramped; the reader will assume that. Describe instead what sets it apart, what distinguishes it from other closets. That's where they should spend your words. Make each word earn its place in their story.

For me, while the wide-angle level of detail usually is preliminary work, either while I'm plotting the story or in an early draft, the zoom lens is one I best employ in the multiple revisions and final draft stages. It seems to me that I can more accurately pinpoint that description of an ancient relic, a garden the heroine works in, the foods at a romantic dinner, once I know and understand my characters, their conflicts, and my plot the best. This usually happens later. I might nail some details early on, but mostly they have to be refined and revised as I plow through endless edits.

Endless edits is probably not the phrase your students wish to hear. But, especially for your more eager writers, it is an absolutely necessary skill to learn. Encourage them with the attitude that worldbuilding takes time, and they don't have to get it right in the first draft. If in an initial round they cannot picture exactly how that threatening death mask sent from their villain to their heroine will look, don't sweat it. They should mark their place, keep the flow of words going, and go back to it in a later revision. When they have fully imagined their characters and story, then the features of the death mask will come to them as if they knew it all along.

Flavorful, Fun Details: Student Handout

Notice that Rowling doesn't pad her world with merely any kind of food, but interesting, fun treats and drinks that will tempt the hungry imagination of her audience. And Rowling doesn't limit her creativity to foods. Here's a sampling of the school books mentioned:

Again, though it may not seem like it, this is a brief sample. I compiled it from a complete one, with notes, at the *Harry Potter Lexicon* (www.hp-lexicon.org/wizworld/books.html). Although almost every

Magical Flavors

- Bertie Bott's Every Flavor Beans
- Drooble's Best Blowing Gum
- Chocolate Frogs
- Cauldron Cakes
- Licorice Wands
- Pepper Imps
- Sugar Quills
- Blood Flavored Lollipops
- Cockroach Clusters
- Fudge Flies
- Butterbeer
- Gillywater
- Ogden's Old Firewhiskey
- Pumpkin Pasties
- Jelly Slugs
- Fizzing Whizbees
- Peppermint Toads
- Acid Pops
- Hagrid's Treacle Fudge
- Mulled Mead
- Elderflower Wine
- Magotty Haggis (served at the Deathday Party)

School Books

- *Advanced Potion-Making* by Libatius Borage (lists instructions for making the Draught of Living Death)
- *The Beaters' Bible* by Brutus Scrimgeour (wonder if he's related to Rufus Scrimgeour?)
- *Blood Brothers: My Life Amongst the Vampires* by Eldred Worple
- *Broken Balls: When Fortunes Turn Foul*
- *Charm Your Own Cheese* by Gerda Catchlove
- *Dragon Breeding for Pleasure and Profit*
- *The Dream Oracle* by Inigo Imago
- **Fantastic Beasts and Where to Find Them** by Newt Scamander
- *Gadding with Ghouls* by Gilderoy Lockhart
- *Guide to Advanced Transfiguration*
- **Hairy Snout, Human Heart**
- *Handbook of Do-It-Yourself Broom Care*
- *Handbook of Hippogriff Psychology*
- **A History of Magic** by Bathilda Bagshot
- **Hogwarts: A History** (a treasure trove of information)
- *Invisible Book of Invisibility* (Flourish and Blotts could never find them)
- *Magical Me* by Gilderoy Lockhart
- **Magical Water Plants of the Mediterranean**
- **Magick Most Evile** (mentions the Horcrux)
- *Men Who Love Dragons Too Much*
- **Moste Potente Potions** (contains instructions for brewing the Polyjuice Potion)
- **Nature's Nobility: A Wizarding Genealogy**
- *One Minute Feasts—It's Magic!*
- *Quidditch Through the Ages* by Kennilworthy Whisp
- **Quintessence: A Quest**
- *Unfogging the Future* by Cassandra Vablatsky

book Rowling created contributed to her worldbuilding in more than one way, those that I bolded either highlighted an important theme, conveyed useful information, or hinted at an ongoing mystery or upcoming plot twist.

While most of the foods listed earlier are thrown in to add flavor, some of them also contain clues or play a role in the story (Chocolate Frog Cards provided a clue to Flamel, Acid Pops were a password to Dumbledore's office). Most of Rowling's details add something extra, whether hiding or highlighting a clue, or providing information on the history or backstory of the characters and setting. If Rowling mentions a flower that Harry passes en route to Hagrid's, she's going to specify the color and variety, and both are probably going to hint at a theme or mystery.

Ministry of Magic and St. Mungo's Floor Charts: Student Handout

Ministry of Magic Level Guide:

Level/Floor	Department
Level One	Unknown
Level Two	Department of Magical Law Enforcement: Improper Use of Magic Office, Auror Headquarters, Wizengamot Administration Services
Level Three	Department of Magical Accidents and Catastrophes: Accidental Magic Reversal Squad, Obliviator Headquarters, Muggle-Worthy Excuse Committee
Level Four	Department for the Regulation and Control of Magical Creatures: Beast, Being and Spirit Divisions, Goblin Liaison Office, Pest Advisory Bureau
Level Five	Department of International Magical Cooperation: International Magical Trading Standards Body, the International Magical Office of Law, the International Confederation of Wizards, British Seats
Level Six	Department of Magical Transport: Floo Network Authority, Broom Regulatory Control Portkey Office, Apparation Test Centre
Level Seven	Department of Magical Games and Sports: British and Irish Quidditch League Headquarters, Official Gobstones Club, Ludicrous Patents Office
Level Eight	The Atrium, fireplaces for arrivals and departures, lifts to other floors, Visitor Check-in, Fountain of Magical Brethren
Level Nine	Department of Mysteries: Circular Room with 12 Doors, Brain Room, Death Chamber, Hall of Prophecy, Locked Room, Planet Room, Time Room. Offices
Level Ten	Courtroom Ten, probably other courtrooms not specified

Note: Level Ten is the lowest, Level One the highest.

(p. 129-136, *Phoenix*)

St. Mungo's Floor Guide:

Floor	Division
Ground	ARTIFACT ACCIDENTS Cauldron explosion, wand backfiring, broom crashes, etc.
First	CREATURE-INDUCED INJURIES Bites, stings, burns, embedded spines, etc.
Second	MAGICAL BUGS Contagious maladies, e.g. dragon pox, vanishing sickness, scrofungulus, etc.
Third	POTION AND PLANT POISONING Rashes, regurgitation, uncontrollable giggling, etc.
Fourth	SPELL DAMAGE Unliftable jinxes, hexes, and incorrectly applied charms, etc.
Fifth	VISITORS' TEAROOM AND HOSPITAL SHOP

(p. 485-486, *Phoenix*)

Giving that Extra Zing

Remember how we talked in prior lessons about giving the reader more? More depth of character, more layers of themes and analogies, more subtext, more clues? As your students build their world, not only should they strive to give more wideness and detail, but encourage them to really kick up a few (a very few) descriptions so that they sizzle with an **extra zing**.

Let me give a few examples, first in a scene where the trio are trying to find their way to Divinations and Harry notices a painting of a fat, dapple-gray pony:

A moment later, a **short, squat** knight in a suit of armor clanked into the picture after his pony. By the **look of the grass stains on his metal knees, he had just fallen off**.

"Aha!" he yelled, seeing Harry, Ron, and Hermione. "What villains are these, that trespass upon my private lands! Come to scorn at my fall, perchance? Draw, **you knaves, you dogs**!"

They watched in astonishment as the little knight tugged his sword out of its scabbard and **began brandishing it violently, hopping up and down in rage**. But the sword was too long for him; **a particularly wild swing made him overbalance, and he landed facedown in the grass**.

"Are you all right?" said Harry, moving closer to the picture.

"Get back, you scurvy braggart! Back, you rogue!"

The knight seized his sword again and used it to **push himself back up, but the blade sank deeply into the grass** and, though he pulled with all his might, he couldn't get it out again. Finally, he had to flop back down onto the grass and **push up his visor to mop his sweating face**.

At this point, Harry asks the knight the way to the North Tower.

"A quest!" The knight's rage seemed to vanish instantly. He **clanked to his feet** and shouted, "Come follow me, **dear friends**, and we shall find our goal, or else shall perish bravely in the charge!"

He **gave the sword another fruitless tug, tried and failed to mount the fat pony, gave up**, and cried, "On foot then, good sirs and gentle lady! On! On!"

And he ran, clanking loudly, into the left side of the frame and out of sight.

They hurried after him along the corridor, following the sound of his armor. Every now and then they **spotted** him running through a picture ahead.

"**Be of stout heart, the worst is yet to come**!" yelled the knight...

"Farewell!" cried the knight, **popping his head into a painting of some sinister-looking monks**. "Farewell, my **comrades-in-arms**!..."

(p. 99-101, *Azkaban*)

This is a long example, but it's a good one for many reasons. Most of the phrases I bolded are because I find them a delightful bit of detailed imagination which bring this pseudo-man within a fantasy world completely to life. Notice how the descriptions pass quickly because they are interwoven with action and dialogue, not dropped in one boring lump. This is detail that moves and sings and gives the reader more than just the minimum needed—a knight in a picture pointing the trio's way.

Rowling's imagination is pure delight. How many of you ever had to find your way to class by following behind a deranged knight on a quest through other paintings? Notice the sweat on his face, the sinister-looking monks (how can monks be sinister looking?). It's this type of imaginative imagery that thrills the readers and makes them obsess over Harry Potter.

"Spot," too, how Harry, Ron, and Hermione go from being "knaves" and "*dogs*" to "good friends" to "comrades-in-arms." With these details in a book that centers on Sirius (Padfoot) transforming from being viewed as a murdering betrayer or the deathly Grim, to loyal friend at the end of *Azkaban*, and comrade-in-arms by *Phoenix*—I hardly think this **dog** reference, or this set-up, is accidental. After all, the reader must **be of stout heart, for the worst is yet to come**! Thus, this bit of worldbuilding packs a powerful clue-filled punch.

Here's a slightly different example from *Goblet*:

The Hogwarts staff, demonstrating a continued desire to impress the visitors from Beauxbatons and Durmstrang, seemed determined to show the castle at its best this Christmas...***Everlasting icicles*** had been attached to the banisters of the marble staircase; the usual twelve Christmas trees in the Great Hall were bedecked with everything from ***luminous holly berries*** to ***real, hooting, golden owls***, and the ***suits of armor had all been bewitched to sing carols whenever anyone passed*** them. It was quite something to hear "O Come, All Ye Faithful" sung by an empty helmet that only knew half the words. Several times, Filch the caretaker had to ***extract Peeves from inside the armor, where he had taken to hiding, filling in the gaps in the songs with lyrics of his own invention, all of which were very rude.***

(p. 395, *Goblet*)

Even though this is a lump of description, it's kept from being boring by the imaginative, unusual imagery and the action within. That last bit, about Peeves filling in rude lyrics, is the zest. Rowling could easily have stopped with the everlasting icicles, the hooting, gold owls, and the singing suits of armor. That would have provided the whimsical Christmas feel she was after. In taking it that extra level—the Peeves factor—she adds an elusive zing to make the whole description come alive...and loads of fun.

One of my favorite descriptions on steroids, which has already been presented in lesson two, was the Christmas tree gnome topping the Weasley tree in *Half-Blood*.

Stupefied, painted gold, stuffed into a miniature tutu and with small wings glued to its back, it glowered down at them all, the ugliest angel Harry had ever seen, with a large bald head like a potato and ***rather hairy feet***.

(p. 309, *Half-Blood*, Bloomsbury)

Those hairy feet add the zing to an already delightful description. I would love to be able to come up with something so clever, amusing, and imaginative.

Challenge your students: What nuance can they add to their perfectly good description to give it that extra sparkle?

Creating with such descriptive flair may come to some of your students naturally, out of the blue, when their mind is at rest, or when they're focused and tapping away at their creation. Or, like many of us, they may have to work at it. Encourage them to talk their story aloud, brainstorm with a friend, keep a notebook beside them when their mind is at rest.

This level of detail comes through many layers of polishing. With practice, your students can learn how to add a special layer to their story, in an appropriate way, to really tie-up their Christmas tree gnomes.

Keep in mind that these details are to be woven in. **A little zing goes a long way**. Emphasize to your students that they don't want paragraph upon paragraph of description without dialogue and action keeping the pace afloat. No matter how interesting the imagery, narrative exposition still slows the pace.

The goal here is compact punch. They should hit their description, hit it hard, and twist it out of the ordinary. Make it sing as brilliantly or raunchy as Rowling's suits of armor.

Rule-Building: Appoint Yourself Minister for Magic

In order for your student's fabulous creation to appear as equally awe-inspiring to their reader as it does to them, it must make sense as a whole. If their reader just sees it as a hodgepodge of attention-grabbing but incongruent elements, she's not likely to buy into their story long enough to keep on reading.

If your student is writing a space opera, have they sufficiently studied the laws of physics and the principles of aerodynamics, not to mention the nature of a laser beam, to create their world realistically? Or, if they've worldbuilt an amusement park where ancient dinosaurs come to life, do they know enough about cloning and dinosaur behavior to have your world make sense? If they've created a matriarchal world of cave-dwellers, do they then have a council of men making the important decisions?

There is real danger among beginning science fiction and fantasy writers to think that just because they are dealing with speculative fiction anything goes. But your student can't simply throw a world on the page because it sounds cool. It has to make sense on some level of the laws of the known universe. Their world has to seem to the reader as if it truly does exist, that it all belongs together and has been in existence for whatever timeline their story calls for. Plus, within the story, they must have an internal guide to what can and cannot happen in their particular world according to the type of story they are telling.

To achieve this level of authenticity, they must appoint themselves Minister for Magic of their world and design and implement all the necessary legalese which will keep their minions running true to form. When we look at Harry Potter, the votes were in place early on from a massive amount of readers that the world Rowling had created made complete, exciting, sense. Fans voted with their wallets. Later, they voted with their involvement, playing in her world with their theories and fan fiction. It was quite evident through the books, and as confirmed through interviews, that Rowling had spent massive amounts of time beforehand planning the elements of her world and how it all worked together. She knew what belonged in her world and what didn't. In her head, she had guidelines to follow for her creation.

> The five years I spent on HP and the Philosopher's Stone were spent constructing The Rules. I had to lay down all my parameters. The most important thing to decide when you're creating a fantasy world is what the characters CAN'T do...
>
> www.accio-quote.org/articles/2000/0700-swns-alfie.htm

Some of her specific rules include:

- The happiest people don't become ghosts.
- No magic power can resurrect a truly dead person.
- Something that you conjure out of thin air will not last.
- The animal one turns into as an Animagus reflects your personality.
- You can do unfocused and uncontrolled magic without a wand, but to do really good magic you need a wand.

www.accio-quote.org/themes/therules.htm

If you'd like to read more of her rules, check out the Accio-Quote's page listed above.

Even though Rowling brought together a vast array of elements to her world—ghosts and poltergeists, trolls and giants, and dragons and merpeople—she gathered them in such a way that worked. Her world of mythic elements had once lived and breathed among Muggles, which is how these magical beings became known to us and passed down in folklore, until the Muggles became too much of a problem to deal with—all those witch burnings. So, the International Confederation of Wizards implemented an International Statute of Wizarding Secrecy. Ever since, the goblins and centaurs and house-elves have been protected underground with the witches and wizards who serve both as their protectors and their paternalistic overlords.

To help your students get into the nitty-gritty of how to create and enforce their own rule-building, it would be helpful to look at a specific subset of Rowling's world and how she did it—her laws of magic.

The Laws of Magic

Rowling draws from traditional motifs in weaving her magic, such as Latin words for the casting of spells, curses, and potions. She weaves in elements traditionally associated with witches in her potion ingredients, animal familiars, and mythical names. Because she uses traditional elements comfortable to the reader (and obviously does quite a bit of research), her magic feels old, mystical, and recognizable.

She creates magic so real that it seems to flow from her characters, an integral part of their personalities and their world. Indeed, that's the key to how she makes magic seem vital, by tying it inherently to the people who use it, varying it by personality and intent.

The wand chooses the wizard and no other wand will work as well for that wizard. Before entering Hogwarts, magic seeps from the magical child's pores, exhibited at times of emotional stress or delight. It works within the natural world—things conjured out of nothing are indefinite, remaining in existence for only a limited time. You can't just pick up any wand and say the words. You must understand the charm, feel the power, focus the mind. More powerful charms require more powerful intent and emotions. According to Pseudo Mad-Eye, the whole class of fourth years could utter an Unforgivable Curse, and he wouldn't get more than a nosebleed.

As Rowling said in the interview mentioned above, she constructed rules, theories, and limits to engineer her magical works. Here are some that come through in her writing (also available on DeepRiver.press as a handout):

1) Magic is intrinsic to the individual. It's as much a part of the witch as her heart or lungs and is not constrained

51

by bloodlines or birth. It can pop up naturally anywhere, among any type of person, though it does tend to run in families. Quite often a Muggle-born child will not even realize the magical abilities they possess (though they will know they are somehow different) until they receive their invitation to Hogwarts. In this way it seems to be like a genetic predisposition, similar to natural hair or eye color, height or eyesight. Something that is beyond the witch or wizard's control.

2) Magic must be nurtured and taught. While the trait occurs naturally, the ability doesn't develop without guidance and training. In this way it's similar to an athletic or musical ability. A person may be born with the physical body or the neuro-programming to make a great athlete or musician, but nothing will come of it if they don't study and train, with discipline. So while the power of a witch or wizard may reflect to some extent on their birthright, its fruition reflects more fully on the work and discipline they put into developing it themselves.

3) Magic varies by the person using it. It is modified or adapted based on the personality of the user or bearer. You see this clearly in the use of the Unforgivable Curses. Bellatrix uses them effortlessly, and it's not just because she's an older, more developed witch. It's also because her dark personality empowers the dark curses. There is also the example of the Amortentia potion, which smelled differently to each person based on what attracted them. Lily was gifted at charms, while James favored transfiguration. Different people possess varying abilities and interests.

4) Related to the above but slightly different, **magic reflects the person using it.** Whereas the rule above shows changes in the effectiveness of the curse or impression of the potion, this rule shows how what certain magic produces varies by individuals, reflecting the personality conjuring it. This is clearly demonstrated in the Animagi, the Patronus, and the Boggarts. All of these magical elements change from individual to individual, no two being exactly alike, demonstrating the power of the personality in projecting the magic. Magic varying by personality is similar to a fingerprint, except the Patronus, Animagi, and Boggart are a lot more interesting.

5) Magic reflects the natural order of the world (or at least our study of it). There is the magic of potions, most like cooking (bet Snape would love that comparison). There is the magic of herbology—gardening or pharmacology. Transfiguration seems an awful lot like engineering. Arithmancy—math. Muggle Studies—Social Studies. The obvious History (of Magic), which really isn't magic itself but the study of those who have used it. Then there are the sciences, which include Astronomy and Care of Magical Creatures—zoology. Charms—involves the discipline of learning any new skill.

6) Anything conjured solely by magic cannot last for long. The leprechaun's gold disappeared, much to Ron's dismay. Magical folk must work for a living, unless they inherit great wealth, just like us Muggles. While a love potion may conjure temporary feelings of love, it will not last once the potion is no longer given—as we saw with Merope Gaunt and Tom Riddle, Sr.

7) Like everything else in the world, magic has a dark and light side, and many shades of gray. It can be used for good, evil, or something not quite either. Magic can save an innocent man from death, or worse, the loss of his soul. It can also rip a soul into seven pieces by taking the lives of others. Magic can bring schools and nations together, as in the Triwizard Tournament and the Quidditch World Cup. It can also tear families and communities apart, as when the Dark Mark appears over a loved one's home or the fallout between Gryffindor and Slytherin. How a person is raised and taught greatly influences how they will use their natural abilities—just as in the real world.

8) Magic has constraints, limitations, and counterbalances—there are boundaries. Magic will not solve your personal issues or the world's ills. It's merely a tool. It cannot give you a Nimbus 2000 if you don't have the money, change a person's emotions indefinitely, or bring a loved one back from the dead to real life. **For each action taken by magic there is usually a counter-effect or balance.**

This last point is one of the most difficult to imagine and use, but one of the most important. As the Muggle Minister asked, why hadn't the wizarding world caught and stopped Voldemort if they could do magic? The true answer is not only because Voldemort can do magic as well, but because magic has its limits. A writer must be careful of creating magic in such a way that it is all powerful—then where is your conflict, where is your growth and development, where is your story? Even Superman must have his kryptonite.

In using magic, encourage your students to think of the repercussions for other parts of their script. Take Apparition for example—a legitimate question from readers is why didn't Lily take Harry and just Apparate out of Godric's Hollow away from Voldemort?[4] Why would any witch or wizard not Apparate out of a dangerous situation?

That's why there must be limitations placed upon the magic and the writer must think through clearly to all the plot holes each magical element will introduce.

This is hard to do. In writing straight contemporaries, it's easier to remember that you have to deal with a heroine-in-jeopardy's ability to make a cell phone call, because most of us use a cell phone every day. But how many of us can Apparate? Thus, that little nuance isn't going to pop into your student's head naturally as they write out a situation in which Apparition might be a possibility. They must think, plan, and set the limits, and they must reflect on all aspects of the story where this bit of magic may occur. Magic has to be carefully constructed and its limits fully fleshed out both in magical theory and in construction of their plot.

STUDENT CHALLENGE

With each piece of magic you create, reflect on what its boundary and opposition is. How can it be counterbalanced? How can it be stopped? What other actions can it possibly affect?

Magic must be figured into the overall theme and conflict of the story. One of the themes Rowling hits hard is that with great power comes great responsibility. It is our choices which determine who we are, not our birthright. Magic will only get you so far, the rest is determined by the choices you make. While magic might make peeling potatoes easier, it does nothing to ease the pain of a beloved son's loss.

You'll need to construct your own rules of magic, not copy someone else's. Be quite ruthless in charting your laws of what magic is in your world, how it is used, and how it is counterbalanced. Create a list of the magical elements you will employ; write your own spellbook. Make sure you understand your magic fully so that you will convey it effectively and not confuse your reader. As much as possible, personalize it to your own characters, plots, and themes.

Encountering a New World: How to Introduce Your Reader

When Harry crosses the threshold of the Leaky Cauldron and enters the Magical World, everyone he meets takes magic for granted. Except for a few Muggle-borns, like Hermione, they've lived with magic their whole lives and it's just part of their natural world. (Hermione makes up for her loss by deliberate over-studying.) Harry's introduction to magic is thus the reader's introduction as well.

Many beginning fantasy writers make it obvious they're using *magic*, something special and out of the ordinary, and intentionally draw the reader's attention to it. Rowling's use is far more casual. She lets us encounter the world as Harry does, since, like us, he's seeing it for the first time. The scene in which Harry meets Draco draws clearly the distinction between those in-the-know and Harry:

"My father's next door buying my books and mother's up the street **looking at wands**," said the boy. He had a bored, drawling voice. "Then I'm going to drag them off to look at **racing brooms**. I don't see why first years can't have their own..."

Harry was strongly reminded of Dudley.

"Have *you* got your own broom?" the boy went on.

"No," said Harry.

"Play Quidditch at all?"

"No," Harry said again, **wondering what on earth Quidditch could be**.

"*I* do—Father says it's a crime if I'm not **picked to play for my house**, and I must say, I agree. Know what house you'll be in yet?"

"No," said Harry, feeling more stupid by the minute.

"Well, no one really knows until they get there, do they, **but I know I'll be in Slytherin, all our family have been—imagine being in Hufflepuff**, I think I'd leave, wouldn't you?"

"Mmm," said Harry, **wishing he could say something a bit more interesting**.

(p. 77-78, *Stone*)

---

[4] Rowling's answer to this was to show in *Hallows* through Voldemort's memory that neither James nor Lily had their wands on them.

Notice, all the bolded words regarding magical elements are casually thrown into the conversation. Harry is a fish-out-of-water, feeling insecure at his lack of knowledge, and grappling with how much he has to learn. His uninitiated POV reflects the reader's. This new world is wonderful and exciting to us, but to those who've lived there all their lives, it's as natural as ours. There's no grand introductory "Everything You Need to Know about Magic 101" nor do the magical characters treat their skills as anything out of the ordinary. Harry learns slowly, gradually, as the need arises, as he encounters new situations. This type of introduction *shows* the reader the new world rather than *telling*.

If your student is using a contemporary, familiar setting, where their character is not a fish-out-of-water, there will be less need to introduce their reader to a Special World. They will still have some level of introduction, as most writers strive to create something unique and interesting in their primary settings.

However, if they're writing in science fiction, fantasy, paranormal romance, historicals, or a foreign locale, encourage them to consider how they will introduce their reader to the world they have created. Will they make the introduction obvious or subtle? How many of their characters will be in-the-know versus the uninitiated? If all their characters are familiar with the setting, but the reader is not, how will they ease the reader into their Special World without whomping them over the head with a lot of explanation disguised as dialogue, or even worse, boring narration?

Rowling's model is to use the fish-out-of-water motif and let the reader discover the Special World through Harry's eyes, learning as he does. Challenge your students: don't draw excess attention to the special powers, or use exposition to explain the world to your reader, just let them discover it for themselves as needed, through action and dialogue, as new situations arise within the plot. In other words, show rather than tell.

In this manner, there is always the feel that a new discovery is just around the Knockturn Alley corner, that surprises lurk behind every Dirigible plum bush, and that the exciting world of Hogsmeade and Hogwarts has not yet been fully explored.

STUDENT CHALLENGE

In worldbuilding, the Dark Lord's in the detail. Add the extra elements, the layers upon layers that turn your descriptions from interesting to zesty. Worldbuild your character interactions as well as your setting because it's those fully fleshed actions that can make your writing take flight.

The final product should view like a movie on the wide screen. Big and full, colorful and sensory packed, detailed and active. Employ all your senses in crafting your details; show them to your reader in action. Then add the extra zings that lets the reader sit back and thoroughly enjoy your story as they would a great movie, viewing fully in their mind's eye all its wonderfully imaginative elements.

And to make sure they're not thrown out of the story, develop rules that help it all fit together. Then introduce them to it naturally. To a world that they will wish to spend time in, and yearn to explore every dark alley and secret passage.

Worldbuilding: Activity

DURATION:
One (1) hour class period followed by possible homework to complete the remainder.

SYNOPSIS:
The worldbuilding activity is a favorite among young writers. In this activity, students should put a silencing charm on their inhibitions and expand their imaginations as fully as Perkins' tent. Students will consider the journey of their protagonist and create secondary characters that will aid and challenge their plight. These secondary characters will inspire the world in which they live—where they work, socialize, shop, etc. Students will choose ONE character that they will portray as they compose an email to the protagonist to apply for a job in this world they have built.

COMMON-SENSE APPROACH TO TEACHING:
Interdisciplinary Creativity

STANDARDS:
Often taken for granted, the composition of emails frightens some students. When they complete part 2 of this activity, have them research online the common practices used in the business world. This will teach them the skill of independence in life-long learning as well as the common-sense approach to teaching we are focusing on in this activity.

BEGIN WITH A STORY:
Hopefully your students have a short story they have developed over several activities in our workbook or a previous work sample from class. If not, they will first need to create a short synopsis of a work of fiction they want to develop further. Once they have a general idea of the main conflict and perhaps an inkling of a resolution, they are ready to begin worldbuilding.

Worldbuilding starts with three key questions:
1) Who will be affected by my protagonist's choices?
2) Who are the necessary support characters to aid my protagonist on his or her journey?
3) Where do these people live, work, socialize, shop, and otherwise interact with others?

Your students will answer these questions through this activity.

Worldbuilding: Student Handout

For this activity, you will create a world for your characters to live in. This is not the time to play it safe. Be daring and bold. Use your creativity to mold an original and intriguing atmosphere—your story depends on it.

IDENTIFYING PLOT POINTS

Consider the journey of your protagonist and choose four (4) points along their story arc that will help pivot or shape continuing events. Plot these points on the handout.

DEFINE YOUR SECONDARIES AND THEIR ACTIONS

The characters that help push events along or hinder their development should be carefully considered. For each plot point, imagine and create unique characters that are essential to that action. These characters can be enemies or friends. They may even be more than one person. Maybe a group of people who form an organization and who share similar views are your supporting characters. Write in their name and a brief description. The chapter on characterization will develop the characters more, but for now we will focus on the world that surrounds them.

HOGWARTS WASN'T BUILT IN A DAY

Worldbuilding takes time. As you expand the conflict and characters in your story, your imagination will grow to expand the world around them—so don't worry. To get started, consider the setting needed to support your characters as you know them now. Be unique and deploy the full capacity of your creativity. Shy away from using imagery you have seen in other works and truly create something of your own imagination. Consider how Rowling twisted elements from the real world into something more interesting. The familiarity of what the reader knows blended with the creativity of the writer is a powerful combination.

Using the chart below, try your hand at building your own world. Then share your world with your classmates in groups.

Protagonist's Plot Points	Secondary Characters and Their Actions	Wide Angle World Element: Where do they live, work, socialize, shoo?	Zoom Angle World Element: What are they eating, reading, buying, driving?	Extra Zing: A short description that packs a punch. Only need 1-2.

Worldbuilding: Continuing with Real-World Skills

In this mini activity, you will choose one of your secondary characters from your worldbuilding practice and compose an email to the protagonist on their behalf. First, use the Internet to research best practices for emails. Using what you find, compose an email using the following directions.

Step 1: Choose your strongest character from the four (4) we focused on in the worldbuilding activity.

Step 2: Consider the relationship between the protagonist and the secondary character you have chosen. Think about any dialogue they might share and how they address one another throughout your story. The language your character uses in the email should represent their feelings (positively or negatively) for the protagonist.

Step 3: The purpose of the email is for your secondary character to apply for a job or request a favor from the protagonist. Challenge your creativity and be sure to reference the complex world you have created. Your character could make mention of places in your world where he has worked before. Or, she could support her request for a favor with how it will benefit part of the community in which she lives. Make sure you mention key items and places that appear in your story. Through your email, your small group should vividly imagine the world in which these characters live.

Have fun with this mini activity! Make jokes and entertain your classmates and teacher.

Lesson Four

Revealing Wormtail
(Mystery Plotting)

In this lesson we'll examine the Harry Potter series as a complex mystery and how your students can learn from Rowling's masterful clue-hiding techniques. Many teachers grew up on Harry Potter and are well familiar with the massive search for clues during the height of the phenomenon. Others maybe not so much. So first, we'll explore how Rowling completely engaged her fans in speculation from one book to the next.

JK Rowling expected a lot from her readers, and she got it. She expected an active participant to pick up on her clues and to follow their trail. What she got was a world full of Harry Potter sleuths who not only jumped in enthusiastically to ferret out the evidence, but also delighted in stringing it together to plaster the Internet with theories of what was yet to come.

The frenzy to share speculation was born not only of the desire to keep the excitement going between books and to share and connect with other HP fans, but also the eagerness to spot a clue before anyone else did. Every fan secretly hoped to have one of her treasured theories confirmed with the next release and to be able to say, "I told you so!" The frenzy at the very end, before *Deathly Hallows* hit the shelves, to post those last-minute theories, was both wildly crazy and astounding.

As mentioned in lesson one, there are three aspects to JK Rowling's writing which were the primary elements that propelled her series from simple bestsellerdom to publishing phenomenon: memorable quirky characters, fabulously detailed worldbuilding, and a well-plotted, engrossing, trail-of-clues mystery. While the characters and the worldbuilding sucked fans into Rowling's magical world, it was when they discovered the trail of clues that they turned from mere fans to truly obsessed fanatics.

In my observation, the readers who question what the hoopla is all about and denounce Rowling as a poor writer are the casual readers who have not yet discovered the world of analogies, myths, clues, and red herrings which live and seethe below the surface.

If you missed out on depth of the Potter phenom and have no idea what I'm talking about when I speak of Rowling's masterful use of dropping clues and withholding secrets, then let me encourage you to first take a dip into the mass hysteria. There are a few archived forums which will give you a thorough indoctrination to the mania with which HP fans searched out and dissected every little nuance of her story (including her interviews). Here are three I recommend:

- The Chamber of Secrets –www.cosforums.com/index.php

- The Leaky Cauldron– www.the-leaky-cauldron.org/features/essays (I used to point to the Leaky Lounge, but unfortunately it is no longer online.)

- Mugglenet– www.mugglenet.com/the-quibbler/the-quibbler-old

Besides the passionate world of fan fiction (which we'll cover in a later chapter) these forums are where fans congregated to feed the frenzy for the next book. The first one listed, Chamber of Secrets, is the official forum of *Mugglenet*, the largest Harry Potter fansite online (by traffic count). The threads you would most want to look at would be "The Stone," located in the "Harry Potter" forum, and "Divination Studies," which is now located under "Harry Potter Archives."

For equal obsession, but a bit more of an adult audience, try the essays on *The Leaky Cauldron*. Both sites have been recognized by Rowling personally with her Fan Site Award. What's even better was that the webmasters were invited after the release of *Half-Blood Prince* to Rowling's home for a personal interview. Melissa Anelli from *The Leaky Cauldron* later obtained more personal interviews with Rowling, which she included in her book detailing the HP phenomenon, *Harry, A History*.

To truly understand Rowling's success, you must experience the obsession for yourself. Especially if you're seeking to inspire your young writers. So, off you go. Take a few minutes, or if you're like me several hours, and immerse yourself in the world of Harry Potter sleuthing. See for yourself what so enthralled the fans that they turned a release party into an event fit for a rock star, what made an eight-year old read an 870-page tome (while praying that *Deathly Hallows* would be even longer). Experience the phenomenon that still has fans writing fan fiction of their own because they can't stand the agonizing separation from Rowling's characters since the series ended. And most of all, see for yourselves the techniques which inspired a whole new generation of writers.

Becoming a Harry Potter Sleuth

Now that you've observed the world of Harry Potter sleuthing, we're going to conduct our own investigation. There are three central questions to the HP mania which drove the search for clues throughout the series:

- What exactly happened in Godric's Hollow?
- Where did Snape's loyalty lay? and
- How would Harry defeat Voldemort?

Although the three questions are simple, the answers are quite complex. Rowling built an elaborate and richly detailed world that is full and complete. What is amazing about her construction is that every aspect of her creation, each character, has something to contribute to these three simple mysteries. Clues are hidden everywhere.

For your students, it will be most helpful to look at a completed trail of clues before tearing apart and analyzing exactly how Rowling created her mysteries. Many initially skeptical readers point to the revelation of Scabbers as Wormtail and the betrayer of James and Lily as their initiation into fandom. It was with *Azkaban*, in the revelation of a three-book trail of clues, that many fans first got the hint of what lurked below the surface in an HP book. They were hooked.

Baiting the Rattrap

The Wormtail thread is also a fairly easy one to analyze, so let's look at how it played out across the three books.

"Hagrid," said Dumbledore, sounding relieved. "At last. And where did you get that motorcycle?"

"Borrowed it, Professor Dumbledore, sir," said the giant, climbing carefully off the motorcycle as he spoke. "Young **Sirius Black** lent it to me. I've got him, sir."

(p. 14, *Stone*)

Here, from the first chapter of the first book, is a key clue to the series and especially to *Azkaban*. Yet the name Sirius Black is thrown in so casually and never mentioned again, that the reader innocently enough would not pick up Sirius Black being at Godric's Hollow as anything important.

We also see from this first chapter Professor McGonagall in her Animagus form, sitting on a wall all day. So we know from the outset that witches and wizards can transform into animals for long periods of time.

Near the beginning of *Azkaban*, Ron is worrying about his pet rat Scabbers, who has been acting unusual since his family's return trip from Egypt (note the reference to Egypt, more later).

"Hm," said the witch, picking up Scabbers. "How old is this rat?"

"Dunno," said Ron. "***Quite old. He used to belong to my brother.***"

"What powers does he have?" said the witch, examining Scabbers closely.

"Er—" The truth was that Scabbers had never shown the faintest trace of interesting powers. The witch's eyes moved from Scabbers's tattered left ear to **his front paw, which had a toe missing**, and tutted loudly.

"He's been through the mill, this one," she said.

"He was like that when Percy gave him to me," said Ron defensively.

"***An ordinary common or garden rat like this can't be expected to live longer than three years or so***," said the witch. "Now, if you were looking for something a bit more hard-wearing, you might like one of these—"

She indicated the black rats, who promptly started skipping again. Ron muttered, "Show-offs."

(p. 59, *Azkaban*)

Rowling flashes three hints here: Scabbers belonged to Percy, he's missing a toe, and he's lived far longer than he should have, but then she immediately distracts us with the entertaining spectacle of skipping black rats. It's also in the very next paragraph when Crookshanks leaps onto Ron's head and chases Scabbers. Now, who would suspect anything out of a cat chasing a rat? So, the reader is immediately thrown into new action, which nicely distracts her from mulling over any clues.

Perhaps the reason Rowling named Percy as Scabbers' former owner, besides showing how Ron always has hand-me-downs, is to hide how old Scabbers really is while at the same time hinting that he's older than he should be. Former ownership also camouflages why Scabbers is missing a toe. Ron doesn't know how Scabbers lost the toe, but that lack of knowledge is not suspect as the pet's not originally his.

A few pages later, Harry overhears Mr. Weasley discussing with his wife the recent escape from Azkaban of Sirius Black and his threat to Harry:

"The guards told Fudge that Black's been talking in his sleep for a while now. Always the same words: *'He's at Hogwarts...he's at Hogwarts.'*"

(p. 66, *Azkaban*)

Something changed recently in Black to make him lose sleep. He's looking for someone at Hogwarts, a male. Through Mr. Weasley, we're led to believe that *he* is Harry. Then there's a crucial scene about mid-way through the book that reveals a ton of clues about Pettigrew, while on the surface condemning Sirius Black. I'm talking about the scene in the Three Broomsticks with Madam Rosmerta:

"Never saw **one without the other**, did you? The number of times I had them in here—ooh they used to **make me laugh**. Quite the **double act**, Sirius Black and James Potter."...

[from McGonagall] "Black and Potter. **Ringleaders of their little gang**. Both were bright, of course—**exceptionally bright**, in fact—but I don't think we've ever had such a **pair of troublemakers**—"

"I dunno," chuckled Hagrid. "***Fred and George Weasley*** could give 'em a run fer their money."

(p. 204, *Azkaban*)

Okay, think. "Never saw one without the other," "double act," "pair of troublemakers," and then the direct connection to the current twin troublemakers. Fred and George just so happened, earlier in this very chapter, to have given Harry the Marauder's Map for him to sneak into Hogsmeade. Coincidence? Not when your name is JK Rowling!

Obviously we're supposed to connect James and Sirius to Fred and George. James and Sirius were "ringleaders of their little gang," "exceptionally bright," and "a pair of troublemakers." Could they have been bright enough to create a map that is turned on by "I solemnly swear that I am up to no good," (p. 192, *Azkaban*) and turned off by "mischief managed?" By juxtaposing the red-haired twins of today to the troublemakers of the past, Rowling gives the reader a hint to the identities of two of the map's original owners. (Note that this type of clue is completely directed to the reader, not the characters within the story).

The Three Broomsticks scene continues as Flitwick talks about what a Fidelius Charm is and how it works, McGonagall reveals that Dumbledore suspected a traitor close to the Potters, and Madam Rosmerta mentions that Peter Pettigrew tagged along after James and Sirius, though not in their league talent-wise. Also, there is some detailed information from Fudge about what appeared to happen between Sirius and Pettigrew:

"I was Junior Minister in the Department of Magical Catastrophes at the time, and I was one of the first on the scene **after Black murdered** all those people. I-I will never forget it. I still dream about it sometimes. A crater in the middle of the street, so deep it had **cracked the sewer below**. Bodies everywhere. Muggles screaming. And Black **standing there laughing**, with what was left of Pettigrew in front of him...a heap of bloodstained robes and a few—**a few fragments**—"

(p. 208, *Azkaban*)

Who would match a rat's missing toe to "a few fragments" left from a long-dead, blown-up wizard? Now, if Rowling had written at this point that the biggest fragment was a finger, then the reader might have had a stronger chance to figure out early on the connection between Scabbers and Pettigrew. Many writers would have written just such a detail here and had their readers guess their secret long before the climax. **However, by not pinpointing the fragment as a finger, Rowling still leaves a clue, just not an easy one.**

Another clue here is that although Fudge was one of the first on the crime scene, he arrived after the murders—and to a gaping hole in the sewer, one a rat could slip through. The only eyewitnesses were Muggles who have since had their memories wiped, and Black was "clearly" out of his mind. If he was such a cold-blooded murderer, why had Black not fled the scene, and why was he standing there laughing? A reader with wits is supposed to pick up on these subtle hints and start stringing the clues together that all was not as it appeared to be, especially to someone as unobservant as Fudge.

Thus, the clues are all there, when you know where to look. As the master magician she is, however, Rowling increases the emotional tension of this scene by having Fudge condemn Sirius as a murdering betrayer. She uses Hagrid's rage to point our attention where she wants it to go, toward Black as the betrayer of Harry's parents, and not toward the clues she's just revealed. That's **sleight of hand**, a technique we'll discuss more in the analysis portion.

The reader is thus left with a story of murder and betrayal, severed body parts, and a double pair of expert troublemakers joined by a map. All this emotional luggage is weighing on Harry when that missing body part is clarified later. Winter break has commenced and Ron and Hermione are trying their hardest to convince Harry not to go after his parents' betrayer himself. Harry shoots back that they don't understand, they don't hear his mum "screaming and pleading with Voldemort" (p. 214).

"You're going to take Malfoy's advice instead of ours?" said Ron ***furiously***. "Listen...you know what Pettigrew's mother got back after Black had finished with him? Dad told me—the Order of Merlin, First Class, and ***Pettigrew's finger in a box***. That was the biggest bit of him they could find. Black's a madman, Harry, and he's dangerous—"

"Malfoy's dad must have told him," said Harry, ***ignoring Ron***. "He was right in Voldemort's inner circle—" (p. 215)

There it is! There's the finger, which is our biggest clue yet linking Pettigrew to Scabbers. But look at the distraction around it. Harry is ignoring Ron, who is furious. Harry is completely focused on his anger, on his desire for revenge, on his mother's voice being murdered. And the reader along with him. All this heightened emotion nicely distracts from the prime clue being laid at the reader's...fingertip.

Shortly after, Harry receives the unexpected gift of the Firebolt, and when Hermione drops in on the boys' dorm room with Crookshanks in hand, the following ensues:

"GET—HIM—OUT—OF—HERE!" Ron bellowed as Crookshanks's claws ripped his pajamas and **Scabbers attempted a wild escape** over his shoulder. **Ron seized Scabbers by the tail** and aimed a misjudged kick at Crookshanks that hit the trunk at the end of Harry's bed, knocking it over and causing Ron to hop up and down, howling with pain.

Crookshanks's fur suddenly stood on end. A shrill, tinny, whistling was filling the room. **The Pocket Sneakoscope** had become dislodged from Uncle Vernon's old socks and **was whirling and gleaming on the floor**.

"I forgot about that!" Harry said, bending down and picking up the Sneakoscope. "I never wear those socks if I can help it...."

The Sneakoscope whirled and whistled in his palm. Crookshanks was hissing and spitting at it.

"You'd better take that cat out of here, Hermione," said **Ron furiously**, sitting on Harry's bed **nursing his toe**.

(p. 225-226, *Azkaban*)

The Sneakoscope sounds an alarm when anyone nearby is untrustworthy. In this scene, the Sneakoscope goes off because of Crookshanks' nefarious plans for Scabbers, correct? At least, that's what Rowling leads the reader to believe by juxtaposing the Sneakoscope's alarm with Crookshanks' attack and his hissing and spitting. However, it was Wormtail's disguise as Scabbers and his attempt to escape from Crookshanks who recognized his falseness that set the Sneakoscope off.

One other little note: notice Ron nursing that stubbed toe. That's a deliberate wink toward Scabbers' missing digit. The reader was just notified that a severed finger fits into the mystery of this story, and now we're given a sly reminder that Scabbers is missing a toe. The reader should be putting two and two together and deciphering that this missing finger resembles a rat's toe. In fact, as Ron seizes his pet by the tail, Rowling is giving us a nudge to think of what a rat tail looks like...a bit like a worm, maybe. *Wormtail* was one of those tricksters named on the Marauder's Map.

However, suspicion is firmly cast onto Crookshanks as causing all the trouble with Scabbers, so the casual reader allows the distraction of her attention without realizing that this particular cat smells an awful lot like red herring.

Later, when Lupin is giving Harry Patronus lessons, Harry discovers that Lupin was friends with his father:

"Why—you didn't know my dad, did you?"

"I-I did, as a matter of fact," said Lupin. "**We were friends at Hogwarts**."

(p. 241, *Azkaban*)

Then a page later:

"If you knew my dad, then **you must've known Sirius Black as well**."...

"Yes, I knew him," he [Lupin] said shortly. "Or I thought I did."

(p. 242-243)

By putting the friend connections together, we can now connect James and Sirius and Lupin and Pettigrew. Four friends at Hogwarts. There were four troublemakers named as creators of the Marauder's Map, one of them called Wormtail. We have a rat who's been acting awfully strange, who has a tail that could be described like a worm.

This masterful trail of clues leads the reader to an emotional revelation in the Shrieking Shack. It starts with Lupin revealing to the Trio that he saw Peter Pettigrew with Ron on the Marauder's Map:

"They didn't see what they thought they saw!" said Black savagely, still watching Scabbers struggling in Ron's hands.

"Everyone thought Sirius killed Peter," said Lupin, nodding. "I believed it myself—until I saw the map tonight. **Because the Marauder's map never lies. Peter's alive. Ron's holding him**, Harry."(p351)

Point to note here: Only the movie shows Harry seeing Peter Pettigrew on the map; it doesn't happen in the book. In the book, the only time Peter is seen on the map is by Lupin revealed in this scene above.

Lupin then gives the backstory on the Marauders and Snape makes his dramatic appearance. Finally, we get to the bit where all the clues come together:

"Fudge," said Black. "When he came to inspect Azkaban last year, he gave me his paper. And **there was Peter, on the front page on this boy's shoulder**...I knew him at once...how many times had I seen him transform? And the caption said **the boy would be going back to Hogwarts...to where Harry was**..."

"My God," said Lupin softly, staring from Scabbers to the picture in the paper and back again. "**His front paw**..."

"What about it?" said Ron defiantly.

"**He's got a toe missing**," said Black.

"Of course," Lupin breathed. "So simple...so brilliant...**he cut it off himself?**"

"Just before he transformed," said Black. ...

"Didn't you ever hear, Ron?" said Lupin. "**The biggest bit of Peter they found was his finger.**"

"... He's been in my family for ages, right—"

"**Twelve years**, in fact," said Lupin. "Didn't you ever wonder why he was living so long?" ...

"Not looking too good at the moment, though, is he?" said Lupin. "I'd guess he's been **losing weight ever since he heard Sirius was on the loose again**...."

"He's been scared of that mad cat!" said Ron, nodding toward Crookshanks, who was still purring on the bed.

But that wasn't right, Harry thought suddenly...**Scabbers had been looking ill before he met Crookshanks...ever since Ron's return from Egypt...since the time when Black had escaped**....

(p. 362-364)

Below I've given a summary of all the clues that were laid in advance to prepare the reader for the revelation of Scabbers as Wormtail as Peter Pettigrew:

List of Clues Planted

1) Wizards can be Animagi.
2) A Fidelius Charm was placed on the Potters' location, which required a Secret Keeper.
3) Dumbledore suspected a traitor close to the Potters.
4) Sirius was first at Godric's Hollow, then shortly after at a Muggle street with Peter Pettigrew.
5) Sirius was imprisoned for the murders of Pettigrew and the Muggles, as well as the betrayer of James and Lily.
6) Sirius made no attempt to escape, appearing to be mad.
7) All that appeared to be left of Pettigrew were a few fragments (a finger) and a bloodstained robe.
8) Scabbers has been in the Weasley family for a very long time, longer than normal for a common rat.
9) Scabbers is missing a toe.
10) Scabbers has been ill since Ron's return from Egypt.
11) Black escaped after the Weasley family returned from Egypt.
12) Black escaped to go after someone, a male, at Hogwarts.
13) The Marauder's Map revealed the pranks and jokes of four friends named Moony, Wormtail, Padfoot, and Prongs.
14) James, Sirius, Lupin, and Pettigrew were all friends at Hogwarts.
15) James and Sirius sound an awful lot like Fred and George, who happened to give Harry the Marauder's Map (juxtaposition, to be discussed later).
16) Peter Pettigrew was considered the weakest of James' friends.
17) The Sneakoscope went off around Crookshanks and Scabbers.

In retrospect, it's easy to see that a significant number of clues were planted to give the reader a chance at figuring out the mystery. However, clues were kept subtle and their solution was not obvious. Wherever a clue was laid, **distraction was provided**. So, many readers were left with that delightful sense of surprise.

Plotting a mystery is a fine balancing act. If the author leaves insufficient clues to give the reader a shot at solving the puzzle, the reader feels cheated. However, if the author makes the clues too obvious, the reader also feels cheated out of the pleasant surprised *gotcha* at the end. The evidence is overwhelming that Rowling walked that tightrope gracefully and masterfully and never cheated her readers.

Overview:

Fourteen Traps for Tricking Your Reader

Let's analyze how Rowling strings along her reader by breaking down her techniques. These are a few I have spotted which we'll spend some time with:

1) Focus attention elsewhere: the magical art of sleight of hand.
2) Divert with a joke.
3) Divert with action.
4) Distract with high emotions.
5) Give meaningful names.
6) Camouflage by use of myths and folklore.
7) Use patterns to mark certain clues.
8) Hide in a list.
9) Discredit the witness.
10) Drop in dreams.
11) Mark with repeated clues.
12) Mirror parallels.
13) Reverse expectations.
14) Juxtapose the villain with the scene of the crime.

Rowling lays some clues close to the surface which she intends for the reader to find easily. Then there are others where she uses sleight of hand to misdirect her fans, while still playing fair by having laid it.

1) Sleight of Hand: The Art of Distraction

In weaving the mystery through her world of magic and myth, Rowling is the master magician. Her technique focuses heavily on that old reliable magician's trick: sleight of hand.

> Misdirection is perhaps the most important component of the art of sleight of hand. Using misdirection, the skillful magician choreographs every movement in a routine so even the most critical and observant spectators are ***compelled to look where the magician wants them to***.
>
> (https://en.wikipedia.org/wiki/Sleight_of_hand)

While laying her most important clues, Rowling diverts the readers' attention elsewhere. There are various methods she employs to force the reader to look in the direction she wishes for them to and away from her clue. We'll look at three in the next sections, but sleight of hand can be used in any way a writer creates to distract readers from what she doesn't want them to notice.

2) Divert with Jokes or Ridiculous Statements

One of the simplest methods of diversion is to place the clue in a line of dialogue that seems unimportant or a joke, which focuses the reader on the humor rather than the clue. Ron and the twins are especially good for the joking bit.

> [Harry] "I wouldn't mind knowing how Riddle got an award for special services to Hogwarts either."
>
> "Could've been anything," said Ron. "Maybe he got thirty O.W.L.s or saved a teacher from the giant squid. ***Maybe he murdered Myrtle***; that would've done everyone a favor..."
>
> (p. 232, *Secrets*)

Ron is joking, but hits the truth dead-on. However, there are two sly Rowling tricks sidetracking the reader from taking note of the clue—not only is it an obvious joke, but it's also third in a list of increasingly absurd ones and therefore the most ridiculous in Ron's point of view.

Dumbledore gave us a clue at the end of *Prisoner of Azkaban* of a similar dialogue misdirection in a non-joke format—stating the obvious but making it seem ridiculous. In the face of Snape's rage over the escape of Sirius Black, Dumbledore calmly and without lying states, "Unless you are suggesting that Harry and Hermione are able to be in two places at once, I'm afraid I don't see any point in troubling them further" (p. 420).

Dumbledore makes the reality of Harry and Hermione truly having been in two places at the same time seem ridiculous, and even though the reader is "in" on this clue, it's a blatant sign-post to pay attention to other such well-laid lines where the reader may not be as *in the know*.

Here are a couple of other one-liners from Ron that actually hint at what's to come, while distracting from current clues. At the end of the Boggart lesson in *Azkaban*, Ron ridicules Hermione, who didn't face it in class:

"What would it have been for you?" said Ron sniggering. "***A piece of homework that got nine out of ten***?" (p. 140, *Phoenix*)

His joke is a distraction from noticing that Lupin's Boggart was the moon. However, it's also prophetic as at the end of this book during Hermione's DADA exam her Boggart turns into Professor McGonagall telling her she failed every course.

In *Phoenix*, after the first Quidditch match where Ron plays brilliantly, he says:

…"Did you see the look on Chang's face when Ginny got the Snitch right out from under her nose?" (p. 704, *Phoenix*)

Something tells me that Rowling is hinting at Ginny getting more than the Snitch out from under Cho's nose.

3) Divert with Action

Previously as we followed the Wormtail trail, we saw how immediately after giving us the crucial clues of Scabbers being too old for a common garden rat and missing a toe, Rowling tossed Crookshanks onto Ron's head and incited a cat-rat chase. The purpose of the action (besides providing a clue to Crookshanks' distrust of Scabbers) was to misdirect the reader with something more actively interesting.

There's a good reason why authors are encouraged to write in action whenever possible—because movement attracts the readers' attention. In throwing Crookshanks at Ron's head, Rowling distracts the reader away from her clues and toward the action.

There's a jam-packed clue-filled scene that takes place at Grimmauld Place in "The Woes of Mrs. Weasley" chapter in *Phoenix*. A crucial question floating through this chapter is why is Dumbledore acting so strangely around Harry? The chapter before, Dumbledore would not look at or talk to Harry during his hearing. In this chapter, Ron and Hermione receive their Prefect badges, with everyone astonished that Dumbledore didn't pick Harry.

Harry overhears Kingsley muttering to Lupin about this very thing:

'…***why Dumbledore didn't make Potter a prefect***?' said Kingsley.

'He'll have ***had his reasons***,' replied Lupin.

'But ***it would've shown confidence in him***. It's what I'd've done,' persisted Kingsley, 'specially with the Daily Prophet having a go at him every few days…'

(p. 157, *Phoenix*, Bloomsbury)

Harry is bothered by Dumbledore's striking change of attitude, and the reader along with him. Surely, like Lupin says, Dumbledore has a good reason for ignoring Harry. But what is it?

Could it be related to why Moody seems to watch Harry's every move?

Moody took a swig from his hipflask, ***his electric-blue eye staring sideways at Harry***.

'Come here, I've got something that might interest you,' he said.

From an inner pocket of his robes Moody pulled a very tattered old wizarding photograph.

'Original Order of the Phoenix,' growled Moody. 'Found it last night when I was looking for my spare ***Invisibility Cloak, seeing as Podmore hasn't had the manners to return my best one***…thought people might like to see it.'

(p. 157, *Phoenix*, Bloomsbury)

Why include that little tidbit about Podmore having Moody's best Invisibility Cloak? Because it's important to the story later when Podmore is caught and imprisoned for spying at the Department of Mysteries. However, the reader is not permitted to dwell too deeply here as a long, detailed, dialogue-driven description of the original Order follows—a description filled with clues and red herrings that had readers speculating until the end of the series.

What to make of Frank and Alice Longbottom, "Better dead than what happened to them," or the presence of Elphias Doge in the same picture with Dumbledore, or Caradoc Dearborn, "vanished six months after this, we never found his body" (p. 158, *Phoenix*, Bloomsbury)?

We'd seen a wizard come back from the dead who had only left "fragments" of himself before. Many fans speculated that someone "not properly dead" would be seen in the last book. Would it be Dearborn? Perhaps the Longbottoms would recover? If so, what memory could they have shared?

However, Harry can't handle this much pain all in one photo. He flees the scene only to encounter a trauma more real, more personal, and completely devastating—Mrs. Weasley sobbing over Ron's dead body. Harry feels himself "falling through the floor," only…that's not Ron. It's a Boggart, who at the feeble flick of Mrs. Weasley's shaking wand, transforms from Ron to Bill to Mr. Weasley to the twins to Percy to…Harry.

The reader starts with a dead Ron and ends with a dead Harry, all the other Weasleys thrown in between, except Ginny and Charlie. Without a doubt, there are clues flying with the crack of the Boggart, but where? Is it the missing Ginny or Charlie? Is Rowling playing with reader expectations that the side-kick (Ron) always bites it in the end? Or is she teasing us once again that Harry just might not survive his final confrontation with the Dark Lord?

By the time Rowling wrote this scene, the mad passion to figure out who would die before series' end had already spurred some to high bets and mad searches for spoilers. With the release of *Half-Blood*, this frenzy to know who died next would culminate with guns and criminal activity![5]

As we see here with Mrs. Weasley's Boggart, Rowling teased her reader with a lot of red herring soup. What is obvious, though, is that in these few pages she flings clues as quickly as the cracking Boggart—from Dumbledore's change of attitude toward Harry, to Sturgis Podmore using Moody's Invisibility Cloak, to possible hints from the former Order of the Phoenix, to who will live or die by series' end. All in four pages!

The action whips from Harry's eavesdropping, to the former Order moving-picture-show, to Harry fleeing and encountering the popping of the dead-body Boggart. Non-stop action, and interesting action at that, prevents readers from dwelling too long on any one clue, and propels their attention to where Rowling wants it to go—ever forward in a frenzied pace to get to the surprise ending, without stopping to think too hard.

Also, note that two of these clue-filled scenarios were presented in listing form (which we will discuss in a later point)—the description of the former Order, and the progression of the dead bodies. Rowling is quite accomplished at multi-tasking her clue-dropping techniques.

4) Divert with High Emotions

If there is one thing that attracts the reader's attention more than intense action, it's high emotion. Jealousy, betrayal, hatred, and revenge. All emotions were rampaging through the eavesdropping scene in the Three Broomsticks discussed earlier. Harry was so caught up in the immensely powerful betrayal by his father's lifelong best friend that he missed the finer points of the clues being laid. Yet there is another scene, one of the most powerful in all of Potterdom, that packs a Whomping Willow of emotion.

The end of *Half-Blood Prince* has been finely picked over by a rabid Harry Potter CSI team. The emotions burning through this ending surely obscured most of our views for anything less pressing than dealing with the murder of Dumbledore at the hand of his trusted confidant Snape. But clues litter the crime scene, and we must push the emotion aside to uncover them. (Below also available on DeepRiver.press Writer's Resource page as a one-page handout.)

> Malfoy stepped forwards, ***glancing around quickly*** to check that he and Dumbledore were alone. **His eyes fell upon the second broom.**
>
> 'Who else is here?'
>
> [Dumbledore says] '***A question I might ask you***. Or are you acting alone?'
>
> Harry saw ***Malfoy's pale eyes shift back to Dumbledore*** in the greenish glare of the Mark.
> (p. 546, *Half-Blood*, Bloomsbury)

Note: Draco instantly notices the second broom, the one belonging to the immobilized and hidden Harry, and correctly surmises someone else is present. Dumbledore, a skilled magician himself, expertly distracts Draco's attention, then keeps him talking for several pages, until three more Death Eaters arrive, including the deadly werewolf Greyback.

---

[5] http://www.guardian.co.uk/media/2005/jun/03/pressandpublishing.uknews

Now compare the above lines with the most over-analyzed scene in Potterdom a few pages later:

'Draco, do it, or stand aside so one of us—' screeched the woman, but at that precise moment the door to the ramparts burst open once more and **there stood Snape**, his wand clutched in his hand as **his black eyes SWEPT the scene, from Dumbledore slumped against the wall, to the four Death Eaters, including the enraged werewolf, and Malfoy**.

'We've got a problem, Snape,' said the lumpy Amycus, whose eyes and wand were fixed alike upon Dumbledore, 'the boy doesn't seem able—'

But somebody else had spoken Snape's name, quite softly.

'Severus...'

The sound frightened Harry beyond anything he had experienced all evening. **For the first time, Dumbledore was pleading**.

Snape said nothing, but walked forwards and pushed Malfoy roughly out of the way. The three Death Eaters fell back without a word. Even the werewolf seemed cowed.

Snape gazed for a moment at Dumbledore, and there was **revulsion and hatred etched in the harsh lines of his face**.

'Severus...please..."

Snape raised his wand and pointed it directly at Dumbledore.

'Avada Kedavra!'

(p. 556, *Half-Blood*, Bloomsbury)

Revulsion and hatred, yes. But...for whom?

From the moment of his entrance, Snape's "black eyes SWEPT the scene, from Dumbledore slumped against the wall, to the four Death Eaters, including the enraged werewolf, and Malfoy." That all important allusion to the second broom is the most critical clue given. Could any astute reader not believe that Snape would have noticed all that Draco saw, and more?

Many writers would have written a line such as, "Snape's gaze lingered on the second broom." But not the extremely devious JK Rowling. No, for her that would be too revealing a clue, or pardon me, a dead giveaway. Instead she slyly hints at the second broom Snape sees with the deliberate use of the coy word "swept." By paralleling Snape's scanning the area with Draco's own discovery and instant understanding of what the second broom meant, Rowling gives a powerful hint but one the reader has to work for.

So what? Snape saw the second broom?

Couple it with another subtle, but potent clue. Dumbledore's pleading. Albus Dumbledore plead for his life? This from the man who said that "to the well-organized mind, death is but the next great adventure?" (p. 297, *Sorcerer's Stone*)

Dumbledore would, however, plead for Harry's life, even if it meant sacrificing his own. Thus the cunningly planted clues tell the alert reader that Snape acted in response to Dumbledore's open plea (and possible silent Legilimency demand) to get the Death Eaters away before Harry could be discovered and Draco's soul imperiled. To sacrifice Dumbledore's life for his students'. For Dumbledore sacrificed himself not just for Harry, but for Draco as well.

Later, fans went crazy debating the Good Snape/Bad Snape, Murderer/They-Had-a-Plan theories. Yet what reader is going to pick up on these nuances in a first read-through when all their attention is focused on the "revulsion and hatred etched in the harsh lines" of Snape's face? Their attention was drawn bewitchingly to where the author wanted it, on Snape murdering Dumbledore in front of our eyes.

For Harry or the reader, there could be no higher emotional scene in the book thus far. Rowling expertly used intense emotion and shocking action to distract her reader from the finely worded clues.

Using emotions to distract a reader is a powerful, magnetic tool and not the easiest to learn. However, if you can help your students grasp this concept, it will empower their writing tremendously. With Rowling's examples, teach them that, when laying a clue, don't draw attention to it, but rather focus their readers' interest elsewhere. Make the obvious look ridiculous "a la Dumbledore" or a Ron-type joke. Don't slow down the action, but rather increase the pace as a distraction. Intensify the emotional reaction away from the clue. Help your students master the magician's sleight of hand, and they'll bewitch their reader.

Sleight of Hand: Mini Activity

Misdirection is perhaps the most important component of the art of sleight of hand. Using misdirection, the skillful magician choreographs every movement in a routine so even the most critical and observant spectators are compelled to look where the magician wants them to.
(https://en.wikipedia.org/wiki/Sleight_of_hand)

Rowling used jokes, high emotion, and intense action to direct her reader's attention where she wanted it to go – away from important clues she was hiding.

Use the chart below to pinpoint your most important clues and what technique you can use to direct your reader's attention AWAY from it.

Clue	Which Fits - Joke/Emotion/Action?	Work out the distraction...
Moaning Myrtle was killed by Basilisk	A Ron joke	"Could've been anything," said Ron. "Maybe he got thirty O.W.L.s or saved a teacher from the giant squid. Maybe he murdered Myrtle; that would've done everyone a favor..." (p. 232, *Secrets*)

5) A Hagrid by Any Other Name

Years ago, when the HP books were new and fans were first beginning to share their enthusiasm online, the main clues discussed were the meanings behind names. Readers quickly caught on that many came from myths, others from British locales. Some characters were named after flowers or stars. Then there were Rowling's own creations, combinations of words with new meanings (such as Umbridge, a portmanteau from umbrage and bridge, as she provided an offensively manipulative connection from the Ministry to the school). All types of names were strikingly relevant to the character or object they represented, and most held a clue regarding that character's role in the series.

Minerva McGonagall is named after the Roman goddess of wisdom and war. She resembles a distant, austere goddess (with a warm side she reveals upon occasion), but a very apt second in command, as shown in *Deathly Hallows*. So, from the beginning we have a name that characterizes McGonagall as well as gives an early indication of the role she is to play in the finale.

Here are some other names with their derivation:

1) **Argus Filch** = Argus Panoptes from Greek mythology. Argus of the 100 eyes made a great watchman, just like nasty old Filch.

2) **Petunia** = flower name meaning anger and resentment. Sounds like petulant.

3) **Lily** = flower associated with death and resurrection.

4) **Bellatrix** = the third brightest star in Orion. Means female hunter.

5) **Draco** = from the constellation Draco. *Draco* means dragon, a reminder of his serpentine Slytherin family.

6) **Grimmauld Place** = definitely a grim old place, but it might also be a play on the brothers Grimm and a nod to their fairy tales.

For a more complex naming example, I'd like to look at three characters together: Sirius Black, Albus Dumbledore, and Rubeus Hagrid. In Latin, Albus means white and Rubeus means red. In alchemy, there are three phases of transformation from lead until gold (we earlier discussed seven stages, but these seven stages are divided into three phases). The phases are, in order, black, white, and at last red. The black phase must "die" for the white to begin, then the white falls away for the red. At last, the red phase produces the gold of the Philosopher's Stone.

The death of Sirius Black culminates the first phase of Harry's personal transformation from child to adult. Likewise, the death of Albus Dumbledore (white) propels Harry from his mentored stage into his last and greatest phase where he has to go it alone. Rowling did not kill Hagrid off in *Hallows* as she wanted the Red Man (an alchemy image) present to the end to bring Harry's "dead" body out of the forest. However, she does symbolically kill him off at the beginning in the "Fallen Warrior" chapter where Hagrid falls to the earth from Sirius' motorbike during Harry's escape from Privet Drive. Note that this happens immediately after the Harrified Polyjuice potion had "turned a clear, bright gold" (p. 50, *Hallows*). Gold, the color of the final phase of Harry's alchemical transformation. Rowling works with tremendous alchemical symbolism throughout the HP series, and you see it reflected even here in the names.

Now, were all these clues apparent by just looking at those names? For most readers, the answer is no. Rowling chose names filled with symbolism and analogies, but the reader had to do some legwork to discover the reference. However, many of the meanings behind the names are much closer to the surface than Rowling's other clues and thus a good intro to the beginning Harry Potter sleuth.

Putting meaning behind the names of characters is a time-honored technique for many writers. Even authors outside of fantasy or mystery like to give their characters names that indicate their personality or fate. However, warn your students to be careful in choosing a name that it also fits the character and time period in which the story takes place. Getting too cutesy or unusual, especially with difficult to pronounce names, can turn a reader off.

6) Drawing Upon Myth and Folklore

Another technique that Rowling employs is to draw from ancient stories to impart and hide clues. She uses both myth and folklore to hide and reveal Lupin's "furry little problem." Take his name for instance—Remus, according to Roman mythology, was one of the twin founders of Rome who was suckled by a she-wolf as a baby. Not only do we have the wolf connection with Remus, but *lupine* in its adjective form means wolfish and is derived from the Latin *lupus*, meaning wolf.

So, Lupin's mythic name should have given the reader a heads-up to his wolfish connections. Then Rowling uses folklore dispersed throughout *Azkaban* to give further hints that Lupin is a werewolf. Hermione figured it out by picking up clues through Professor Snape's essay:

> Lupin stopped dead. Then, with an obvious effort, he turned to Hermione and said, "How long have you known?"
>
> "Ages," Hermione whispered. "***Since I did Professor Snape's essay***..."
>
> "He'll be delighted," said Lupin coolly. "He assigned that essay hoping someone would realize what my symptoms meant.... Did you **check the lunar chart** and realize that **I was always ill at the full moon**? Or did you realize that the **boggart changed into the moon when it saw me**?"
>
> "Both," Hermione said quietly.

(p. 345-346, *Azkaban*)

The reader had been given Lupin's wolfish names, seen him sick about monthly, and had his Boggart described as "a silver-white orb" (p. 138, *Azkaban*). Notice it wasn't described as a moon directly; that would have been too obvious a clue. That Snape assigned the werewolf essay when he taught Lupin's class (even though they were on hinky-punks), coupled with Snape's obvious hatred of Lupin, are two proximity or juxtaposition clues. Together, these present strong hints using various techniques.

Rowling is also quite adept at drawing upon ancient beliefs to weave in thematic subtext, which hints at multiple clues. Egyptian mythology, in my opinion, provided subtextual support for one series theme—the mysteries surrounding death and eternal life.

For ancient Egyptians, Thoth was the moon god of learning and writing and was often associated with monkeys (or baboons) and, at the Temple of Osiris at Abydos, with two snakes in the form of a caduceus. He was believed to be the writer of the *Book of the Dead*, an ancient Egyptian funerary text that provided the deceased directions on how to cross through the obstacles in the land of the dead to arrive at the Egyptian afterlife, the Field of Reeds. Thoth was also credited with writing many other books, sometimes referred to as the Book(s) of Thoth. One that he was credited for in a later manifestation as Hermes Trismegistus is *The Emerald Tablet*. This Hermetic manuscript was recognized as the most ancient, primary source of alchemical knowledge—and provided a guide for creating the Philosopher's Stone. Indeed, Thoth/Hermes Trismegistus was considered the father of alchemy.

Now, look closely at the descriptions of the Chamber of Secrets:

> [Harry] was standing at the **end of a very long, dimly lit chamber. Towering stone pillars entwined with more carved serpents rose to support a ceiling lost in darkness, casting long, black shadows through the odd, greenish gloom that filled the place**...
>
> He pulled out his wand and moved forward between **the serpentine columns**. Every careful footstep **echoed loudly off the shadowy walls**...
>
> Then, as he drew level with the last pair of pillars, **a statue high as the Chamber itself loomed into view, standing against the back wall.**
>
> Harry had to **crane his neck to look up into the giant face above**: It was **ancient and monkeyish**, with a long, thin beard that fell almost to the bottom of the wizard's sweeping stone robes, where two enormous gray feet stood on the smooth Chamber floor. And **between the feet, facedown, lay a small, black-robed figure with flaming-red hair.**
>
> "Ginny!"

(p. 306-307, *Secrets*)

The description of this chamber just breathes ancient temple, from the towering stone pillars, to the sense of echoing vast, cavernous space, to the colossal god-like statue filling the inner sanctuary. From its serpentine pillars that look just like a giant caduceus to the monkeyish statue reminiscent of Thoth as a baboon, my guess is that the Chamber of Secrets is an allegorical temple of Thoth. Alchemy is the primary metaphorical subtext of the series, and Rowling has provided a strong setting for it here in her underground temple.

These themes started with the Philosopher's Stone from the first book, which Harry obtained in an underground chamber like this one. Rowling continues to weave in subtle hints to alchemy and Egyptian myths related to death and eternal life as the series progresses. Finally, Harry's transmutation from base metal to gold culminates in *Deathly Hallows*. From his self-sacrifice in the Dark Forest to his enlightenment at "King's Cross," Harry not only achieves victory over Voldemort, but becomes the Master of Death as well.

Rowling's use of images, stories, and characters that directly reflect myths and folklore is deliberately designed for just such speculation as I've done above. She wants to see if her readers have their wits about them and to put those wits to use to follow her trail of clues.

Don't let this last analysis throw you off teaching such craft skills to your students. From the simple technique of choosing names of mythic meaning, to a more moderate one of weaving in hints of folklore, to the advanced skill of layering a deep meaning of subtext into a story, Rowling's work provides examples for creative writing students at various stages of development. They can:

- Name certain characters after mythic heroes or heroines.
- Design their settings similar to places where appropriate mythic stories transpired.
- Employ the use of folkloric creatures or magical items.
- Weave in plot points that mirror a classic story.

As your student challenges the reader, they will be challenging themselves as a writer!

Myths and folklore provide a wealth of universal knowledge and familiarity a reader can connect to in order to draw deeper into a story. Reader involvement is a powerful tool. Your student doesn't have to weave in every detail of the myth they employ. Just enough to alert the reader and engage their minds in how the stories relate.

7) Seeing Spots and Spotting Cameos

One technique Rowling used in the early books to note when a character was in disguise, was less than truthful, where she'd hidden a clue, or information was being withheld was to mark it with a "spot." The chart on the next two pages gives a few examples.

Not all "spotted" mentions are represented here. This is just a sampling. I bet she had great fun playing with the reader as to whether they could "spot" a few of her clues and disguises.

Book	Page #	Quote	Camouflaged Item or Clue Spotted
Stone	5	As he pulled into the driveway of number four, the first thing he saw—and it didn't improve his mood—was the tabby cat he'd **spotted** that morning.	Professor McGonagall in Animagus form
	55	"You was just a year old. He came ter yer house an'—an'—" Hagrid suddenly pulled out a very dirty, **spotted** handkerchief and blew his nose ...	Hagrid is withholding info regarding what happened at Godric's Hollow and intimate knowledge of Tom Riddle.
Secrets	50	Harry looked quickly around and **spotted** a large black cabinet to his left...	The vanishing cabinet. Doesn't come to fruition until Half-Blood.
	155	Under a large, cracked, and **spotted** mirror were a row of chipped sinks.	The bathroom entrance to the Chamber of Secrets.
	156	Moaning Myrtle was floating above the tank of the toilet, picking a **spot** on her chin.	Moaning Myrtle was the girl killed 50 years before by the basilisk.
Azkaban	303	He peered out at the grounds again and, after a minute's frantic searching, **spotted** it. It was skirting the edge of the forest now...It wasn't the Grim at all...it was a cat.... Harry clutched the window ledge in relief as he recognized the bottlebrush tail. It was only Crookshanks...	Red herring—trying to throw suspicion on Crookshanks when it is really Scabbers, aka Wormtail. Also, the Grim is not who he appears to be.
Goblet	472	"Course Dumbledore trusts you," growled Moody. "He's a trusting man, isn't he? Believes in second chances. But me—I say there are **spots** that don't come off, Snape. **Spots** that never come off, d'you know what I mean?"	Refers to Snape's Dark Mark, but also Barty Crouch's own Dark Mark, concealed by his cover as Mad-Eye.
	604	"Harry," he said as Harry reached the door. "Please do not speak about Neville's parents to anybody else. He has the right to let people know, when he is ready." "Yes, Professor," said Harry, turning to go. "And-" Harry looked back. Dumbledore was standing over the Pensieve, his face lit from beneath by its silvery **spots** of light, looking older than ever. He stared at Harry for a moment, and then said, "Good luck with the third task."	Dumbledore is hiding his thoughts here from Harry regarding Neville's parents, but also others. We find out in Hallows just how much information Dumbledore has withheld throughout the series.
Phoenix, Blooms-bury	540	Marietta gave a wail and pulled the neck of her robes right up to her eyes, but not before the whole room had seen that her face was horribly disfigured by a series of close-set purple pustules that had spread across her nose and cheeks to form the word 'SNEAK'. 'Never mind the **spots** now, dear,' said Umbridge impatiently, 'just take your robes away...'	Marietta had definitely disguised herself as a friend to Dumbledore's Army, but the main person in disguise here is Umbridge, acting as a concerned professor.
Half-Blood, Blooms-bury	343	'So the Ministry called upon Morfin. They did not need to question him, to use Veritaserum or Legilimency. He admitted to the murder on the **spot**, giving details only the murderer could know	Morfin appeared to be the murderer, when in reality it was Tom Riddle.
	396	The girl did not say thank you, but remained rooted to the **spot** and watched them out of sight...	Either Crabbe or Goyle in Polyjuiced disguise.

Another cute little trick Rowling plays is to give each book's villain a cameo appearance in chapter 13 (unlucky number). While Voldemort is the series' villain, each book has its own antagonist in disguise. To help the reader along in unmasking this book's villain, she established a pattern that provided her observant readers with a clue, once they latched onto it.

Book	Chapter 13 Title	"Villain" in Disguise	Their Cameo Role
Stone	Nicolas Flamel	Quirrell	Quirrell and Snape's confrontation in the Forest. Snape appears to be the traitor, but that's through Harry's biased POV.
Secrets	The Very Secret Diary	Ginny Weasley	As a result of her Valentine, Ginny sees that Harry has Riddle's diary and is terrified.
Azkaban	Gryffindor versus Ravenclaw	Sirius Black and Wormtail	Sirius breaks into the Gryffindor boys' dormitory, trying to find Wormtail. But Pettigrew has pretended death and fled the scene.
Goblet	Mad-Eye Moody	Barty Crouch/Mad-Eye Moody	Moody transfigures Malfoy into a ferret. He appears to be Harry's protector, but in reality, reveals the Dark side of Barty Crouch.
Phoenix	Detention with Dolores	Umbridge	Through sentences carved in blood, Umbridge's self-righteous mask is blasted away to reveal her sadistic, power hungry core.
Half-Blood	The Secret Riddle	Tom Riddle	Riddle appears to be a poor, defenseless orphan, but Dumbledore and Mrs. Cole see through him.
Hallows	The Muggle-born Registration Commission	Umbridge	She's back! You can't sink much lower than nailing Mad-Eye's eye to your door.

Rowling's definitely got a bit of Fred and George about her when it comes to laying her clues. She likes to see if you've got your wits about you.

Obsessed fans took tremendous pleasure in discovering one of Rowling's patterns and then hunting out clues which related to it. This play with patterns is a powerful tool for those writing in genres where the concealing of secrets and reader involvement in unmasking them is appealing. Mysteries are an obvious choice, but this technique could work on a subtextual level with almost any genre that employs a hint of mystery, suspense, or concealed secrets.

Although all the above analyses and tables are my own, I should gratefully acknowledge that I learned about the spots and chapter 13 cameos from Galadriel Waters at Wizarding World Press. Her *Ultimate Unofficial Guides to the Mysteries of Harry Potter* are the books that first started me searching out the clues within Rowling's world.

8) Hide in a List

We've already analyzed a few examples of how a clue can hide in a list, including the listing of the members in the Order photo, Mrs. Weasley's cracking boggart, and Ron's joke about Riddle murdering Myrtle. Here's another list that hides clues from *Phoenix* when Harry and friends are cleaning out Sirius' "black" house:

They found an unpleasant-looking silver instrument, something like a many-legged pair of tweezers, which scuttled up Harry's arm like a spider when he picked it up, and attempted to puncture his skin. Sirius seized it and smashed it with a heavy book entitled *Nature's Nobility: A Wizarding Genealogy*. There was a musical box that emitted a faintly sinister, tinkling tune when wound, and they all found themselves becoming curiously weak and sleepy, until Ginny had the sense to slam the lid shut; *a heavy locket that none of them could open*; a number of ancient seals; and, in a dusty box, an Order of Merlin, First Class, that had been awarded to Sirius's grandfather for 'services to the Ministry'.

'It means he gave them a load of gold,' said Sirius contemptuously, throwing the medal into the rubbish sack.

(p. 108, *Phoenix*, Bloomsbury)

That heavy locket is a Voldy-Horcrux, which R.A.B, aka Regulus Black, brought back home for safe-keeping and destruction. Slytherin's locket is first mentioned in *Half-Blood*, but notice how it's hidden here in an earlier book among a listing of many interesting items, all with curious descriptions. In fact, its description is the least intriguing. The locket is not even listed as the first or last item of the list, where the eye tends to naturally fall.

Help your students hide clues in a list by not making it the only item of interest that stands out. And if they want to be really deceptive, they should embed the clue in the middle of the list and not the beginning or end.

9) Discredit the Witness

Another way your students can hide a clue is to make the person who reveals it look like a complete idiot. For Rowling, Trelawney and Luna seem to be the biggest target for this deception. They simply spout so much nonsense, each in her own way, that you don't expect them to ever get anything right. Fudge is a similar character. So, once a character has been discredited, he or she becomes a prime candidate for hiding an important clue.

What Trelawney is most famous for are her two "true" prophecies, but she also makes an accurate prediction in Harry's first lesson:

"My dear," Professor Trelawney's huge eyes opened dramatically, "***You have the Grim.***"

"The what?" said Harry.

He could tell that he wasn't the only one who didn't understand...

"The Grim, my dear, the Grim!" cried Professor Trelawney, who looked shocked that Harry hadn't understood. "***The giant, spectral dog that haunts churchyards***! My dear boy, it is an omen—***the worst omen—of death***!"

Harry's stomach lurched. ***That dog on the cover of Death Omens in Flourish and Blotts—the dog in the shadows of Magnolia Crescent***...

(p. 107, *Azkaban*)

Trelawney is presented as a charlatan; McGonagall discredits her entirely and tells Harry she's predicted a death every year. Plus, the reader knows quite well Harry's not going to die in book three of a seven-book series (which Rowling had already announced). So, who would pay attention to the very real clue that death is attached to the Grim? It's not Harry's death that's being foretold, however, it's the dog's death...it's Sirius'. The Grim, Sirius' Animagus alter-ego, finally catches up to him at the end of *Phoenix*.

Taking Trelawney seriously is one thing...but Luna...? Still, Luna was on to something big. With her father, her accusations ranged from "Fudge's dearest ambition is to seize control of the goblin gold supply" (p. 174, *Phoenix*, Bloomsbury), to Scrimgeour being a vampire (p. 294, *Half-Blood*, Bloomsbury), to the Aurors as part of the Roftang Conspiracy to "bring down the Ministry of Magic using a combination of Dark magic and gum disease" (p. 299, *Half-Blood*, Bloomsbury). She hammered home that something was rotten within the Ministry and a battle for power was imminent. In *Deathly Hallows*, one of the first things to happen was the fall of the Ministry, toppled from within.

So, if your student has done the work to create an outlandish character, they can utilize one of Rowling's techniques and put the character to extra work by giving her an outlandish clue to hide that the reader will never suspect. They should make sure she truly does spout nonsense most of the time, or the reader will catch on and start taking their character seriously. Remember, it's always sleight of hand, distraction, that mesmerizes the reader best.

10) Drifting off to Dreamland

Dreams play a prominent role in the Harry Potter series, illuminating both Harry's fears and dropping clues for things to come. Many dream scenarios revealed vital information. It was obvious from the start that the dream of Wormtail and Voldemort in "The Riddle House" in *Goblet* was a vision of a scene actually taking place, and thus it was riddled with clues.

Others were not quite as obvious. Harry dreamt about doors upon doors before he and the reader understood that there was a particular door in the bowels of the Department of Mysteries that Voldemort desperately wanted access to—and why.

Because dreams can take on an abstract, disjointed, mixed-up quality, they're an excellent tool for hiding images and hints of what is yet to come. There are several dream sequences in the series where clues lurk, but here's one from *Sorcerer's/Philosopher's Stone* that we can analyze fairly easily:

> Perhaps Harry had eaten a bit too much, because he had a very strange dream. He was wearing ***Professor Quirrell's turban, which kept talking to him, telling him he must transfer to Slytherin at once, because it was his destiny. Harry told the turban he didn't want to be in Slytherin***; it got heavier and heavier; he tried to pull it off but it tightened painfully—and there was ***Malfoy, laughing at him as he struggled with it—then Malfoy turned into the hook-nosed teacher, Snape***, whose ***laugh became high and cold—there was a burst of green light*** and Harry woke, sweating and shaking.

(p. 130, Sorcerer's Stone)

This dream provides several connections between people that will play out through the rest of the series. Quirrell's talking turban is an obvious connection to Voldemort, and the series' three chief antagonists are all lumped together: Draco, Snape, and Voldemort. Here, from Harry's first day at Hogwarts, is a dream-like mirrored image of the final confrontation scene of *Stone*, with Voldemort a la turban offering Harry a place by his side and Harry refusing.

After experiencing the climactic scene of *Half-Blood*, Malfoy's transformation into Snape preceding a "burst of green light" in this early dream is especially frightening—when you consider how much detailed fore planning Rowling puts into her series. At the end of *Half-Blood*, the last time Snape and Malfoy are together, there was a murderous burst of green. Could Rowling have dropped a clue about the ending of *Half-Blood* all the way here near the beginning of the series?

Dreams have long been a popular tool of writers for weaving secrets and deeper meaning into stories, but they also have long been criticized for being poorly written, used to insert info dumps or too much introspection, or too obvious foreshadowing. So a beginning writer should approach a dream scene with great caution.

A dream scene should only be written if it is necessary to the plot, forwards the action, and should be kept short. Done in a subtle manner, a dream can foretell action to come without sacrificing a surprise ending. Keep in mind that dreams highlight emotions and patterns, but don't always need to make sense logically.

11) Repeated Clues and Running Bits

Before getting started with this section, let me recommend an excellent, older series of books written for fans to seek out and uncover many of Rowling's hidden clues. I was fortunate to edit one of Wizarding World Press' *Ultimate Unofficial Guide to the Mysteries of Harry Potter* series books by Galadriel Waters, E.L. Fossa, and Astre Mithrandir. However, the whole series was my introduction to HP sleuthing. Wizarding World Press approaches the hunt totally from a fan perspective, but gave me the idea of studying Rowling's technique from a writer's. These fan guides also helped me see how creatively Rowling colors outside the lines when devising ways to torture...I mean, tease...her reader-sleuth.

One thing the Ultimate Unofficial Guide books emphasize is what Wizarding World Press calls "running bits." Like a running gag, a running bit is a small reference that pops up repeatedly throughout the story or series. It's another trick in Rowling's arsenal that she uses to identify certain types of clues by colors, story elements, or other themes. The UUG books cover several; I'll only hit a few.

We've already seen how Rowling uses "spots" to point out a clue or someone acting deceptively. She also used pink in a similar method. There's an essay in Wizarding World Press' *The Plot Thickens...Harry Potter Investigated by Fans for Fans* called "Pink Stinks" by Julie Maffei (age 13). In it she links several pink items from the series and theorizes that pink is considered a color of concealment.

Here's a list of pink items Ms. Maffei mentions that conceal or disguise:

1) **Hagrid's pink umbrella**—conceals Hagrid's snapped wand
2) **Lockhart's pink robes**—conceals a completely false man
3) **Pansy Parkinson's pink Yule Ball robe**—disguises a mean-spirited girl
4) **Tonks' pink bubble gum hair**—disguises a Metamorphmagus
5) **Umbridge's pink Alice bands and sweaters**—disguises a cold-hearted woman masquerading as a teacher who cares

6) **The Fat Lady's pink dress**—conceals the opening into the Gryffindor dormitory

7) **Petunia's pink cocktail dress**—she's definitely hiding a secret in her knowledge of the wizarding world.

Just like with spots in an HP novel, once you've been alerted to this running bit, then the next time you see pink, you should guess that something is not as it appears to be.

Another running bit Rowling used was the number seven. Seven is a theme within the series that holds magical significance. It's also used as a marker for major clues.

"Oh that's my Foe-Glass. See them out there, skulking around? I'm not really in trouble until I see the whites of their eyes. That's when I open my trunk."

[Mad-Eye] let out a short, harsh laugh, and pointed to the large trunk under the window. It had *seven keyholes* in a row. *Harry wondered what was in there, until Moody's next question brought him sharply back to earth.*

(p. 343, *Goblet*)

Here we have a running bit (seven) marking a major clue: the fact that the real Mad-Eye is hidden beneath those seven keyholes. However, Moody distracts Harry and the reader from reflecting too deeply.

Seven marks many other major clues throughout the series:

- The seventh floor of Hogwarts holds the Room of Requirement as well as the entrance to Dumbledore's office

- The prophecy is on row 97 in the Department of Mysteries

- Harry (and Neville) are born as the seventh month dies

- Voldemort's soul is in seven pieces

- There were seven books to the series.

Some of Rowling's most interesting running bits, however, are the frequent use of items that relate to a key mystery in the story. In *Secrets*, we had numerous mentions of roosters, frogs, and running water before entering the Chamber of Secrets. Clocks clicked ominously throughout *Azkaban* as well as finger and toe references. There were eyes staring us in the face all over *Goblet* where Mad-Eye had such an interesting role to play.

This is a playful technique Rowling employs to have fun with her reader. Whereas some clues she tries hard to distract you from, others she wants to draw the reader's attention to. The clues are still not obvious, until you've figured out the running bit, but then you can use your new key to unlock several more.

Help your students get creative with marking their clues. Plot out clever ways to distinguish between types of secrets and how to mark those. If reader involvement in their story is important, encourage them to seek fun ways to engage their reader in the clue hunt. After all, the whole purpose of a mystery is to involve the reader as a sleuth. Giving them the key to hunt down and unlock a string of clues is an excellent technique for encouraging their engagement.

12) Mirrored Images

Remember how in the Wormtail trail of clues we analyzed the scene in the Three Broomsticks where Harry first learns about the relationship between Sirius and his father? There was a definite parallel drawn between James/Sirius and Fred/George. The twins mirrored the troublemaking best friends of old in a deliberate ploy to force the reader to reflect on who designed the Marauder's Map. Not only were characteristics mirrored to help us draw the link, but proximity was used as well. Rowling had Fred and George give Harry that map *immediately* before the revelations in the Three Broomsticks so the mapmakers would be uppermost in our mind when the parallels were noted between the two sets of troublemakers.

Your students can juxtapose or mirror many aspects to draw parallels and hide clues: symbols, characters, and plots. Patterns from days gone by have been repeatedly mirrored in the contemporary world of Harry. Here are a few that were considered possible clues prior to series end:

- Would the Hogwarts' Houses work together, or would they divide, as reflected in Slytherin's disagreement and departure from the school he helped found?

- Were Harry, Hermione, Ron, and Neville a modern version of the Marauders, and if so, would Neville betray Harry?

- And perhaps one of the greatest reflections of all—Harry looked a bit like Tom Riddle, including having

76

similar backgrounds, but they acted entirely opposite with their choices. How would Harry defeat his shadow without reflecting him?

Even whole scenes can be mirrored to hint at possible connections or tease your reader:

> For one brief moment, the great black dog reared on to its hind legs and placed its front paws on Harry's shoulders, but Mrs. Weasley shoved Harry away towards the train door, hissing, 'For heaven's sake, act more like a dog, Sirius!'
>
> 'See you!' Harry called out of the open window **as the train began to move**, while Ron, Hermione and Ginny waved beside him. The figures of Tonks, Lupin, Moody and Mr and Mrs Weasley shrank rapidly but **the black dog was bounding alongside the window, wagging its tail**; blurred people on the platform were laughing to **see it chasing the train**, then **they rounded a bend**, and SIRIUS WAS GONE.
>
> (p. 166, *Phoenix*, Bloomsbury)

Keep in mind this image of Sirius chasing after the departing Hogwarts Express train, and remember how Sirius "was gone" by the end of *Phoenix* as we study this scene from *Half-Blood*:

> 'Now, dear, you're coming to us for Christmas, it's all fixed with Dumbledore, so we'll see you quite soon,' said **Mrs. Weasley through the window**, as Harry slammed the door shut behind him and **the train began to move**. 'You make sure you look after yourself and...'
>
> **The train was gathering speed**.
>
> '...be good and...'
>
> **She was jogging to keep up now**.
>
> '...stay safe!'
>
> Harry waved until **the train had turned a corner** and Mr. and **Mrs. Weasley** WERE LOST TO VIEW...
>
> (p. 130, *Half-Blood*, Bloomsbury)

That's a great example of a mirrored scene, with Molly reflecting Sirius' actions of the prior year. Molly did not die, and thus this is a bite of red herring, but it seems that Rowling deliberately mirrored Molly's actions to Sirius' to put that very thought in her reader's mind. She wanted us to question whether this beloved mother who worried so for all her children would live or die.

Your students can mirror their scenes to not only drop clues and hints of secrets, but to show plot changes and character development as well. It's a great technique to revisit an earlier scene through someone else's POV to distinguish between characters, or through the same eyes as before to show how that character's perspective has changed or developed. Once a scene's structure has been established, its mirrored reflection can point to distinctions that hint at clues, secrets, and changes and help involve the readers deeper into the story as they analyze the parallels and differences.

13) Reversing Expectations

Barty Crouch as Mad-Eye Moody is a prime example of hiding a clue by reversing expectations. Mad-Eye was an Auror, a man reputed to have spent his life fighting Dark witches and wizards. He's got the scars and missing chunks of his nose to prove it.

He's also a totally cool guy. He taught some of the best Defense Against the Dark Arts classes Harry and friends had experienced and personally worked with Harry until he was able to totally throw off the Imperius Curse. Most importantly, he watched out for Harry throughout his fourth year, acting as his prime supporter from the faculty in the Triwizard Tournament. Who'd ever expect such a cool guy, who'd helped Harry in so many ways, of being in league with the Dark Lord?

And yet, Rowling turns these deep-seated reader expectations on their head. She doesn't just sweep those expectations aside, she uses them as the direct reason for why Moody *is* the book's villain. It's *because* he's Harry's #1 supporter in the tournament that makes him the *most* suspect. Readers had been alerted by Snape to the use of Polyjuice, which was deliberately shown to the reader in a prior book. We'd seen Moody constantly drinking from his flask (a running bit). However, even without these hints, the reader should have a clue that something was amiss with Mad-Eye due to reverse expectations.

Another example of how Rowling reverses assumptions is with the surprising relationship between Tonks and Lupin. Some readers guessed their hook-up early in *Half-Blood*, but it came as a complete shock to me. My attention was not focused there, and one of the main reasons is because it went against my expectations.

First, I didn't suspect Tonks of having a love interest. It was obvious something was going on with her, but it was also clear that Rowling was setting her up as a red herring for the book's villain in disguise. I thought it was entirely possible that Tonk's change in Patronus and metamorphmagus was just as presented, because of the trauma she'd recently experienced, and that more was only being hinted at to tease the reader.

One reason I didn't suspect a love interest with Lupin is because of his age. Lupin is of Harry's parents' generation, and Tonks, though older, we associate with Harry's generation. Their relationship went against my social assumptions for pairing, and so I didn't see it coming.

There's also the bit of Lupin being an ostracized werewolf, and so I wasn't anticipating a romantic involvement for him. Though any romance reader should have because he's the perfect tortured hero.

So, because the Lupin-Tonks hook-up reversed reader expectations in regard to age and social connections, it was a masterfully laid mystery.

14) Returning to the Scene of the Crime

We saw how juxtaposition worked in that mirror analogy with James/Sirius and Fred/George. Because the scene of Fred and George giving Harry the map was juxtaposed with the scene in which Harry hears about the dual troublemakers of Sirius and James, the reader should make that map connection between both sets of troublemakers.

For another simple example of how to juxtapose two supposedly unrelated elements to hint at a clue, let's look at *Goblet*. Early on, Rowling tells the reader straight-up what to look out for in this book. In Chapter 9 after the Quidditch World Cup, some unseen person near the Trio casts the Dark Mark into the air. Wizards pop in all around, shooting stunning spells at Harry, Hermione, and Ron.

> "Do not lie, sir!" shouted Mr. Crouch. His wand was still pointing directly at Ron, and his eyes were popping—he looked slightly mad. ***You have been discovered at the scene of the crime!***"
>
> (p. 130)

Discovered at the scene of the crime! Get that? We're supposed to watch out for it.

Then Bagman pops onto the scene:

> "Where have you been, Barty?" said Bagman. "Why weren't you at the match? ***Your elf was saving you a seat too—***"
>
> (p. 133)

Take note! Although "Barty" was at the World Cup, he had his elf saving him an empty seat that he never used.

Bagman's comment reminds us of what Winky had told Harry back in the stands. She was a good house-elf, not a shameful one like Dobby. Winky always obeyed her master...even to the point of saving a seat for him in the highest box when she was deathly afraid of heights.

So when Mr. Diggory asks her impatiently, "Elf? Did you see anyone?"

> Winky began to tremble worse than ever. Her giant ***eyes flickered from Mr. Diggory, to Ludo Bagman, and onto Mr. Crouch.*** Then ***she gulped*** and said, "***I is seeing no one, sir...no one...***"
>
> (p. 137, Goblet of Fire)

Ludo Bagman is placed in that sentence for a purpose. He is a reminder that Winky's belief above all is to obey her master, who her eyes flicker to next before she gulps and fudges the truth. The juxtaposition of Bagman to Crouch in this sentence is supposed to remind the reader as to where Winky's loyalties lie...and how committed she is to carrying his orders out.

The criminal returning to (or being present at) the scene of the crime is also a type of clue juxtaposition. At Hogwarts, Mad-Eye appeared on the scene immediately after the discovery of Barty Crouch, Sr.'s disappearance. A similar thing occurs in the Pensieve scene with Riddle "discovering" Hagrid as the person behind the monster in the school, Quirrell at Diagon Alley the day Gringott's was broken into, or young Harry feeling his scar hurt from that first banquet at Hogwarts.

The hook-nosed teacher looked *past Quirrell's turban* straight into Harry's eyes—and a sharp, *hot pain shot across the scar on Harry's forehead*.

(p. 126, Sorcerer's Stone)

Notice how Rowling uses Snape as a distraction from Quirrell. It is Snape with his obvious dislike for Harry who is shown to be the most suspect. Indeed, the whole Quirrell being bullied by Snape set-up not only juxtaposes Quirrell into the necessary scenes, but plays with reader expectation as well. "Who would suspect p-p-poor, st-stuttering P-Professor Quirrell" (p. 288, *Sorcerer's Stone*) when Snape is swooping about, angry and showing nothing but hatred toward Harry?

This whole reversal of expectations worked so well with Quirrell, that Rowling was able to reverse the reversal in *Secrets* and still take the reader by surprise. Lockhart, the pompous new Defense Against the Dark Arts teacher, was a prime candidate for causing the disruption in the school in *Secrets*. Although he was definitely a fraud, he wasn't substantial enough to even be the tool of Slytherin's heir. That role was left to a new student, a young girl, Harry's best friend's sister, someone the reader would never suspect because it went against all expectations...Ginny Weasley.

With these examples, you can teach you students to juxtapose their villain with the necessary scenes without giving him away, or juxtapose a clue next to its meaning without casting a spotlight onto it. After all, the reader loves to be surprised, as long as the writer played fair.

Playing Fair

As a final note to baiting a trail of clues, it should be emphasized that before dropping a major mystery twist that involves a magical element, Rowling first shows the reader how that element works beforehand. For example, we see the trio use Polyjuice in an unsuccessful attempt to find out if Draco is the heir of Slytherin two books before Polyjuice is used as a major plot device to hide a Death Eater as a trusted teacher at Hogwarts. Likewise, we'd been told about the Imperius Curse and even seen it performed on Harry in *Goblet* before it was used to twist Madam Rosmerta two books later in *Half-Blood*.

Even aside from magical elements, writers must always play fair with their readers. Give them the necessary clues on one hand, while distracting them by sleight of hand with the other. Ask your students to remember a story where they'd totally figured out its mysteries well before the end against one where they were pleasantly surprised. Consider too, have they ever read a book where they felt cheated that clues were not given, and how did that make them feel toward that author? Challenge them to make a game of playing with their reader, inviting them along on a clue hunt...but to play that game fairly.

The Game's Afoot Again: On Cursed Child and Fantastic Beasts and Where to Find Them

To fans who fell in love with the secrets and mysteries of Harry Potter, it came as no surprise that JK Rowling's first series afterward was a mystery. While the Cormoran Strike detective novels are great stories, they fall outside the scope of this guide as they are set in a completely different world.

However, two new works were released in 2016 that take place in Rowling's wizarding world. *Harry Potter and the Cursed Child*, a play in two parts, has been performing in London since July. The first in a five-film series, *Fantastic Beasts and Where to Find Them*, is set to release at the time of this guide's publication. *Cursed Child* takes places after the epilogue at the end of *Deathly Hallows*. Its cast is made up of the old crew, now older: Harry, Ron, Hermione, Ginny, Draco, along with their children and some new faces as well. The plot involves a twist on the storyline fans are already familiar with.

While being set in the familiar wizarding world, *Fantastic Beasts* involves a totally new cast of characters (though some may be ancestors to those we've already met, and there may be a couple of surprises thrown in) and takes place in the United States. So, new faces, new setting, and a new story.

What is most curious to me about both projects is that Rowling has decided to release script books for each. Scholastic (US) and Little Brown (UK) is offering the print book editions of *Cursed Child* and *Fantastic Beasts*, while Pottermore is publishing the electronic.

It may seem perfectly natural for this huge franchise to market itself in as many ways as possible, but I have a different take on it. Rowling has said in prior interviews that she prefers the novel form over films. She cut her clue-laying teeth through the Harry Potter novels. Even though she is now also a script writer, I wonder if she has not also hidden some Easter eggs into the upcoming storylines, especially *Fantastic Beasts* as she is the writer, that will be easier to find in her favored print format.

It will be most interesting to see how the new storylines and formats will change Rowling's mystery techniques. Something tells me that for *Fantastic Beasts*, at least, the games are about to begin! As a teacher, this can provide you with fresh resources for years to come to engage your students in actively seeking out possible clues and theorizing where they shall lead while learning to utilize this technique in their own writing. Perhaps a new generation can thrill to the discovery of Rowling's mysteries as she unveils a fresh wizarding world for her fans' obsession. (See our Writer's Resources page on DeepRiver.press for fun activities involving *Fantastic Beasts and Where to Find Them* after the movie is released.)

Take Away

In creating story questions and character secrets, a writer should be the master magician. People love to be surprised. Like opening that beautifully wrapped package at Christmas that we've stared at under the tree for weeks, the moment of ripping off the wrapping and seeing what has been hidden inside is a thrill.

Tell your students: don't cheat your readers out of this discovery! Help them learn sleight of hand. Encourage them to hide their mysteries well and distract from the clues they've planted. The tools for hiding and distracting are as many as there are clues to plant. For students who take up this challenge, however, I believe they will have just as much fun in planting their clues as their reader will have in finding them.

Hiding Your Clues: Activity

DURATION:

Approximately one (1) hour. Also to be reapplied as students continue their work.

SYNOPSIS:

In this activity, students will identify a series of clues they would like to hide throughout their work and note them in their journals. For a short story, it would be a group of clues that indicate coming actions, the main villain, truths about the characters, or twists in the plot of the single journey.

COMMON-SENSE APPROACH TO TEACHING: Collaboration & Reflection

STANDARDS:

Most state and national standards require students to produce clear and coherent writing with strong development, organization, and style. Their writing should be appropriate for the task at hand and should engage the audience. Students will plan, revise, edit, rewrite, and try new approaches as a way of focusing on a specific purpose and audience. Students will use the Internet to research, produce, publish, and update their writing products.

STUDENT WORK:

This activity can be completed as students are initially working out the details of their story or later once they have a work in progress and are returning to hide additional clues. It is recommended that you encourage students to reflect upon their clues throughout the process to foster a healthy mystery between their story and their readers. Reapplication is key. Have them apply this principal every step of the way as they develop their work to the fullest.

STUDENT DIRECTIONS:

There are three (3) essential steps to hiding clues in your work: identify the clues you would like to shroud, decide on how difficult you want the clue to be, then determine the technique to trick your reader. As an added bonus, you can consider having similar clues work together in a pattern to alert the reader to further clues or revelations.

In your journals, create a list of clues you would like to hide. Use the following handout of techniques to help hide your clues.

The handout includes concise examples of each technique we have covered in depth through this chapter (aside from the Sleight of Hand covered in the above mini exercise).

PATTERNS OF CLUES (Optional):

Students who have developed a series of clues revolving around the same theme—for example, all the clues point to uncovering the hidden villain—can use a pattern to engage the reader even more. Rowling marks many clues with the word "spot." Once the reader has determined this pattern, it is easier to "spot" more clues. How can students create a similar link between closely-related clues? Challenge them to engage their creativity to find a subtle means of accomplishing the same effect.

Techniques for Hiding Clues: Student Handout

1) **Give meaningful names**. (**Bellatrix** = the third brightest star in Orion. Means female hunter.)

2) **Camouflage by use of myths and folklore**. (Remus, according to Roman mythology, was one of the twin founders of Rome who was suckled by a she-wolf as a baby.)

3) **Use patterns to mark certain clues**. ("Moaning Myrtle was floating above the tank of the toilet, picking a *spot* on her chin.")

4) **Hide in a list**. ("There was a musical box that emitted a faintly sinister, tinkling tune when wound, and they all found themselves becoming curiously weak and sleepy, until Ginny had the sense to slam the lid shut; *a heavy locket that none of them could open*; a number of ancient seals; and, in a dusty box, an Order of Merlin, First Class, that had been awarded to Sirius's grandfather for 'services to the Ministry'.")

5) **Discredit the witness**. (McGonagall discredits Prof. Trelawney, saying she's predicted a death every year. So all Trelawney predicts must be suspect.)

6) **Drop in dreams**. (All the doors Harry dreams about in *Order of the Phoenix*, pointing to the Department of Mysteries.)

7) **Mark with repeated clues**. (Number seven marking many important clues in the series, such as the keyholes to Mad-Eye's trunk.)

8) **Mirror parallels**. (Sirius, as Padfoot, chasing the train in *Order of the Phoenix*, followed by Mrs. Weasley doing the same in *Half-Blood Prince*. Would she meet Sirius' fate?)

9) **Reverse expectations**. (Mad-Eye Moody in *Goblet of Fire*, the coolest Dark Arts teacher and support of Harry, revealed as the villain.)

10) **Juxtapose the villain with the scene of the crime**. (Quirrell in Diagon Alley the day Gringotts is robbed.)

Lesson Five

Put a Fidelius Charm On Your Godric's Hollow
(Holding off Backstory)

I once heard literary agent Donald Maass give a workshop on his *Writing the Breakout Novel*. One thing he said I will always remember—**backstory is called backstory because it belongs in the back of the story**.

This lesson follows on the heels of how to leave a trail of clues because one of the most important mystery techniques you should encourage your students to discover is the power of withholding backstory. Remember the three central questions I asked at the beginning of the Wormtail chapter, the ones that drove Rowling's trail of clues?

1) What exactly happened in Godric's Hollow?
2) Where does Snape's loyalty lie? and
3) How will Harry defeat Voldemort?

The first two out of three of these are primarily concerned with backstory, and even the third is built upon it. The reader is compelled to read more because they don't know the answer to these questions—they don't know the backstory.

Overview:

In this lesson we'll help your students discover:

1) The benefits of holding off the protagonist's backstory.
2) How to backstory even their secondary characters.
3) When to reveal backstory to pace plot.

Awaiting the Baggage Claim

What happened at Godric's Hollow is obviously all backstory. It's ancient history, but incredibly important to Harry's present because it reveals answers about who Harry is and what he must do to survive.

Why does genealogy or history consume so many people? We want to know where we came from to better understand who we are and our place in the world.

Consider, however, do you understand your family history, your own personal backstory completely? Aren't you still trying, to some extent, to understand yourself, your life, the kin who spawned you, and especially where you are going?

Consider, too, the people you encounter daily. When you meet a new teacher at school or the parent of one of your students, do you know all about them the moment you meet? Yet, does that lack of knowledge keep you from communicating and conducting business? You probably start off most acquaintances with just the basic facts: name, appearance (if meeting face-to-face), occupation, and the goal that brings them into your sphere (i.e., coordinating a class together, a volunteer opportunity for parents).

So, too, with the character on the page. The reader does not need to know every little detail of personal trauma about your student's hero or heroine in the first paragraph, first chapter, of even first half of the book. Just the basic facts will do. Name, a hint of appearance, an identifying characteristic (the hooks discussed in the first lesson), and a gripping current goal. Fundamentally, what the reader needs is a point in common, a compelling, interesting, character—a reason to continue reading.

Share the following handout with your students to help them reflect on how to create and withhold backstory for their characters.

Withholding Backstory: Student Handout

As a creative writing student, you'll learn about the need to create a *sympathetic* character. The word "sympathetic" just doesn't work for me. It's too easily confused with compassion or pity. If you have no problem understanding sympathy as "with understanding," or having a mutual association, then okay, a sympathetic character is fine. Too often writers carry this sympathy to the page by creating a protagonist bordering on perfect, noble and heroic from the get-go, or even worse, someone who needs our sympathy, as in pity. Sympathetic just does not carry the spellbinding quality which I believe to be the true center needed for character introduction.

What I think is a better word for defining character set-up is **compelling**. You want a protagonist who will draw in your reader's attention. Someone that intrigues, fascinates, and almost addicts your reader to the point that they cannot look away (like the power of high drama on good TV). You want your readers completely controlled by your Imperius charm, bound and determined to read onward to learn more, to see what your protagonist will do, so that eventually the reader will discover what makes him tick...just not at the beginning.

With this understanding of compelling, you'll see more clearly why backstory needs to be cut from the beginning as drastically as possible. Because one element people find completely compelling is mystery. If your reader knows, understands, and is totally in sympathy with your character from the start, then that's not a compelling character. However, consider presenting the reader with a character who is powerful in his passions, obsessed with a certain goal, completely intriguing in the way he thinks, acts, views the world—and the clincher—has an air of mystery about him. This is a character that your reader will latch onto and must read on to uncover his mysteries and see what he will do.

Consider the withheld Godric's Hollow backstory. In our introduction to Harry, we learn that a powerful wizard wanted to kill this harmless little baby, was unable to do so, and that somehow the baby survived and the uber-wizard lost his powers. We also know that the baby's parents died and he's off to live with his aunt and uncle.

We know just enough backstory to generate a ton of questions—why did this powerful wizard want to kill an innocent baby? How exactly did the baby survive? What happened to the wizard? How does Dumbledore know all this? How could that scar prove helpful?

So, although some backstory is revealed at the beginning, it is revealed from a limited third source (we never see Godric's Hollow directly), and only enough to inform and orient the reader to what they absolutely must know at that point to begin the story. What little is revealed keeps the reader guessing, thereby creating an air of mystery.

Harry is compelling from the start because he fascinates. Again, how was he, as a baby, able to survive a curse no one else had ever survived before? That's an intriguing, compelling mystery. Also, we meet an eleven-year-old child who has magical powers and is not aware of it. *How interesting.* What other powers might he have? *How mysterious.* He feels put upon, put down, misunderstood, bereft, and alone, but he's able to talk to snakes and even sic one on his bully cousin. *How cool.* Finally, the clincher—he gets an invitation to leave his dreary life behind and go to a school with other witches and wizards to learn magic. *We are so there!*

That's how to create a character with a minimal use of backstory. It was quite deliberate. Rowling said in a TV interview:

> Discarded first chapters of book one: I reckon I must've got through fifteen different alternative chapters of book one. ***The reason for which I discarded each of them were: They all gave too much away. And in fact if you put all those discarded first chapters together, almost the whole plot is explained.*** This is an old notebook in which I worked out—and again, I don't want you to come too close on this—[flashes paper] That is the history of the Death Eaters!

(http://www.accio-quote.org/articles/2001/1201-bbc-hpandme.htm)

Rowling understood clearly that the appeal of her mystery was in the backstory she cut, and she guarded her mysteries well. All obsessed fans knew that she'd written the end to book 7 since nearly the beginning and had it locked away in a vault. Indeed, the withheld backstory is probably the key to what made her the first career author billionaire.

Too many times I've read a first chapter or critiqued a work with too much backstory upfront and the author has defended herself saying, "But I need that to set it up right, for you to understand the complex situation or my troubled character." Hogwash. *Hogwarts*. You don't need it. Truly.

The reader only needs to understand enough to keep on reading. That's it.

We don't need to know that Voldemort came after Harry Potter having determined that he was the child of the prophecy because not only was he born at the end of July to parents who had defied him thrice, but he was also a half-blood, like himself. That he entered Godric's Hollow with his yew wand, having been told by his faithful servant Wormtail, betrayer of Lily and James Potter, the secret to their hideout. We don't need to learn from the start that Pettigrew was the fourth member of the group of Marauders, a little, weak man, feeling left out and unappreciated, and clinging to the new bully about town because he was too scared not to. That Voldemort then entered the Potter home, and that James, Lily's husband, who had tried to date her throughout their school years, but only managed to catch her interest during their seventh year at Hogwarts, then married and had baby Harry a year before, with his best friend Sirius as godfather, tried to hold Voldy off at the door, shouting at his wife to save herself and their child, but put up a brave struggle and was killed. We don't need to know that Lily, a very talented witch who was quite skilled at charms and a favorite of her Potions Master Slughorn, was offered the chance to live by Voldemort, due to the secret lifelong love of double-agent Severus Snape, but refused to abandon her baby and was killed. We don't need to know that her loving, chosen sacrifice thus protected her son in ancient magic, so that when Voldemort tried to kill him, baby Harry survived the curse no one had before, or that the scar Harry was left with connects him psychically to Voldemort and holds a piece of his soul, one of seven. That Voldemort has killed many times before and with certain deaths has severed a piece of his soul and placed it in a prized receptacle, all of which must be destroyed before he can be finally defeated. And we especially don't need to know that the betrayer, Pettigrew, in his Animagus form scurried through the rubble, retrieved Voldemort's wand and kept it hidden so he could present it to his master years later after having lived for twelve years as a rat in a wizard family whose son will eventually become Harry's best friend.

All we need to know is that Voldemort, the most powerful Dark Lord of 100 years, killed Harry's parents, then tried to kill Harry and failed, losing his powers in the process.

See the difference?

Yes, I know my little example is a bit ridiculous, but trust me, it's out there. Or, if you take an honest look at your own, my own, work-in-progress, you'll probably see a tendency toward the former rather than the latter.

So much of what we've studied about the success of Rowling's techniques involve giving the reader more—more detail in worldbuilding, more clues to follow, more in-depth characters to enjoy. **But when it comes to backstory, what the reader wants is less**. Rowling masterfully held off backstory until the reader was beyond curious to know, until the readers were begging, screaming in cyberspace, dying to know what happened. Until they felt compelled to hunt out the clues for themselves or write their own fanfic because they just could not tolerate the wait.

Let me put in one word of caution lest you stray too far to the other side. There is a difference between being pleasantly strung along and unpleasantly befuddled and downright lost. Make sure you include just enough backstory, as Rowling did, to orient your reader at the beginning. They should know the important basics: where your character is coming from, why they are here, and what they are hoping to accomplish (for now). Hit your GMC (Goal, Motivation, and Conflict) and hit it hard. The rest should be doled out sparingly like cheese along the maze of a mousetrap.

Hook your reader by hiding the bait. Make them come after it. Give them more by giving them less—especially when it concerns the backstory of your protagonist.

Backstory Even Your Secondaries

Look now to the second central question of the series—where do Snape's loyalties lie? For many, Snape is the most compelling character of Potterdom, even more so than Harry. If you visit the HP forums online, you'll note the threads that garnered the highest hits. Or if you attend a fan conference, it's impossible to miss the avid Slytherins dressed in their silver and green, discussing and debating their misunderstood Potions Master. Fans of all types, whether priding themselves on their House of Gryffindor or Slytherin, obsessed over Snape.

And what do we know of him half-way through the first book? That he's the Potions Master, seems to loathe Harry on site, and wants the Defense Against the Dark Arts job. That's it. The major key to Snape's success is his complete air of mystery. We know so little about Snape, and yet what we know is totally compelling.

Even though Snape is most definitely an antagonist to Harry, he's exactly the opposite of Voldemort. Whereas Voldy is always described as cold and calculating, Snape is passionate and emotional—hateful, yes, cruel as well, and rather slimy, but volatile in his emotions. He's got a goal we understand—to become Defense Against the Dark Arts professor—but we don't know either why he wants it or why Dumbledore will not let him have it. (Please note the classic goal and conflict).

Again, with Snape, Rowling set up just enough backstory to create more questions in the reader's mind. Why does Snape want the DADA job so badly? Why does he hate Harry? Why did he owe James Potter a life debt? And where do his loyalties lie?

Rowling does not limit herself to intriguing backstory about her hero and main protagonists, she's got detailed, intriguing backstory woven into the story at appropriate times for a large number of her characters...and more was dangled before our noses as the series progressed. Weren't you eager to know the relationship between Albus and Aberforth and why the brothers were never together? What were the horrific visions wakened in Dumbledore's head as he drank that potion in the Inferi cave? What type of tortuous backstory did that hint at?

Were you not on the edge of your seat to find out whether Hagrid, in his fascination with monsters, had accidentally killed a student and that's why he was expelled? Can you imagine how many readers would have lost interest if everything revealed about Tom Riddle in *Half-Blood* was flung at them at the beginning of *Stone*?

Rowling is famous for keeping notebook upon notebook of detailed backstory for her characters. She's chronicled the histories of most of her secondaries, and even flashed one of her notebooks at the screen during a TV interview[6] that afterward kept many Harry Potter sleuths busy. She kept those notes to herself and remarked that much of that information would never find its way into the book, though it is now creeping out in Pottermore.

It's all details she had to know, however, in order to create a full world. In this way, backstory is very much related to worldbuilding. Backstory is worldbuilding for characters.

Just because your students shouldn't whack their reader over the head with a personal history lesson upfront does not mean they shouldn't create it and know it themselves early on. Encourage them to fully prepare their backstory. Fill their notebooks. Analyze every detail of their characters and their backstories—not just their GMC, but how they relate to each other and their world. Create detailed, rich, compelling histories for each character that weaves in and out with their other characters.

Then, as an added bonus, encourage them to make their backstories do double-duty. Not only does Snape's personal history answer why he is fascinated with the Dark Arts, it also explains why he hates Harry, why he became a Death Eater in the first place, why he was eager to turn Black over to the Dementors, why the Dark Lord trusts him, and especially why he's loyal to Dumbledore. Simplistic backstory that only relates to that one character, or only answers one question, does not contribute to a full, rich, well-rounded character or world.

Above all, encourage your students to go against their natural instincts to tell all from the start. Where backstory is concerned, *less is more*!

Revealing the Backstory

How would Harry defeat Voldemort? This question was not pure backstory, but definitely involved it. How Harry would defeat Voldemort was a combination of backstory mixed with forward plot that drove the reader to the climax of

---

[6] http://www.hp-lexicon.org/about/sources/source_hpm.html

the story. The backstory must be added in the correct amounts to fuel the forward motion of the plot at just the right pace.

When is the right time to reveal backstory? Yes, we've discussed part of the answer to this question—when the reader is beyond dying to know. The full answer, however, goes deeper. Reveal backstory only when it's necessary to the plot. Don't ever tell the reader more than they need to know right now, in the current situation, to understand what is happening. Finally, don't ever give the protagonist more information than he needs right now to make his choice as to what he will do next.

Think about *The Da Vinci Code*. One reason that book hit such a high note of success was its compelling mystery and the rate at which it was revealed to the reader and to Sophie, the female lead. Sophie represented the reader in the story, having no clue as to the mystery behind Da Vinci's *Last Supper*. With the ending of each chapter, one clue was solved at the same time another was formed. The reader, or Sophie, never went without a driving, intriguing question related to plot or backstory.

Teach your students to reveal their mysteries, their carefully constructed backstories, at the demand of the plot. Even then, they should not reveal everything in one lump. String hints out, with new questions forming, to build up reader expectations and tension before they reveal the full answer. Dribble the hints and clues temptingly through their story. Parse them out in interesting doses so that the reader never goes without a driving question.

As they reveal these secrets, they should do so in an exciting manner. Nix the scenes of characters sitting over tea, at dinner, or driving in a car discussing their innermost secrets. Instead, they should consider flinging their hero's tortured past and mistakes at him from the poisonous words of his most despised enemy as they race through a chase scene (as Snape did to Harry following Dumbledore's death). Or, give their heroine the information she's craved just *after* she's made a huge mistake due to her lack of knowledge. Create their own version of the Pensieve, their own way to impart backstory in a non-boring method.

The reader, and Harry, were only given the final piece of necessary backstory—the full knowledge of how the elder wand works, that Dumbledore once possessed and now awaits in Voldemort's hand, which makes it completely under Harry's control—immediately before Harry struck. Because once Harry had earned all the information which had been withheld from him, he is finally prepared to rise with the pressure which has been building since the beginning and meet his chosen fate.

Take Away

For compelling backstory, teach your students to:

1) Create detailed, rich, interesting, compelling backstory for all their main characters and most of their secondaries.
2) Hold their backstory off until the reader is dying to know it.
3) Weave the backstory in by snippets through imaginative means that doesn't bore their reader and is apace with the forward plot.

> **STUDENT CHALLENGE:**
> If you remember nothing else from backstory, remember this—trim, trim, trim. Cut, hack, and chainsaw out any backstory that you absolutely do not need at the front of the book. Revise fifteen times until you start off with only a compelling character and an intriguing mystery or story question.

Postponing Backstory: Activity

NOTE: This activity should be completed near the end of the course. Our recommended pacing uses this activity as a means for your students to reflect on their completed drafts and improve their stories by reworking the amount and location of backstory. This activity is not counterproductive. It is vital to plot and character development that students write in backstory as they develop their characters so they can root conflict in a well-developed fictitious world, even if they have to rework the location and amount of that backstory later.

DURATION:
One (1) hour and possibly revisited again.

SYNOPSIS:
Using their short stories, students will comb through their work to remove unnecessary backstory and weave it in later where appropriate.

COMMON-SENSE APPROACH TO TEACHING: Collaboration & Reflection

WHERE IS YOUR BACKSTORY? WHERE COULD IT BE? According to literary agent Donald Maass: *Backstory is called backstory because it belongs in the back of the story.*

Postponing Backstory: Student Handout

Now that you have a completed draft of your story, reflect on it as a whole. Look closely at your characters and consider the backstory of each person.

Our goal is to preserve the mystery of certain key characters for the reader as long as possible. What could you remove or postpone to make that character more intriguing throughout the story?

Use the chart below to identify where you have inserted too much or too early backstory for your protagonist, antagonist, and main secondary characters. Then plan how to cut it from there and weave it in at the appropriate place later in the book. Be sure that you don't go too far, however. You never want to leave your reader confused.

Character	Where is your backstory now?	Where is the latest place it needs to be inserted to avoid reader confusion?

Lesson Six

Pulling the Sword Out of the Hat
(Mythic Structure, Archetypes, & Themes)

With her education in the classics, Rowling is quite adept at making use of myths throughout her series in a variety of ways. We've already seen how she taps into myths to name characters and to plot clues, but her use of these ancient stories of human understanding flows much deeper. She employs:

1. Classic mythic structure—the Hero's Journey
2. Mythic archetypes for storytelling and characterization
3. Mythic conflicts and themes, (i.e. the battle of good against evil, the journey through the Underworld, and the antagonist as the protagonist's shadow, the shadow of one's soul).

We'll need to discuss what myths are and why they are powerful as tools in writing, but that particular discussion will be deeper and more meaningful after we've seen myths in action in a contemporary story. After that, we'll explore how myths, their characters, conflicts, and themes, can be used to help your student improve their own storytelling abilities.

Overview:

Help your students discover:
1) What exactly is the Hero's Journey?
2) What are its twelve steps?
3) A chart outlining all twelve steps in all seven Harry Potter books.
4) An analysis of each of these steps from the chart in Harry Potter.
5) Using your Guiding Theme to hone your story.
6) Why use mythic structure?
7) What are character archetypes?
8) What are storyline archetypes?
9) What are personality archetypes?
10) How to make sure your archetypes are fully rounded peop;e.
11) Using classic myths to enhance your story.
12) Using mythic themes.
13) A final note on genres.

First, let's dig in by examining how Rowling utilizes classic mythic structure to plot her Harry Potter series.

The Monomyth, aka The Hero's Journey

Many of you will already be familiar with the theories of comparative mythologist Joseph Campbell. His seminal work, *A Hero with a Thousand Faces*, presented the idea of the monomyth, also known as the Hero's Journey. Or you might be more familiar with the book *The Writer's Journey* by story consultant and screenwriter Christopher Vogler. Vogler studied Campbell's work and presented the mythologist's complex theories in a condensed and more accessible form for writers.

Campbell's comparative studies of hundreds of myths showed striking commonalities among stories separated by centuries, cultures, and continents. Like Jung, he theorized that these points of congruence thrive due to archetypal knowledge and understanding, which exists in all peoples, and that bridges separation of time and space. Thus the monomyth is a universal pattern of story structure that transcends human boundaries. It bubbles up in myths from ancient Greece, to medieval courtly romances, to today's commercial fiction. To put it simply—the Hero's Journey is the story plot which has lasted the longest because it strikes a universal human chord of truth.

As such the Hero's Journey is the archetypal outline for a blockbuster plot. Since the 1940s when its modern face was reinterpreted by Campbell in *A Hero with a Thousand Faces*, many books and movies have been based on it, most famously the *Star Wars* series by George Lucas.

The summaries of the steps of the Hero's Journey provided below are based on Vogler's presentation of Campbell's work. I'm going with Vogler because he simplifies the steps, which makes it a bit easier for students to understand. Please note that Vogler wrote a whole book on this journey, and we're covering it in one chapter. Thus my presentation will be simplified. I will not be able to discuss all the variations and nuances of style. I highly recommend you read Vogler, or if you love mythology and esoteric studies as I do, try Campbell.

Also, I'm adding a thread at the beginning that is not part of Vogler's twelve-step Hero's Journey, even though he discusses it. **Theme, or the Central Question of the Work,** is to me the hub of the wheel around which all elements of the story revolve, including the plot. Each step of the Hero's Journey will pull from and flow back into the theme or the central question. You'll see it clearly in my analysis of Rowling's work and could be viewed as the impetus for the beginning of the Hero's Journey and in the character fulfillment at the end, coming full circle.

Vogler's Twelve Steps to the Hero's Journey

First we'll look at brief summaries of each of the twelve steps of the Hero's Journey, then a table summarizing all seven Harry Potter books according to the Hero's Journey, and finally a break-down analysis of how Rowling implements each of the steps throughout the series.

The Hero's Journey in All Seven Harry Potter Books

Across the next several pages is a chart detailing the Hero's Journey for Harry Potter. For easier reading, there is a pdf version available at the publisher's website www.DeepRiver.press on the Writer's Resource page.

The chart is coded with *italics*, **bold print,** and ALL CAPS is to help your eye follow similar items across the seven columns of the table.

Note: These steps do not always happen sequentially. For example, Harry first crosses the threshold of Platform 9¾ into the magical world before he meets the key mentor, Dumbledore (though he has met Hagrid, who serves as a mentor as well). Also, Rowling tends to have the Resurrection before the Road Back. The specific structure of the journey is not fixed in stone. It is also quite open to interpretation. You may analyze certain key aspects differently than I have.

Twelve Steps of the Hero's Journey: Student Handout

(modified from Christopher Vogler's *The Writer's Journey*)

Ordinary World—The home base of the hero, his normal everyday world. The Ordinary World should be in sharp contrast to the world he's getting ready to venture into, the Special World. Usually, the problem the hero will face already exists in his Ordinary World, but lies dormant.

Call to Adventure—A discovery or arrival that hints at a new world and calls the heroine within, a challenge or wrong done that must be answered. The Call to Adventure prompts the heroine to leave her Ordinary World for the Special World. It could be something that threatens the peace of the Ordinary World if the heroine does not go off to deal with it.

Refusal of the Call—The moment in which the hero hesitates, not sure whether he wants to change. By refusing the Call, the hero shows that he fully understands the serious nature of the Adventure, that his life will be threatened or seriously altered. Does he want to take that risk, or stay safe with the status quo? Can he truly make a difference?

Meeting with the Mentor and Gift—The mentor serves as the guide for the Hero's Journey. He's the old wise wizard who trains and tests the hero, and gives gifts to enable the completion of the hero's quest (not do it for him).

Crossing the First Threshold—The portal from the Ordinary World to the Special World, usually guarded by a Guardian or Gatekeeper. It is symbolic of the heroine having made a firm commitment by taking that first major step to begin her quest. Gatekeepers serve to test whether the heroine is worthy to pass.

Tests, Allies, Enemies—This is where the hero is prepared for the Ordeal to come by developing skills and facing tests, meeting and accepting allies, and learns who his enemies are. A hero cannot simply enter the Special World and triumph. There would be no growth arc. He must be challenged, learn, and grow in order to succeed. This is where you get to truly torture your hero!

Approach to the Inmost Cave—As the heroine approaches the Inmost Cave, the place of her greatest challenge, she will face new and more difficult obstacles and guardians to overcome to prove herself worthy for that ultimate battle. The Inmost Cave represents the classic Underworld, and the heroine must be prepared to journey through it, face death, and be reborn. Often, the heroine may pause, tempted to turn back, knowing the horrors she's about to face.

The Ordeal—In the Inmost Cave the heroine must face her deepest fears. Using all the skills she's learned up to now, she confronts the antagonist/villain and faces the ultimate test, the culmination of the trials that have prepared her for this final battle. Here she faces either literal or symbolic death. She must face some form of death in order to experience resurrection.

Reward (Seizing the Sword)—The reward is something the hero wins or steals from the Ordeal that is a trophy of sorts, marking his triumph over the antagonist. The Reward is personal, and most powerful as a symbol of the book's theme or central question. It may not always be material, but could be presented as a celebration or a love scene.

The Road Back—The bridge from the Special World to the Ordinary World. Here the hero crosses another threshold that may include a reassessment and rededication of goals. The Hero must decide whether to return to the Ordinary World rather than to remain in the Special World. Oftentimes, the hero may be chased out of the Special World by those he opposed, or may find the defeated Villain rallying for a second round.

Resurrection—That moment when either literally or symbolically the heroine is reborn. This may be brought about by a rebounding villain who must be conquered once more. The heroine awakens to a new world and a transformed life. Generally speaking, it happens on the Road Back because a bit of reflection is usually necessary to understand the transformation that occurred as a result of the Ordeal. It conveys the idea of cleansing, of baptism. The stench of the Ordeal, of death, must be washed away for the heroine to reenter the community.

Return with the Elixir—The Elixir is like the reward except it benefits someone beyond the hero. Sometimes the two may be combined, but the Elixir is usually a gift that has the power to heal the hero's wounded community. It can also heal or benefit an individual. The important aspect is that it is something the hero has gained from the Special World that benefits others beyond himself (whereas the Reward after the Ordeal benefited the hero, or was a trophy of the hero's triumph).

Twelve Steps of the Hero's Journey: Page 2

Journey	Stone	Secrets	Azkaban	Goblet	Phoenix	Half-Blood	Hallows
Guiding Theme; **Central Desire or Question**	Power; **Desire to know parents**	Bravery; **Where do I belong?**	Identity; **Who am I, & where do I come from?**	Self-worth; **Am I worthy?**	Love; **Desire to be included**	Compassion and trust; **How can I trust and understand others?**	Resolve and self-sacrifice; **How can I do what I am called to do?**
Step 1 Ordinary World	Muggle World; #4 Privet Drive, locked in cupboard	Muggle World; #4 Privet Drive, in bedroom pretending he's not there	Muggle World; #4 Privet Drive; doing homework in secret in bed	Muggle World; #4 Privet Drive; asleep in bed, dreaming of the Riddle house	Muggle World; #4 Privet Drive; lying on back in flowerbed listening to the news	Muggle World; #4 Privet Drive; sitting in chair by bedroom window waiting for Dumbledore	Muggle World; #4 Privet Drive; packing, preparing to leave it forever
Step 2 Call to Adventure	Letters from Hogwarts; Hagrid's hand delivery	Dobby's warning: Harry must not go back to Hogwarts	News report on Muggle TV about escaped convict Sirius Black	The dream of Voldemort and Wormtail in the Riddle house; Harry's scar hurting	Dementors in alley between Magnolia Crescent and Wisteria Walk	Dumbledore's arrival at #4 Privet Drive; announced by a letter ahead of time	Arrival of Harry's bodyguards (the Order); all willing to risk their lives for him
Step 3 Refusal of the Call	Vernon Dursley's withholding letters; "I don't think I can be a wizard." (p. 58, *Stone*)	Denies Dobby and tries to shut him up	Blows up Aunt Marge; denies he's seeing anything important with Sirius	Refuses to write to Dumbledore about his scar; denies its importance	Uses his Patronus on Dementors; denies how the Ministry will look at his actions	Refuses to prepare himself for Dumbledore's arrival so he won't be disappointed	Harry refuses to give hairs for the Polyjuice, does not want to endanger his friends
Step 4 Meeting with the Mentor and **Gift**	Hagrid: **knowledge of Fluffy**; Dumbledore: **knowledge of Erised, Invisibility Cloak**	Riddle through Diary: **diary, Parseltongue**; Dumbledore: **hat and sword**	Lupin: **ability to cast Patronus; belief in himself**	Mad-Eye: **ability to throw off Imperius Curse**	Sirius: **two-way mirror; love; knowledge and connection with his parents**	Dumbledore: **understanding of Voldemort, faith in Snape**; Snape: **Potions book**	Aberforth via fragment of mirror; **feeling of Dumbledore watching; gifts from his will**
Step 5 Crossing the First Threshold; **Guardian**	Diagon Alley as an initial dip; **Tom/The Leaky Cauldron**; Platform 9 ¾ the full commitment; **the train guard**	Ford Anglia; **Dobby, Whomping Willow**	Knightbus; **Stan Shunpike**	Dursley's boarded up fireplace via Floo Network; **George, Mr. Weasley, Fred, Ron;** Portkey to Quidditch World Cup; **Amos & Cedric Diggory**	Grimmauld Place; **the Advanced Guard and Dumbledore**	Slughorn's home; **Slughorn**	Tonks' family home; **Tonks' mother and father, the mother a sister to Bellatrix and Narcissa**

Twelve Steps of the Hero's Journey: Page 3

Journey	Stone	Secrets	Azkaban	Goblet	Phoenix	Half-Blood	Hallows
Step 6 Tests; *Allies*; ENEMIES	**Troll, Mirror of Erised, Nicolas Flamel**; *Ron & Hermione*; QUIRRELL & SNAPE	**Polyjuice Potion, Aragog, learning Parseltongue**; *Moaning Myrtle & Dobby*; LOCKHART, GINNY, RIDDLE	**Dementors, Patronus lessons**; *Fred & George*; PETTIGREW, DEMENTORS	**Triwizard Tournament**; *Sirius, Pseudo Mad-Eye, Cedric*; BARTY CROUCH JR.	**Occlumency lessons, Thestrals**; *DA especially Neville, Luna, Ginny*; UMBRIDGE	**Riddle/ Pensieve lessons, Felix Felicis**; *Slughorn, Ginny*; DRACO, RUFUS SCRIMGEOUR	**Wandering through wilderness, hunt for Horcruxes**; *Ron, Hermione, Snape)*; VOLDY, UMBRIDGE, BELLATRIX
Step 7 Approach to the **Inmost Cave**	The labyrinth of tests miles under Hogwarts; **the final chamber**	From the bathroom, down the pipes; **Chamber of Secrets**	Through the Whomping Willow; **Shrieking Shack, the lake**	The Maze; **Graveyard**	Department of Mysteries; **Atrium**	Tom Riddle's Cave; **the island in the underground lake**	Back to Hogwarts, Shrieking Shack; **the Dark Forest**
Step 8 Ordeal: **Opponent faced**; *Triumph over opponent*; DEATH EXPERIENCE (MAY BE SYMBOLIC)	**Quirrell / Voldemort**; *Denies Voldemort's demand to join him, prevents him from getting Philosopher's Stone*; DEATH AT HANDS OF QUIRRELL	**Riddle, Basilisk**; *Prevents Riddle from taking over Ginny, kills Basilisk*; DEATH AT BITE OF BASILISK	**Marauders, Dementors**; *Learns personal history and corrects wronged history, saves godfather*; DEATH BY DEMENTORS	**Voldemort, Death Eaters**; *Overcomes Imperius curse and stands proud, maintains wand connection until claims portkey*; CEDRIC'S DEATH AND HIS DUEL WITH VOLDEMORT	**Bellatrix. Lucius, Death Eaters, Voldemort**; *Prevents them from obtaining prophecy, "loves" Voldemort out of his body*; SIRIUS' DEATH, DEATH BY VOLDY'S POSSESSION	**Voldemort's Horcrux, Death personified by blood offering, Inferi, Dumbledore's weakness**; *Breaks through Voldy's defenses and takes locket*; INFERI ATTACK	**Death and Voldemort**; *Sacrifices self, then travels through Death (King's Cross) and chooses life to save others*; KING'S CROSS
Step 9 Reward (Seizing the Sword)	Philosopher's Stone	Sword of Gryffindor	Godfather: Sirius Black	Cedric's body; Triwizard Cup	Knowledge of the prophecy	Locket and Dumbledore's trust: "I am with you." (p. 540, Bloomsbury)	Claims the Elder Wand through Expelliarmus
Step 10 The Road Back	Hospital	McGonagall's and Dumbledore's Offices	Time-turner sequence	Mad-Eye's office/ hospital	Dumbledore's locked office	McGonagall taking charge	From King's Cross back to the forest, then to the castle.
Step 11 Resurrection	At Dumbledore's hands; talk with Dumbledore	Fawkes' tears	Harry's Patronus	Fawkes' song	Harry's heart, his ability to love	Fawkes' lament	Narcissa's hands on his chest; Portrait: Dumbledore's tears
Step 12 Return with the Elixir	Feast; earned back points lost for Gryffindor	Dobby's freedom	Pettigrew's life saved (life debt), Sirius' as well	Galleons for Fred and George	Alerting the world to the return of You-Know-Who	Dumbledore's funeral: for a moment, the union of the magical world	The celebration and mourning in the Great Hall; Voldemort's dead body

Analysis of Each Step

Harry's Ordinary World changes somewhat from book to book. His story always begins at the Dursley home in the Muggle world. However, through the course of the series, he goes from being locked in his cupboard, to having his own room, to getting presents from friends for his birthday, to having more freedom to move about his Ordinary World, to finally leaving it forever.

Except for the last book, he always starts out dormant and hidden in each book—asleep and locked in his cupboard, pretending he doesn't exist, dreaming in his bed, lying on his back hidden by flowers, sitting in a chair in his bedroom waiting. He does not start off active. He jumps into action after the Call to Adventure.

Harry's Call to Adventure directly reflects the primary focus of *that book's* story.

1. *Stone*—The letters from Hogwarts signify Harry's initiation into Hogwarts and the wizarding world.
2. *Secrets*—Dobby's warning is spurred by the Diary of Tom Riddle, which Dobby's master, Lucius Malfoy, will pawn onto Ginny Weasley.
3. *Azkaban*—The newscast regarding Sirius' escape starts the immediate focus on Sirius and his mystery.
4. *Goblet*—Voldemort and Wormtail at the home of Riddle's father foretells the climactic scene at the graveyard using his father's bone for Voldemort's rebirth.
5. *Phoenix*—The Dementors sent by Umbridge reflect the intensifying discord between Hogwarts under Dumbledore and the Ministry under Fudge as manipulated by Umbridge.
6. *Half-Blood*—Dumbledore's arrival at Privet Drive sets the stage for the private lessons into the Pensieve, which form the core of this book.
7. *Hallows*—The sacrifice Harry's friends are willing to make for him by drinking his Polyjuice is directly reflected in the self-sacrifice Harry will make for them all in the end.

Harry's Refusal of the Call—Except for the last book, Harry's refusals all seem to revolve around one theme—his own importance. He refuses to believe that he is someone of consequence, therefore he hesitates to make any change. He can't be a wizard, his life can't be seriously in danger, his scar pain isn't important, the Ministry won't use any excuse to come after him, and maybe Dumbledore won't consider him important enough to show up as promised. So Harry is essentially denying the Call by denying himself. This hints at Harry's ultimate quest—to believe in himself. Yes, he does have the power to make a difference, and he must believe in himself to accomplish his destiny.

However, in *Azkaban*, the Call to Adventure and Harry's subsequent refusal is a bit more complex because Rowling intertwines Harry's own search for identity with Sirius' mislabeled identity. Harry is forced to play along with Uncle Vernon's lie about attending St. Brutus' Secure Center for Incurably Criminal Boys, a parallel for Sirius being falsely locked in the Prison of Azkaban for twelve years. When Harry blows up Aunt Marge, not only is he refusing her assessment of his parents, but also silently acknowledging (hence his loss of control) how little he knows about his own Mum and Dad, and himself.

Note, too, the Refusal of the Call can take the form of having the call refused for the hero, as what happens when Vernon Dursley takes Harry's letters in *Stone* and then imprisons Harry in his room in *Secrets*.

In *Deathly Hallows*, Harry finally believes in himself and his ability to act, but still refuses to accept the help he needs. He's still trying to go it alone.

Harry's Mentor and Gift—Dumbledore is the primary mentor throughout the series. But he's not the only one. I believe that each book also has another person who serves as mentor to Harry. Each of these mentors gives a special gift that enables Harry to triumph over that book's particular antagonist.

1) Hagrid serves as a mentor in ***Sorcerer's Stone,*** giving Harry his first knowledge of the magical world and his parents as well as the information about Fluffy and the flute by which to calm him. Dumbledore gives Harry the knowledge of Flamel (through his Chocolate Frog Card), his Invisibility Cloak, and a preview of how to work the Mirror of Erised. Finally, Hagrid also gives Harry the photo album of his parents (which is more a reward).

2) In *Secrets*, while Dumbledore is still the primary mentor, with his gifts of the Sorting Hat and Gryffindor's Sword, Riddle by way of his diary serves a mentor role as well. It is through the diary that Harry learns about the Chamber of Secrets and what happened to Hagrid years ago. It is also through Riddle/Voldemort's "gift" of Parseltongue that Harry is able to enter the Chamber and save Ginny.

3) In *Azkaban*, Lupin is Harry's role-model, connection to his parents, and teacher of the Patronus. Harry uses the Patronus to save himself and Sirius from the Dementors—Harry's main antagonists through this intensely personal soul-searching book.

4) In *Goblet* his mentor is the pseudo Mad-Eye. Harry is not aware of Mad-Eye/Barty's duplicity until the end of the story, when Mentor transforms into Antagonist. However, throughout the book, pseudo Mad-Eye encourages Harry, points him in the direction of the skills and tools he'll need to complete his quest, and gives him the main gift he needs to defeat Voldemort in the graveyard scene—the ability to throw off the Imperius Curse and stand his own ground.

5) In *Phoenix*, with Dumbledore conspicuously absent, Sirius serves as Harry's mentor. While Sirius is in many ways a personality Harry does not wish to imitate, he does provide Harry with a strong connection to his parents, new information about himself and his abilities, and the unshakable love that helps him to once again overcome Voldemort in the end.

6) In *Half-Blood*, we return to Dumbledore as the primary mentor, giving insight into how Riddle became Voldemort and the unwavering faith in Snape that Harry will need to complete his quest at the end of book 7. Note that this last gift continues into *Hallows* because book 6 and 7 are in many ways one book. Snape, however, has served as an unwitting second mentor throughout *Half-Blood* by way of his potions book.

7) In *Hallows*, we have a curious device of Dumbledore remaining a mentor to Harry through his brother Aberforth. It's Aberforth's blue eyes, looking remarkably like his brother's, that gives Harry solace and hope through the story. It is also Dumbledore's portrait at the end that guides Harry in his disposal of the elder wand. Finally, Snape gets his full due as mentor, and with his last memories, gives Harry the final knowledge he needs to go into the Dark Forest and completely vanquish Voldemort.

Harry's Crossing the First Threshold—There are several symbolic thresholds between Harry's Muggle World and his Special World of magic. He crosses three in the first book alone—The Leaky Cauldron and its brick gate to Diagon Alley, Platform 9¾, and finally, the boat ride over the lake to Hogwarts. However, I think Platform 9¾ is the most significant for the first book because it truly carries Harry away from the Muggle World for his full immersion into the wizarding one. It's significant to note that the Platform's Guardian is called a "guard" (p. 91, *Sorcerer's Stone*).

Even though Harry uses Platform 9¾ in later books, Rowling deliberately chooses other portals between the worlds so that the gateway isn't always the same, and Harry is exposed to larger, newer parts of the wizarding world. In *Secrets*, he arrives by flying car, thus learning more about the role of the Ministry of Magic as well as the Whomping Willow, which will play a huge role in *Azkaban*. Likewise, in *Azkaban*, the Knight Bus gives Harry a fuller sense of the magical world nationally. The portkey to the Quidditch World Cup enlarges his view internationally; Grimmauld Place deepens his understanding of good people versus bad people (the world is not divided between good people and Death Eaters). The same is true for Slughorn, extending Harry's understanding of the Slytherin nature. Finally, in *Hallows*, through the gate and guardians of Tonks' home and parents, Harry is made to realize just how many people in the wizarding world are willing to make sacrifices for him, even those he doesn't know personally.

Harry's Tests, Allies, and Enemies—It would take too much space to list every test Harry faces as well as every ally he gains. What I've tried to do in my chart above is to list the biggies. For allies, after *Stone*, I've assumed Ron and Hermione as Harry's greatest allies for the rest of the series, and, until *Hallows*, only listed the new noteworthy ones for that book. Likewise with the enemies—Voldemort is assumed to be the head honcho, but each book has a particular antagonist closer to Harry who provides many of the tests and obstacles Harry must overcome for that book. Also, Snape is assumed on the level of Voldemort, an antagonist present in each book. It was not until near the end of *Hallows* that Snape switched in Harry's eyes from being an antagonist to mentor.

Harry's Approach to the Inmost Cave—The Inmost Cave, the part that is bolded, is the Underworld. Notice that in each book, the Inmost Cave is underground, either literally or symbolically. Even the Shrieking Shack, although itself not underground, must be reached through an underground method via the Whomping Willow, a metaphorical tree of life with its roots in the Underworld. What's more, the Shrieking Shack is symbolically underground as it's believed to be a haunted refuge of the Dead. Likewise, while the graveyard in Goblet is not underground, it is without doubt symbolic of Death, and the Dark Forest of *Hallows* is where you face your darkest fears.

The Approach to the Inmost Cave, the first part of this table not bolded, is where Harry and his friends face the final obstacles, tests, and guardians to prepare Harry for his journey through the Underworld. However, Hermione and Ron always leave Harry before the Inmost Cave as Harry must face that final Ordeal on his own.

> ## Harry's Journeys Through the Underworld:
> - *Stone*—Maze under Hogwarts; Death at Quirrell's hands
> - *Secrets*—Chamber of Secrets: Death by Basilisk
> - *Azkaban*—The Shrieking Shack & by the Black Lake; Death by Dementor
> - *Goblet*—Riddle's Graveyard; Death of Cedric and then the duel
> - *Phoenix*—The Arch; Possession by Voldemort
> - *Half-Blood*—Tom Riddle's cave; Death by Inferi
> - *Hallows*—King's Cross; Death by Voldemort

Azkaban is a complex example as there are two major themes going on, search for identity and recognition of personal strength. With the aid of the time turner, there are also two Inmost Caves. Even though Ron and Hermione are with Harry in the Shrieking Shack, it is Harry who alone determines to save Pettigrew's life. Harry is also alone when he conjures his Patronus by the lake.

In *Phoenix*, even though Dumbledore is present in the Atrium when Voldemort possesses Harry's body, it's as if Voldemort and Harry are isolated with Dumbledore powerless to help. Likewise, Harry is the strongest one standing on the island in Voldemort's Cave at the end of *Half-Blood*. It is Harry's strength that must rescue Dumbledore.

And in *Hallows*, Harry must walk into the Dark Forest completely alone, with only the "ghosts" of his deceased loved ones for comfort, but dropping even them with the final steps.

Harry's Ordeal—Harry experienced a death/resurrection within each book. However, the answer to each book's Theme/Desire/Central Question that Harry gains is what carries him through his Ordeal, helping him triumph over his confrontation with Death.

1) *Stone*—Harry denies Voldemort's offer to reunite with his parents as he realizes that putting his desires over others' lives is not the right choice.

2) *Secrets*—Harry channels incredible bravery in confronting the monstrous Basilisk to save Ginny's life and shows by actions that he's not Riddle's shadow.

3) *Azkaban*—Harry learns a lot about his own personal history and identity, gaining understanding deeper than public beliefs and opinions. He uses this knowledge of self and family to save both Pettigrew and Sirius.

4) *Goblet*—As the youngest and least experienced Triwizard Champion, Harry conquers his jealousy to prove his worthiness alongside the true Hogwarts Champion. He then proves his worthiness further by bringing Cedric's dead body home to his parents.

5) *Phoenix*—It is Harry's growing love and his desire to be loved which drives Voldemort out of his body.

6) *Half-Blood*—Harry's new ability to look below the surface with compassion and understanding is what helps him release the locket and then guide Dumbledore back home.

7) *Hallows*—With his greatest sacrifice yet, Harry firms his resolve to do what no one else can do, and makes the same loving, knowledgeable sacrifice to save others which his mother made for him.

In fact, this last ordeal not only serves as a step in the Hero's Journey for *Death Hallows*, but also as the final ordeal for the complete series. From *Stone* all the way through to *Hallows*, the books had an overarching Hero's Journey as well. At the end of *Deathly Hallows*, Harry experienced his greatest death and resurrection of all.

Finally, while Voldemort is most definitely the series' overarching Antagonist, each book presents a different face of opposition to Harry. Those are the ones I've noted in the table.

Harry's Reward—What is interesting to note is that in each book, Harry's Reward is also a symbol of that book's overarching theme or central question.

1) Philosopher's Stone—is very much a symbol of power for Voldemort and the only way Harry is able to lay claim to it is by not choosing power for himself. Because he will not grasp power at the expense of others, he also denies his desire to be with his parents.

2) **Sword of Gryffindor**—a strong example of Harry's courage and where he truly belongs, in the House of the Brave.

3) **A Godfather**—this is a touching, sentimental reward in that the orphan can finally claim a parental figure, one who knew and loved his parents, can provide Harry some personal history, and has risked life and limb to save his godson.

4) **Triwizard Cup**—I had the hardest time deciding on what Harry's reward was in *Goblet* because I see two possibilities, and they're both related to complex themes in this story. Although you wouldn't necessarily consider a dead body a reward, it is Cedric's and Harry's cooperation at the last that symbolizes Harry's worthiness and fair-play (as well as Cedric's). While the Triwizard Cup demonstrates how Harry has mastered advanced skills to be able to stand on his own in front of the Dark Lord and his crew of Death Eaters, it is Harry's risking his life to honor Cedric's last request and return his body to his parents that truly shows the noble merit of Harry's character.

5) **The Prophecy**—Harry's "reward" in *Phoenix* is bittersweet. In many ways, he'd much prefer to return to his ignorant, innocent state. Unfortunately, Harry and his world will never be at peace until he has faced, accepted, and accomplished his mission. He must embrace his ability to love to defeat Voldemort, and knowledge of the prophecy is a powerful tool in his quest.

6) **Locket and Dumbledore's Trust**—While serving as a powerful Horcrux in *Deathly Hallows*, at the end of *Half-Blood*, the locket represents the role-reversal between Dumbledore and Harry that is the most appealing and most relevant to the book's theme of compassion and trust. At his weakest, Dumbledore must rely totally on Harry, and Harry delivers. Harry is rewarded with beautiful words which I'm sure will warm him in the year to come, "I am not worried, Harry...I am with you." (p. 540, *Half-Blood*, Bloomsbury)

7) **The Elder Wand**—How can a young, rather innocent wizard defeat the greatest Dark Lord of all time? Through the most powerful wand of all time, one that has been won to Harry's loyalty through his great compassion and desire not to harm or to kill, and which he calls to his service by a simple charm to disarm—*Expelliarmus!* A charm which Voldemort would never use. But, once again, Harry rejects this ultimate power and simply uses the Elder Wand to restore his old and trusted one.

Harry's Road Back—In my analysis, Harry's Road Back is not the Hogwarts Express that returns him to the Dursleys and the Muggle World, but rather that intermediary scene between the inmost cave and the feast, often with Dumbledore where understanding is reached. Often set in an office or the hospital wing, this scene more accurately captures the feel of the Road Back than the Hogwarts Express because Harry's true new community is the Wizarding World, not the Muggle, and because it is in this scene that Harry understands his recent quest and his transformation. Likewise, in *Hallows*, it is from the Dark Forest to the Castle, carried in Hagrid's loving arms, where Harry fully understands his resurrection, how he has broken through the bonds of death and his own attached Horcrux, and how he can now defeat Voldemort and save his friends' lives.

Harry's Resurrection—Fawkes serves as the tool, or symbol, of resurrection in three of the books (*Secrets*, *Goblet*, *Half-Blood*, and even hinted at in *Hallows*). In *Secrets*, it is Fawkes' tears which quite literally bring Harry back from the verge of death, whereas in *Goblet*, *Half-Blood*, and *Hallows* it is his music which enters Harry's soul giving him strength, warmth, and rebirth symbolically.

At the end of *Stone*, we learn that Dumbledore yanked Harry out of Quirrell's grasp, saving him from death. In *Azkaban* we have the first instance of Harry saving himself by conjuring his most powerful Patronus. Even though this resurrection is from Harry, there is the hint that his father had a part through the identification of Harry's stag Patronus with his father Prongs.

In *Phoenix*, it is Harry's heart that saves him, his ability to love. Whereas in *Hallows*, not only do we get the Phoenix song at the end, in front of Dumbledore's portrait, but we also, surprisingly, get the gentle hands of a loving mother and long-time enemy on Harry's chest as Narcissa searches for and feels his tell-tale beating heart—and then lies to cover for him.

Harry's Return with the Elixir—The ending to *Stone* is a classic example of a return to the community with the elixir. Harry and friends win back all the points they lost for Gryffindor, plus more. They enable their House to triumph, and Harry has delayed Voldemort's return to power, at least for now.

Notice that in my assessment of the return sequence throughout the seven books, I have Harry's community as the Magical World, not the Muggle. I believe that once Harry passed through that barrier at Platform 9¾, the Muggle World ceased to be his true home. Although by saving the Magical World from Voldemort he also saved the Muggles, the immediate communities for Harry are Gryffindor House, Hogwarts, and the Magical World.

Also, though the Leaving Feast occurs in the first four books (and *Phoenix* without Harry attending), after *Stone*, Rowling no longer uses it as the scene for gifting the Elixir. Most of the elixirs become more personal, benefiting an individual...until they come together in the final book to save the whole wizarding community.

At the end of *Secrets*, Dobby, with his release from house-elf slavery, benefits the most powerfully and directly from Harry's return. By series' end, free Dobby saves Harry et. al. from Malfoy Manor, playing a pivotal role in aiding Harry on his quest to defeat Voldemort.

For *Azkaban*—Pettigrew gains his life and owes Harry. When Pettigrew repays this life-debt, although it loses him his life, it aids Harry in the defeat of Voldemort.

For *Goblet*—Fred and George get the gold and thus their shop. At the end, the Weasley's joke shop is a powerful center of rebellion against Voldemort, as well as Fred and George being personal supporters of Harry throughout.

For *Phoenix*—while the magical world didn't *want* to know Voldemort had returned, ignorance was not power. Finally, that brief moment of unity at Dumbledore's funeral in *Half-Blood* set the waves in motion for that stronger show of unity paralleled at The Battle of Hogwarts.

Thus, Rowling utilized each elixir and its recipients in her series to build toward the final, greatest elixir of all.

Guiding Theme, Central Desire or Question

As you can see, the central core of each of Rowling's stories acted as a hub of a wheel, around which her plot revolved. The central desire or question drove Harry's forward action, and then, once answered, guided him through his ordeal. That's tight plotting.

In my experience, it seems that many writers may not know when they begin a new project what is the core of that story. As writers, we sometimes have to discover what we're all about by exercising ourselves through the physical act of writing. Or as Rowling said in an interview with Oprah, "Sometimes I know what I believe because of what I've written."

However, if the art of writing is in the revising, once your student has a rough draft, then the fine tuning begins. This is when they must roll up your sleeves and start asking the necessary questions to sharpen their plot and hone their guiding theme.

Have your students go over each of these Hero's Journey plot points. Where is the theme in their story? Can it be defined or sharpened better? How does each point relate to their overall theme? These are the types of questions which can transform their first draft into a polished story that resonates deeply with their reader.

STUDENT CHALLENGE

The best way to learn how to use the Hero's Journey is to study contemporary stories and diagram their flow. You've got examples of seven books in this lesson, but they're all fantasy. The Hero's Journey is not limited to fantasy by any means. It can apply to any type of story.

Chart out your favorite movie or book based on the Hero's Journey. Do this with a partner, if possible, because these definitions are open to interpretation and it would help to see someone else's slant of the same story. Then, chart out your own story. See how your hero's quest flows with mythic structure, then analyze where it can be strengthened or tightened. The overall theme/central question should be somehow reflected in each step along the way.

Last, and perhaps most important—**don't sweat it**! Seriously. By its very definition of myth, as projections of the collective subconscious, the Hero's Journey is going to come naturally to you. It lives inside your imagination. You've absorbed its essence each time you've read a book, watched a movie, or listened to your grandpa's tall tales. It lives in the world around you, and you know it instinctively.

Plotting A Hero's Journey: Activity

DURATION:
One (1) hour. Including a short discussion and explanation of the Hero's Journey shared in the chapter.

SYNOPSIS:
This is an activity that aims for students to think both broadly and in detail of their protagonist's actions. They are to consider the overall story arc of their protagonist and decide on milestone events to push the development of that character and how he responds.

COMMON-SENSE APPROACH TO TEACHING: Collaboration and Reflection

STANDARDS:
Students will create a meticulous plan of fleshing out their protagonist's journey through their story. They must consider their choices carefully as their initial decisions will strongly affect how they develop their story. They should work in groups to brainstorm their respective Hero's Journeys.

DELIVERY & GROUP ELEMENT:
Have students break into pairs and assist one another with their journey. Use a timer to ensure each student is given equal amounts of time. Using our handout* from earlier in this chapter that explains the steps of the Hero's Journey, allow students time to plot their own story along the chart. Allow them to reference their charts as they develop their plot and secondary characters through our other activities.

Handout: Twelve Steps of the Hero's Journey from page 92.

Your Hero's Journey Chart: Student Handout

Using the chart below, plot out your story's Hero's Journey:

Guiding Theme; **Central Desire or Question**	
Step 1 Ordinary World	
Step 2 Call to Adventure	
Step 3 Refusal of the Call	
Step 4 Meeting with the Mentor **Gift**	
Step 5 Crossing the First Threshold; **Guardian**	
Step 6 **Tests**; *Allies*; ENEMIES	
Step 7 Approach to the **Inmost Cave**	
Step 8 Ordeal: **Opponent faced**; Triumph over opponent; **Death experience** (may be symbolic)	
Step 9 Reward (Seizing the Sword)	
Step 10 The Road Back	
Step 11 Resurrection	
Step 12 Return with the Elixir	

Why Use Mythic Structure?

So, what does this Hero's Journey mean for your creative writing students? What does it matter how Rowling constructed each book of her series? You probably already know the answer to this—it's important to learn from the best. Learn from the story mentors who have come before, just as Rowling did. Tap into the power of myths that have guided humanity for thousands of years...because they lasted for a reason.

The best way to learn the Hero's Journey, and how to use it, is by studying the works of others, both contemporary commercial fiction, as we have done here with Rowling, and ancient mythic bestsellers.

Myths are collective, shared stories that come to us from virtually all civilizations which have existed for the last 7,000 years. They describe the deeds of the gods, goddesses or other supernatural beings. They explain the "why" of some practice, belief, institution, or natural phenomenon. Or in the words of Joseph Campbell, "Myth is the secret opening through which the inexhaustible energies of the cosmos pour into human cultural manifestations." (THWATF, p. 3) Myths are outwardly projected fears, hopes, and dreams of the collective subconscious that point toward universal Truth.

Jung believed that myths are the means to bring us back in touch with our inward forces. They serve as vehicles to the great collective unconscious, with their universal archetypes and themes, which ultimately lead to the transformation of self.

Freud defined myths on the psychological order of dreams. Campbell took Freud's position further when he said, "The myth is the public dream and the dream is the private myth."[7]

What Joseph Campbell taught follows in a long line of mystics, prophets, alchemists, and visionaries—people who recognized that myths merely changed their outward clothes when they transferred their inward truths, transforming from century to century, people to people. Underneath it all, human desire remained one and the same—the push for betterment, the quest for redemption. The need for love.

What the mythic hero has always done and will continue to do is show us the way to fulfillment. The mythic hero accomplishes what the human heart longs for—renovation of self and transformation of our world. Writers possess a powerful medium to participate in this creative, redemptive process.

Why does myth affect us so profoundly? Why do we want to change our world so badly? Because most humans are dissatisfied with our lot in life and want the world to change. Our hero is the person who can improve the world for us. Our heroine is the person who can teach us to re-invent ourselves.

What the reader wants in a storyteller is someone who can reflect our real world back at us and yet provide us hope for a better tomorrow. After all, in the words of mythic heroine Scarlett O'Hara, "Tomorrow is another day."

Bottom line, myth has power. Deep archetypal power. When your students employ mythic structure and themes, they immediately increase the power and universality of their work. A writer who taps into myth, dips into a deep well that many before have dipped into before. With each sip they take from that well to nourish their own story, they immediately draw upon all those who have dipped in beforehand.

I once edited a young adult fantasy for a debut novelist. After I'd read the story the first time through, I complemented him on his powerful use of the Hero's Journey. He said, "*What?*" He'd never heard of Joseph Campbell, Christopher Vogler, and didn't know much about myth. So, I outlined his twelve steps for him, much as I did with *Harry Potter* above, showing him how he'd hit each step within his story. He was amazed.

That's the power of myth. It lives inside you even if you haven't been formally introduced.

Character Archetypes

Archetypes—you know them well. You recognize these recurring people instinctively whether you meet them on the page, on the screen, or on the face of your next-door neighbor. There's the loving and nurturing grandmother down the street who always gives your toddler a fresh-baked cookie when he visits. There's the angry and aggressive type-A, who flipped you off when you tried to merge in front of him in heavy traffic. Then there's the resourceful librarian who helps you find just the book your students will love.

Myths have their stock archetypes as well. Heroes and mentors, formidable guardians of secret passages and

---

[7] From *The Power of Myth* with Bill Moyers; http://www.mythsdreamssymbols.com/mythanddreams.html

laughing tricksters of chaos, heralds who bring challenges, and shadows who bring death. These types serve as what I call **storyline archetypes**—their form is designed as a function of telling the story.

Another set, which I call **personality archetypes**, are related to those mentioned above but suit a different purpose—to describe the traits of that character rather than the role they play in the story. In myth (and modern stories) we meet the spunky kid, nurturer, bad-boy, wounded hero, best friend, crusader, librarian, scientist, antihero, and many others. Indeed, the field of personality archetypes is almost as limitless as the world is filled with personalities.

In describing these common character types, symbols, and relationships the Swiss psychologist Carl G. Jung employed the term ***archetypes, meaning ancient patterns of personality that are the shared heritage of the human race***.

(p. 29, *The Writer's Journey*, Vogler)

Rowling molds her characters with a wide variety of archetypes, both storyline and personality. We'll look at examples of each and which characters represents those archetypes within her series.

Storyline Archetypes

There are five storyline archetypes I wish to discuss in detail in this section—Threshold Guardian, Herald, Shapeshifter, Trickster, and Shadow. I'm skipping the Hero and the Mentor to focus on those less familiar to students.

Each of these archetypes serves a distinct purpose in conveying the story. However, as an archetype is not limited to one character, neither is a character limited to one archetype. Even in a single book, but especially in a series as long and complex as Rowling's, archetypes can switch between characters and characters can merge and flow between archetypes. It would be impossible for me to cover all archetypes presented at all stages through the entire HP series, so we'll focus on a few of the more interesting and strong.

A) Threshold Guardians are placed at portals to new worlds or gateways to new challenges to keep the unworthy out. A Guardian may be a good-hearted ally of the hero, looking out for his best interest, or he may be an accomplice of the villain, seeking to harm or hinder the hero from completing his quest. Either way, a test of the hero is the ability to overcome or win over the many Threshold Guardians he will encounter along the way.

From the Portrait of the Pink Lady, to Dobby sealing the entry to Platform 9¾ in *Secrets*, to the grindylows guarding the "treasures" in the lake during the Triwizard Tournament, Harry encounters numerous thresholds and their Guardians throughout the series. I'd like to focus on one type of threshold and Guardian to look at closer.

Vogler talks about the Law of the Secret Door (p. 112-113). Many myths include a set-up whereby the heroine is told she must never eat from a certain tree, never open a certain box, or never pass through a certain door, upon pain of death. Of course the myths I'm referring to are Eve in the Garden of Eden, Pandora with her box, and Belle in *Beauty and the Beast*. We all know what happens, what is sure to happen anytime this sort of forbidden situation presents itself in a story.

The power of curiosity is universal. In the words of the immortal Dumbledore, "Curiosity is not a sin.... But we should exercise caution with our curiosity... yes, indeed" (p. 598, *Goblet*). Whereas later in the series Harry develops his own driving need to set the world right by stopping Voldemort, in the first three books, curiosity is one of the prime motivators urging on Harry, Ron, and Hermione.

It seems to me there is a forbidden door in each book, and a guardian to go with it. This forbidden door leads directly to the Inmost Cave where the Ordeal occurs:

Stone—right hand side of the third floor corridor that they are forbidden from entering, with Fluffy as the Guardian.

Secrets—haunted girls' restroom (with Percy forbidding Ron to go anywhere near it); Percy and Moaning Myrtle as Guardians.

Azkaban—The Shrieking Shack; Whomping Willow as Guardian (and Crookshanks leads the way).

Beyond these first three books, the secret door and its guardian gets a bit murkier, but they're still there.

Goblet—Portal to the Graveyard: Pseudo Mad-Eye as Guardian. This is an interesting one because not only is Pseudo Mad-Eye the portal's guardian, he's also a shapeshifter in disguise. Talk about combining your archetypes!

Phoenix—Harry's mind holds the secret door in this book. His dreams show him clearly the secret door to the Department of Mysteries, and his mind holds the "forbidden" and dangerous connection to Voldemort.

Snape, through Occlumency lessons, guards the door to Harry's mind.

Half-Blood—Tom Riddle's cave is symbolic of the secret door which was forbidden him as a youth, and he has explored fully as an adult. Voldemort has set many protections on his cave to protect his Horcrux, but it seems to me that the Inferi serve as the classic Threshold Guardians.

Hallows—I would argue that the secret door in this book is one that Harry, in the end, refuses to break into. It is the door into Dumbledore's tomb that holds the Elder Wand. Voldemort violates this sacred space, stealing the wand, whereas Harry finally gets control over his fears and ambitions and follows Dumbledore's wishes by focusing on the Horcruxes and leaving the Elder Wand to Voldemort. Dumbledore would thus be the Guardian of the last secret door.

B) Heralds bring news about impending change, challenges to overcome, and calls the heroine to adventure. As with most storyline archetypes, the character of the Herald can be presented positively or negatively, an ally of the heroine, or a tool of the antagonist. Or, the Herald role can be fulfilled by an inner call within the heroine and not take on the role of an outside person at all.

Although multiple Heralds can, and do, occur throughout the books, we'll look at the first Herald in each book who brings the news of the initial challenge for that year.

1) *Stone*—**Hagrid** serves in the first role of Herald, breaking down the door to bring Harry his letter from Hogwarts.
2) *Secrets*—**Dobby** foretells the doom which awaits Harry should he return to Hogwarts.
3) *Azkaban*—**Aunt Marge**, in a round-about way, serves as a Herald by forcing Harry to consider all he does not know about his parents, his identity—the prime theme of the story, and pushing him out of the house.
4) *Goblet*—**Mrs. Weasley**, through her letter inviting Harry to the Quidditch World Cup, invites Harry to explore the Magical World more fully.
5) *Phoenix*—**The Dementors**, then the letters from the Ministry of Magic. The Dementors force Harry into the action which precipitates the flurry of letters and his call to the hearing. We later learn that the Dementors were envoys of Umbridge.
6) *Half-Blood*—**Dumbledore**, through his advance letter and then in person. Dumbledore arrives to take Harry to Slughorn and starts him on his new quest to delve below the surface of important Slytherins, such as Slughorn, Voldemort, and even Snape.
7) *Hallows*—There are two sets of early heralds in this last book. Both *Daily Prophet* biographies regarding Dumbledore serve to alert (and alarm) Harry to his need to reconsider his pedestaled opinion of Dumbledore. Then the arrival of the Phoenix guard, willing to risk their lives for him, call Harry to his need to accept the help of others in his quest to eliminate Voldemort.

C) Shapeshifters are one of the harder archetypes to understand precisely due to their changing shape and function. By their ability to transform, they keep the hero off-guard and always on the alert. Shapeshifting is often played by the love interest, but could also be found as a role of the villain in disguise.

> Shapeshifters change appearance or mood, and are difficult for the hero and the audience to pin down. They may mislead the hero or keep her guessing, and their loyalty or sincerity is often in question.
> (p. 65, Vogler)

In Harry Potter, the most obvious shapeshifters are all the Animagi running about, each serving a different role depending on which form they're in. As Scabbers, **Wormtail** serves as Ron's pet rat before transforming into the betrayer Pettigrew and back to servant of Voldemort as Wormtail. **McGonagall** appears first as the watchful guardian over Harry's new home before transforming into the strict, but fair, professor Harry is most familiar with. She makes another shift during *Deathly Hallows* as she takes on her divine namesakes' role (Minerva) by leading her troops into battle. Of course, **Sirius** went from being the Death Stalker in his Grim/Padfoot form to loyal best friend as Padfoot/Sirius. Finally, we saw him in *Deathly Hallows* in a new form as a psychopomp (along with James, Lily, and Lupin), guiding Harry on the final leg of his journey through the Underworld.

On the romantic side, **Cho Chang** and **Ginny Weasley** serve as shapeshifters. Cho Chang transforms, in Harry's POV, from a beautiful, out-of-reach star of the Quidditch field, to Cedric's girlfriend, to Harry's girlfriend, to girl whose heart is buried in the past. Ginny morphed from somewhat-annoying-best-friend's-younger-sister, to casual friend, to good friend, to hands-off-unrequited-love-interest, to soul mate.

Snape, however, is the series' ultimate shapeshifter. That's why he's so hard to pin down. One minute he seems to be the most despicable, hate-filled man at Hogwarts, and the next it's revealed he spent the whole of Harry's first year saving his life. He flits between loyal Order member to Death Eater in his role as spy. At the end of *Half-Blood*, he transforms from healer of Dumbledore's Horcrux-damaged wound to murderer. The last major shift, actually the pulling away of all the masks, is to the true face underneath—the unrequited lover. Snape is such a complex character, however, that he deserves his own chapter and will get it in "The Ambiguity of Snape."

D) Tricksters are usually the center of fun, mischief, and mayhem in the story. They delight in upsetting the status quo or in "taking the mikey" out of other characters or the hero. For tricksters we need look no further than Fred and George Weasley. They fit the Trickster description to a Weasley sweater embroidered T. Their spiritual counterpart is Peeves, which is why it was so delightful at the end of *Phoenix*, when they passed their mischievous torch to Peeves, and he seized it wholeheartedly.

Like many fans, I find Peeves and the twins' antics totally amusing, and I fully understand why Dumbledore keeps Peeves about the place. In holding a reader's attention, it's important to have someone kick things up a bit, to foster a constant element of surprise.

Without the Trickster upsetting the status quo, life would not only be duller, but the hero's path more mundane. Tricksters provide aide for the Hero, even if indirectly. Not only can they poke the hero's flaw (*oh Potter you Rotter*) quite painfully, but by showing clearly a different mindset, an opposing world view, an alternate way of being, they enable the hero to do the same. As Ginny says:

> "The thing about growing up with Fred and George...is that you sort of start thinking anything's possible if you've got enough nerve."
>
> (p. 655, *Phoenix*)

Rowling magnificently uses her Tricksters to not only upset the status quo, but to propel her hero onward in his quest. Only Fred and George could have snitched the Marauder's Map from Filch, figured out how to operate it (seriously, who else would come up with "I solemnly swear I am up to no good"?), and then bequeathed it to Harry. But where would Harry have been without that map? You think Rowling doesn't know her archetypes? Think again.

E) The Shadow, and it's usually singular, represents the dark side of the hero, even though it's frequently projected outward into the villain or antihero. Thus the Shadow reflects the negative qualities of the Hero which must be overcome and defeated for the Hero to attain the ultimate quest of personal transformation. In other words, when the Hero overcomes the Shadow, he is symbolically overcoming his own dark side.

Tom Riddle is most definitely Harry's shadow. This role is never more apparent than during Harry's encounter with the shadowy memory of younger Tom Riddle in the Chamber of Secrets.

> "There are strange likenesses between us, after all. Even you must have noticed. Both half-bloods, orphans, raised by Muggles. Probably the only two Parselmouths to come to Hogwarts since the great Slytherin himself. We even *look* something alike..."
>
> (p. 317, *Secrets*)

When Harry is most "in touch" with his shadow are the times when Harry is the most angry and vengeful—like, throughout all of *Phoenix*! He's reflecting his Shadow, but his Shadow does not have the ability to reflect the light of Harry.

Having Harry's chief antagonist as the shadow of Harry's soul suits the major theme of the series—who we are is a result of the choices we make, not our birth. Riddle shows one side of choice while Harry shows the other. In the end, Harry must conquer his own dark side, his inability to understand that the world is not divided into Slytherins and Gryffindors, and that, indeed, the Slytherins are not all bad. He's forced to look with some amount of tolerance at people like Draco and Snape and find a way to work together with people he truly does not like in order to harness the full energy of love to conquer Voldemort. In other words, he needed to learn to trust like Dumbledore, something Tom Riddle could never do, before he could fully vanquish his Shadow.

Teachers, use the mini handout below, along with the archetype description handout that comes later in this chapter, to help your students begin to chart their storyline archetypes.

Storyline Archetypes: Mini Activity

Many of these storyline archetypes aid the telling of a story. Use the chart below to diagnose which of your characters fit which archetypes, and how you can sharpen their role in the story to better fit the needs of the archetype.

Archetype	Your Character
Hero/ine *(Harry)*	
Threshold Guardian *(Guard on Platform 9 ¾)*	
Herald *(Dobby)*	
Shapeshifter *(Cho Chang)*	
Trickster *(Fred and George)*	
Shadow *(Tom Riddle)*	
Antihero *(Snape)*	

Personality Archetypes

Personality Archetypes are not quite as fluid as their storyline counterparts. This is because characters tend not to change their personalities as easily as they change their roles. Think about it in real life—you may be a mother, sister, daughter, wife, teacher, consumer, and a friend, but you're probably not a waif, free spirit, seductress, crusader, librarian, and nurturer equally. Once you reach a certain age, your personality is just not as fluid. That does not mean it's set in cement either.

While we're rarely a deep mixture of many archetypes, we're also never a single one. People are usually a complex mixture of at least two or more. Trauma or drastic changes in our lives can signal a change in our personal archetype as well. This carries through to people on paper and was well represented in *Half-Blood* by Tonks' change of appearance and Patronus. Once her personality changed, her metamorphmagus appearance and Patronus (projected personality) had to change with it.

One excellent guide to character archetypes is *Heroes and Heroines: Sixteen Master Archetypes* by Tami D. Cowden, Caro LaFever, and Sue Viders. They cover sixteen heroic archetypes, eight for male and eight for female, but I've seen other analyses where archetypes are charted with different breakdowns and titles. Their list is by no means complete, but is a great starting point. Three of the five archetypes I mention below are described in their book.

While there are many character archetypes represented within Harry Potter, we'll explore five of the more intriguing:

1) Snape as Antihero: the antihero is a hero with a dark side.

> The spice of a story, the element that makes it more than simple heroes and villains, lies within the character of the Antihero. The Antihero is someone with some of the qualities of a villain, up to and including brutality, cynicism, and ruthlessness, but with the soul or motivations of a more conventional Hero.
>
> (http://www.flowerstorm.net/disa/Gallery/anti-explain.html)

Snape has done terrible things in his past, repented from them, and was redeemed by the series' end, but throughout the series, at least in Harry's eyes, he was a hateful, slimy, mean hearted, double-crossing git. One who happened, in the end, to have his loyalties in the right place.

Antiheroes are often cruel, arrogant, and obnoxious, or selfish, alienated, and weak. Their story role is to be a foil to the hero and other characters in the story, to make them deal with the alternative reality presented by this flawed character. Antiheroes, like a well-drawn villain, will think of themselves as the true hero, living according to their own belief system, even if that system is believed wrong by those they consider beneath them.

In other words, Snape is the perfect description of the antihero.

The antihero best projects the need for balance between the dark and light sides of human nature and the need to restore harmony and peace through repentance or forgiveness. With his outlaw image and distrust of the Force, Han Solo is another great example of an antihero.

Snape can most definitely be a nasty piece of work—the way he insults his students, plays favorites, punishes them unfairly—but he stops short of causing serious harm or injury. *He* never had them write their lines in their own blood. He uses his tongue as a whip to point out and rub salt in any wound of those he detests—all while risking his life in work for the Order. While he's eager to once more take points from Harry at the end of *Phoenix*, he's also the first to greet the returning injured McGonagall with a sincere note of welcome (p. 751, *Phoenix*, Bloomsbury).

Yes, without a doubt, Snape killed Dumbledore. Consider, though, that it took an antihero to pull off the less-than-heroic agreement between Dumbledore and Snape.

The Filk Challenge: Mini Activity

Filks are a wonderful and fun medium for channeling your creativity. A filk is a musical composition, often set to a previously existing tune, based in a science fiction or fantasy fandom. Or, according to writer and filker, Gary McGath, filk music is:

...a musical movement among fans of science fiction and fantasy fandom and closely related activities, emphasizing content which is related to the genre or its fans, and promoting broad participation. Filkers are people who participate in this movement.

http://www.mcgath.com/filkdef.html

With the below Harry Potter filk as an inspiration, your challenge is work in a small group to create your own filk. Your team can choose from any fandom you wish, but you must be willing to perform it live for the rest of the class.

Have fun!

I Am the Very Model of the Anti-Hero Archetype
By Marina Frants
to the tune of "I Am the Very Model of a Modern Major-General," from *The Pirates of Penzance*.

Scene: Enter SNAPE, swirling his cloak, followed by a chorus of SLYTHERINS

SNAPE
I am the very model of an Anti-Hero Archetype,
My condescending manner's guaranteed to make the heroes gripe,
I hang out in a dungeon that a nicer guy would wither in,
It doesn't bother me at all because I am a Slytherin.
I always dress in black with a theatrical and stylish flair,
It makes up for the fact that I don't brush my teeth or wash my hair.
I work with smelly potions in an underground laboratory
And have a gift for sarcasm and other snarky oratory.

SLYTHERINS
He has a gift for sarcasm and other snarky oratory,
He has a gift for sarcasm and other snarky oratory,
He has a gift for sarcasm and other snarky oratory!

SNAPE
I'm biased toward Malfoy and the other kids in Slytherin,
I terrorize Longbottom into quiverin' and ditherin',
In short I can assure you that I more than live up to the hype
Of being the very model of an Anti-Hero Archetype.

SLYTHERINS
In short we can assure you that he more than lives up to the hype
Of being the very model of an Anti-Hero Archetype.

SNAPE
I have an evil history that's murky and mysterious,
I have a vicious grudge against that bloody bastard Sirius,
I torment Harry Potter every opportunity I get,
But when he is imperiled I am always there to save the brat.

I was a double-agent in the previous Death Eater war,
And now I go again to risk my scrawny neck for Dumbledore,
Exactly what I'm doing, only JKR can say for sure,
But if I'm caught I'll probably get Crucio'd by Voldemort.

SLYTHERINS:
But if he's caught he'll probably get Crucio'd by Voldemort,
But if he's caught he'll probably get Crucio'd by Voldemort,
But if he's caught he'll probably get Crucio'd by Voldemort.

SNAPE
I'm capable of standing up to hazards occupational,
I'm capable of carrying a grudge cross-generational,
In short I can assure you that I more than live up to the hype
Of being the very model of an Anti-Hero Archetype.

SLYTHERINS
In short we can assure you that he more than lives up to the hype
Of being the very model of an Anti-Hero Archetype.

SNAPE
In fact, when we discover the true history behind the Prank,
And learn the real reasons for my quitting the Death Eater ranks,
And why I knew Dark Magic by the time I first showed up at school,
And whether I'll make Dumbledore look like a genius or a fool,
And if Karkaroff mentored me the way he mentors Victor Krum,
And if I ever really had a crush on Harry Potter's mum,
In short, when Jo reveals the truth behind my nastiness and rage,
You'll say a better archetype has never stalked across a page.

SLYTHERINS
In short, when Jo reveals the truth behind his nastiness and rage,
You'll say a better archetype has never stalked across a page.

SNAPE
I'm complicated and intense, heroic and despicable,
My motives are so twisted, some would say they're inexplicable,
In short I can assure you that I more than live up to the hype
Of being the very model of an Anti-Hero Archetype.

SLYTHERINS
In short, we can assure you that he more than lives up to the hype
Of being the very model of an Anti-Hero Archetype!

Many thanks to Marina Frants for her permission to reproduce her amazing filk here.

2) Sirius as Bad Boy— "The Bad Boy struts into every room, daring one and all to knock the chip from his shoulder" (p. 10, *Heroes and Heroines*). Because he's been believed to be the black sheep all his life, he's decided to live up to his reputation. He flaunts or ignores societies' rules, while living by his own code of conduct. Women often find him irresistible. Think of Fonzie in *Happy Days*, Sawyer from *Lost*, and who could ever forget Jack Sparrow, *Captain* Jack Sparrow, that is.

Sirius, who's reckless but good-hearted, was framed for a crime he didn't commit. He was believed for twelve long years to have been the betrayer and murderer of his lifelong best friend. Before that he was looked down upon for having come from a dark-magic family, while at the same time being outcast from the family itself for not being Black enough. The girls in the Pensieve scene definitely found Sirius attractive. And hey, when we first hear of him in the series, he's even lending his motorcycle to Hagrid. Sirius is without a doubt the bad boy with the heart of gold, though later he also morphs into a father-mentor archetype for Harry.

3) Mrs. Weasley as the Nurturer—The Nurturer is the loving, caring, usually mother-like figure who takes care of all those around her. She's the one who puts a band-aid on the scabbed knee, always passes around a plate of fresh-made cookies, and lends a sympathetic ear for the one with a hurting heart. Think of Julie Andrews as Mary Poppins.

Mrs. Weasley is a Nurturer with the claws of a tiger when it comes to rearing and protecting her young. She'll send each of her children, including her "adopted" son Harry, a homemade sweater for Christmas, but woe to Ron should he do something stupid, like steal the car. Woe, too, to anyone who would put her children in harm's way, like Mundungus bringing stolen cauldrons into Order headquarters. Bellatrix learns about the claws of this nurturing tigress the hard way!

Mrs. Weasley will always have plenty of food around the house, but Ron and Harry will have to peel the spuds. She has an open ear for Tonks' unrequited love woes, but has her claws out for her own son's fiancée, until she's proved herself worthy. Her worst nightmare is of course the injury and loss of those she loves best, and she shows herself more than strong enough to do whatever it takes to protect her cubs.

4) Ginny as Spunky Kid—The Spunky Kid is often a bit of a tomboy, but that doesn't make her less feminine. She's strong, resourceful, and willing to do whatever necessary to help her friends out.

> She sometimes hides behind her sarcastic wit, and her lack of confidence may make her play down her best attributes, but she is spirited, cheerful and the most loyal of friends. Quick with a wide grin and a good word, she knows and likes everyone, and the world likes her right back.

(p. 65, *Heroes & Heroines*)

Princess Fiona in *Shrek* made a great Spunky Kid.

With her impressive Bat Bogey Hex, sneaking into the broom closet when her brothers aren't looking, and befriending those outcasts others make fun of, such as Luna and Neville, Ginny's the Spunky Kid. She's incredibly loyal to her friends, even when it means coming down hard on Harry for "taking orders from something someone wrote in a book" (p. 182, *Half-Blood*, Bloomsbury).

5) Lupin as Wounded Hero—A Wounded Hero is a character with a serious flaw not entirely of his own fault. He's been hurt by society, another person, or perhaps a love interest. Because of his wound, he believes himself to be unworthy, or either doesn't trust the world to not hurt him again. Though living as a loner, the wounded hero is just crying out to be healed, usually through the love of a good woman. *Shrek* is also a good example for this archetype as Shrek himself is a Wounded Hero.

Lupin suffers a secret curse that makes him "unlovable," or so he thinks. His *furry little problem* keeps him outside of society, while his innate good nature makes him equally unfit for the company of other werewolves. He's afraid to love and to hurt those who get too close. It takes a lot for Tonks to break down the walls he erected to protect others, and his own heart.

Personality Archetypes: Activity

DURATION:
Ongoing—perhaps as a series of homework assignments. Two (2) in-class writing times where they will develop a character archetype.

SYNOPSIS:
Intended to cover the span of several weeks, students will identify personality archetypes in a TV series of their choosing. They will focus on one particular archetype, such as an antihero, and track the character's development over the length of the series.

STANDARDS:
The personality archetype activity is a great interdisciplinary practice that is fun and requires students to apply their schooling to the outside world. They will engage the use of technology and try their hand at cinematic and literary analysis.

PART 1: IDENTIFY THE ARCHETYPES:
Using the following student handouts, have students identify archetypes in their choice of a Netflix, TV, or book series. Students should use a series they have already watched or one they will complete before the end of the activity. Some archetypes may not exist within the show they chose—just find all they can.

PART 2: AN ARCHETYPE STUDY:
Select the character with the strongest portrayal of an archetype. Use the handouts to plot pivotal events that happen to the character that help shape their views, personal journey, or even their personality. Watch the first episode where the character appears and then the last episode where they have been featured. What is the character arc?

Character Archetypes, a Netflix Study: Student Handout

DURATION:
Ongoing—to be done independently.

DIRECTIONS:
For this assignment, you will watch Netflix, or a series similar to those found on Netflix.

Through this activity you will discover an array of characters that embody different personalities and functions in the story—character archetypes.

There are two types of character archetypes: personality archetypes and storyline archetypes.

Personality Archetypes: This archetype is defined by the nature of the character's personality.

Storyline Archetypes: This archetype is defined by the character's function in telling the story.

Popular Personality Archetypes:

Wounded Hero	Librarian	Spunky Kid
Leader	Free Spirit	Bad Boy
Nurturer	Warrior	Waif
Pirate	Crusader	Antihero*

Popular Storyline Archetypes:

Hero	Antihero*	Threshold Guardian
Herald	Shapeshifter	Trickster
Shadow		

*The antihero falls between the two charts because, while he serves a role in the storyline as a foil to the hero, the antihero archetype also describes his personality.

Personality Archetypes, a Netflix Study: Student Handout

PART 1:
You will use a series of your choosing to identify characters that best represent these popular archetypes. You may not find all the archetypes within your chosen series, but several, both storyline and personality, should appear as you conduct your work—find all you can. In your analysis, you should clearly explain the actions that confirm their archetype. **Use the attached explanations of each archetype to help you through the assignment.**

Character	Archetype	Proof and Justification

Personality Archetypes, a Netflix Study: Student Handout

PART 2:

Now that you have plotted your common archetypes, let's focus on a single personal archetype to study. Choose one that comes across strongly through the course of the series.

Use the boxes to plot pivotal events that happen to the character that help shape their views, personal journey, or even their personality. Watch the first episode where the character appears and then the last episode where they have been featured. What differences do you notice?

Character of Focus:		
Pivotal event that shapes them…	How do their views change?	Who is affected by their actions in response to the event?

Understanding Personality Archetypes

Use these descriptions to help you understand the most popular personality archetypes as you complete your assignment.

Wounded Hero	Has a serious flaw not entirely of his own fault. He's been hurt by society, another person, or perhaps a love interest.
Leader	Always the one to take charge. May not often listen to the advice of others.
Nurturer	The loving, caring, usually mother-like figure who takes care of all those around her.
Pirate	Always ready for adventure, but off on a new one as soon as responsibility presents itself.
Librarian	Neat and organized and considered rigid in her approach to others. Methodical and bookish.
Free Spirit	Floats from one idea to the next. Not burdened by material possessions or society's expectations.
Warrior	Willing to fight anyone opposed to him or his people.
Crusader	Concerned with righting injustice and improving lives for those left out by others.
Spunky Kid	Has lots of spirit and is strong, resourceful, and willing to do whatever necessary to help her friends out
Bad Boy	Has a bad reputation, but underneath is, usually a heart of gold.
Waif	An innocent, gentle, and usually not physically strong character.
Antihero	A hero with a dark side: may act like a villain but has the motivations of a hero.

Understanding Storyline Archetypes

Use these descriptions to help you understand the most popular storyline archetypes.

Hero	The protagonist of a story who overcomes adversity to bring about positive change in himself and his community.
Antihero	A hero with a dark side: may act like a villain but has the motivations of a hero.
Shapeshifter	By their ability to transform, they keep the hero off-guard and always on the alert.
Threshold Guardian	Placed at portals to new worlds or gateways to new challenges to keep the unworthy out.
Trickster	Usually the center of fun, mischief, and mayhem in the story. They delight in upsetting the status quo.
Shadow	Represents the dark side of the hero, even though it's frequently projected outward into the villain or antihero.
Herald	Bring news about impending change, challenges to overcome, and calls the heroine to adventure.

Rounding Your Archetypes

One important aspect to keep in mind when discussing with your students how to apply archetypes to their work is that **archetypes should not equal stereotypes**. Just because they choose an archetype to base their character's personality and motivation, does not mean that their character should not be well-rounded and complex. For this reason, I often like to work with two archetypes, one dominant and one subordinate.

For an example of how to use archetypes to round out a character, take a look at Hermione. Although Hermione starts off the series as the goody-two-shoes know-it-all, she is tempered with the less aggravating characteristics of the studious, organized, inwardly uncertain Librarian. As she matures she also develops into the passionate Crusader campaigning for elves' rights.

Students can work with one predominant archetype, then add in another to complement and contradict, forming a nice round character. Add all the complexities we discussed in the first lesson on characterization. In such a way, they'll still play to the reader's need of archetypal characterization while providing well-rounded characters that spring to life.

On Respect of Cultures

I cannot conclude a segment on myths, archetypes, and stereotypes without discussing the recent controversy surrounding JK Rowling's release of some worldbuilding for *Fantastic Beasts and Where to Find Them*. As of this writing, there is tremendous discussion online about whether Rowling appropriated Native American culture for her own benefit in developing the "History of Magic in North America." Some Native Americans scholars fault her for the misappropriate use of their living beliefs.

In writing, cultural appropriation is where a writer draws from a culture not their own to establish the identity of their character in a way that is not respectful. Does this mean as teachers guiding young writers that we must discourage them from writing outside their own culture? This is a topic discussed frequently and often divisively on social media. What I'm about to write is my own deeply personal opinion.

Many writers feel damned if you do and damned if you don't when tackling a character of a culture not their own. In a world full of people who all have their own distinct opinions, this is unavoidable in almost any debate on any subject, as reading a wide range of reviews on almost any book will show you. However, if you shape your opinion thoughtfully through personal connections and dialogue and then research deeply, you can present yourself confidently while still listening respectfully to opinions not your own.

I firmly believe that teachers and their students stunt themselves when they choose not to include diverse cultures in the classroom, either through the stories they read or the ones they write. We live in a diverse world; why should it not be addressed in all its beautiful complexities and colors in our stories? Surely, for most teachers, they only have to look within their class to find a wide variety of cultures and belief systems represented. Each student deserves to see themselves in the stories they read.

My husband is from Turkey and we lived there together, raising our young children, until my son was five. Coming from a family of mixed ethnicity, culture, homeland, and religion, I speak to my own views of writing and cultural appropriation from this experience. I wince every time I see a Muslim portrayed in what seems the only faces they can wear in mainstream media—that of a terrorist or Muslim apologist. Yet do I believe that no one but a Muslim or Middle Easterner should write characters of this culture? Absolutely not. To me, it is imperative that writers of good conscience include alternative and realistic images of people normally portrayed in a limited or stereotypical manner. It helps not only the readers of their stories but the writer themselves.

Stories are the only experience that allow us to get deeply into the head of another human being. This is both a beautiful opportunity and an awesome responsibility. By getting deeply into the POV of the character they're creating, a writer expands their own mind as well as the reader's. However, when mistakes are made, it can do more harm than good.

Therefore, writing of another culture must be done respectfully and in partnership with the culture represented. I feel comfortable portraying characters who are Turkish or Muslim because I have lived in Turkey and have been married into the culture for many years. I have numerous family members and friends I can turn to whenever I have a question.

But when I'm writing a character from a culture that I don't have an immediate connection to, I do my best to find someone from that culture who will talk to me as I shape my ideas and then afterward read what I have written and advise me. *Then I take the advice.* To help explore these cultural issues within your classroom, please share the handout on the next page.

Respect of Cultures: Student Handout

What can you do as a writer of good conscience who wants to explore characters of diverse backgrounds?

1) **Do it!** Write across cultures. It is imperative for people, but especially children, to see themselves addressed in the stories that they read. It is also imperative for people outside these culture to read stories that reflect the full reality of our world. Our story culture should not be mono.

2) **Do it respectfully!** Two key questions can guide you to a respectful approach: 1) How would I like to see myself, my family, my culture portrayed? And 2) How can I find out what *I don't know I don't know*? Ignorance is what will trip you up the most.

3) **Connect with those you know.** It is harder to disrespect people you have met face to face. Whenever possible, draw upon the cultures you have a personal connection with. We live in such a diverse world that this should not be difficult.

4) **Do your research.** Because it *is* so easy to connect with people different from yourself, there is no excuse for not doing your research. This kind of research does not come from books, though that may be a good jumping-off point. The best part of writing cross-culturally is the chance and opportunity to meet other people. Take advantage of it. Talk face to face with people from the cultures you're writing about before you begin to help you shape your story. Have a beta reader who will be honest with you, to tell you where there was something you just didn't understand properly or where you were offensive. Then take their advice!

5) **Expect diverse reactions.** We should not be surprised by this as writers. Even when writing monoculturally, a writer still gets diverse reactions to any story made public. Some people are going to love your story, some will hate it. Why should this one aspect be any different? The trick is, as with other reviews, be judicious in your response.

6) **Learn from your mistakes and make amends.** When in the criticism received you discover an error you made, the best response is to acknowledge your trespass, to apologize for it, and to make amends. Defensiveness does not help to improve your perspective, deepen your writing, or repair a connection you just frayed. If you were sincere in wanting to portray unique, underserved voices in your stories, defensiveness does not attain that objective either.

7) **Bottom line:** You can't write respectfully from a culture not your own without the participation in some significant way of that culture.

If writing cross-culturally still scares you, take some encouragement from Dumbledore. Writers make mistakes. Sometimes this is the reward of taking a valuable risk. Do not let any embarrassment you experience make you hide in your cabin and never come out, for as Dumbledore said to Hagrid, "If you are holding out for universal popularity, I'm afraid you will be in this cabin for a very long time" (p. 454, *Goblet*).

We may never be able to please all the people all the time, and indeed that should not be our objective. In some situations, the reality may boil down to people simply having different opinions. There is no universally correct answer to every subject. But, if we are not striving to speak strongly through our stories, to connect with diverse audiences and people with point of views other than our own, then what is the point of writing?

Base Your Story Conflict on a Classic Myth

Let me tell you a story.

There once was a god-king named Osiris, who ruled over ancient Egypt. He was powerful and intelligent and brought many blessings to his land and people. He took to wife the most beautiful and magical goddess Isis, who was both compassionate and wise and ruled often in his absence. Together they brought forth their son Horus.

But the evil god Set, Osiris' brother, fought Osiris for power and control of Egypt. He killed Osiris, then tried to kill Horus. Isis, however, saved the life of her son and hid him on an island where Set could not find him, until he grew old enough to face his father's murderer.

When Horus became a man, he fought his father's killer, Set, to regain what was rightfully his and to avenge his father. He eventually triumphed over Set and ruled Ancient Egypt justly and fairly, whereas Osiris descended to the Underworld and ruled there. Forever after, Osiris was seen as the embodiment of the deceased Pharaoh and Horus as the Pharaoh who lived.

For a fuller rendition of one of the versions of this myth see: touregypt.net/godsofegypt/legendofosiris.htm. The author of the version presented on this website calls the archetypal story of Osiris, Isis, and Horus one of the Great Stories:

> The Great Stories are part of the core human experience and never change except in the most superficial ways. They defy any attempts to rewrite them with drastic changes, always returning to their original forms. The setting might be modified depending on who's telling it, the characters have different names, but fundamentally, it's still the same story. A version of the Osiris myth exists in every culture: the just king murdered by his cruel brother, only to be avenged by the prince who follows in his father's footsteps.

As a teacher of literature, you are probably very familiar with this archetypal story. It lives on in the Greek myth of Orestes, sworn to avenge his father Agamemnon's murder at the hands of Aegisthus, to Shakespeare's Hamlet, the young prince of Denmark who feels he must act to avenge his father's murder at the hands of his uncle Claudius, to the *Lion King*'s Simba, to Amsterdam Vallon played by Leonardo DiCaprio in the movie *Gangs of New York*.

Each author using myth as a basis for her story will mold and tweak that myth to suit her particular beliefs and presentation. Rowling has fashioned the classic "son avenging his father's murder" myth to include not only a murdered father but the mother as well, and even more importantly to focus the son's action on the liberation of the good world rather than his need for vengeance (even though Harry definitely wants revenge).

The conflicts of the myths we remember to this day speak to human nature as it has been and as it still is. As writers, your students can tap into these older stories to give their contemporary ones a level of depth and universality. There are so many myths to choose from, each with its own timeless conflicts, themes, and characters. Here are a couple examples with their conflicts, but your students can find many more through reading myths and folktales.

The Love Story of Eros and Psyche: Venus, the goddess of love, is jealous of the mortal woman Psyche (Soul) because of her great beauty. She commands her son Eros, or Cupid, to prick Psyche with one of his arrows so that she will fall in love with a loathsome creature. However, gazing on Psyche's beauty, Eros accidentally pricks himself and falls in love with the mortal woman.

After some troublemaking by Venus and quests by Eros, Eros eventually wins his mother's approval to take Psyche away to live in his castle in the sky. Forbidding his bride to look on his face, he only visits her under cover of darkness so that she does not know who her bridegroom is. Psyche's jealous sisters, however, hinting that he is a serpent and will eat her or their babe, persuade Psyche to gaze upon her husband's face. When Psyche does this, Eros, feeling betrayed, leaves her. Psyche must then search high and wide and face many tests set for her by Venus in order to win Eros back.

Classical conflicts that can be picked out of this old story include the human soul's longing for union with the divine, the battle of the sexes and the need for individuation in romantic love, and conflict between mother-in-law and daughter-in-law!

The Wedding of Sir Gawain and Dame Ragnell: In the legendary days of the Round Table, a fearsome knight known as Gromer Somer Joure confronts King Arthur for usurping some of his lands. He issues a challenge that King Arthur must discover what it is that every woman desires most. If the king fails to do so within a year and a day, Joure will kill him.

Sir Gawain, who was the recipient of the usurped land, vows to find the answer and save Arthur's life. He searches out the answer among all the women of the land, but does not find the true one. However, as Arthur rides into the forest near the end of the allotted time, he encounters a hideous hag who introduces herself as Dame Ragnell, the sister of Gromer Somer Joure, and insists she knows the answer to his question. Her price for the info?—to become the bride of Sir Gawain.

Arthur reluctantly conveys the request to Sir Gawain who instantly agrees. Anything to save the life of his king. The confrontation approaches and Joure is given the correct answer—what every woman desires most is the right of sovereignty over herself, to decide her own fate. Joure howls in rage at his sister, knowing only she could have informed the king.

Gawain is true to his oath and marries the hag—to the great pity of the court that such a handsome man is to be paired with such a hideous beast. However, after the festivities and alone in the bridal chamber, when Gawain gulps down his revulsion to bestow the obligatory kiss, he encounters a maiden most fair. How could this be?

Dame Ragnell informs him that she has been cursed. She can either be lovely during the day in front of his friends and a hag in his bed at night, or appear as loathsome to his friends and a beauty to warm him at night. Which would he prefer?

Showing his true nobility and rare intelligence, Gawain answers, "That is for you to decide, my lady."

And with those words, her curse was broken and she was lovely all the rest of her days.

I love this medieval story. It demonstrates clearly some modern-day themes and conflicts, such as the conflict between male and female understanding, the dance of desire between the sexes, and the need of women to control their own destinies.

The power play between men and women in a relationship is universal. Even if your student's story is not a romance, they may have romantic elements that can be deepened by exploring these classical themes of the battle between the sexes. If their story IS focused on the romance, use classical myths to plumb the depths of how two can become one and yet still remain a healthy, independent two.

STUDENT CHALLENGE

Help your students recognize myths that have a similar conflict to the story they are writing. Encourage them to then engage the myth through creative means. Some writers do this above text, writing contemporary retellings of classical myths and folktales. Others choose to write below the surface, using hints and analogies linking their themes, conflicts, and characters. Have them share the points in common between their story and the myth they chose.

Take some time to become familiar with the more popular myths. See how they are still portrayed in today's bestselling novels and blockbuster movies. Then you'll be better able to help your students reflect on which conflicts are still battling it out in our stories today and how they can use them to deeper their own stories.

Mythic Themes

Classic struggles of good against evil, brother pitted against brother, the heroine battling to conquer her own shadow, the Hero's Journey through the underworld...death and resurrection—all are themes that resonate deeply in the Universal Reader's heart because of their archetypal, mythic conflict.

We understand these stories. We know how they must end. Good must win out over evil. Brothers must reconcile. The heroine must conquer her own dark side. The hero must cross through the valley of death and live again.

From the ancient Egyptian journey through the dangers of the Underworld to their Field of Reeds, to Orpheus' journey through Hades for his dead wife Eurydice, to Lyra and Will's journey through a parallel world of the dead in Philip Pullman's *The Amber Spyglass*, heroes have faced their ultimate challenge by passing through the Underworld and lived to tell the tale. Variations of the theme will vary slightly, but the end result is the same—heroes must die in order to be reborn to a new life. Death, resurrection, and transformation are inexorably entwined.

This theme is the most powerful for the reader because most of us, like Voldemort, fear our own death and know that our life on earth can be better. We look to our heroes to reassure us that not only is there life after death, that we can follow their path to eternal life, but also that we too can triumph in making our present life much more fulfilling, whole, and new again.

These repeated myths are comforting to us. We know the stories; we know how they must end, but because the world around us does not often show the results we desire, we must seek reassuring success through our entertainment over and over, time and time again.

The long-enduring, oft-repeated mythic themes resonate because they tap into the universal subconscious that flows between peoples of all centuries, all continents, all cultures. If your student can tap into these themes in their writing, they will deepen the effect of their story for themselves as well as their reader.

STUDENT CHALLENGE:
Have each student identify a key mythic theme or conflict within the story they are writing.

Take Away

Harry Potter fans go crazy seeking out all the mythic references within Rowling's world. They can find connections to almost any myth ever recorded. Did Rowling intend all the mythic references that fans find and thrive on? Of course not! Did she intend many of them? Without a doubt.

The brilliance of using myth is that by using one, your student can instantly gain links to all the others who have come before and referenced that myth as well.

By tapping into her own deep well of human subconscious, Rowling dove into the ever-flowing lake of mythic human consciousness with all its rich diversity and interconnectedness. Once a writer dips their bucket into the eternal flow of myth, they bring up not only the myth they sought, but all the variations which generations before you have tapped into, pouring from that same story. The wealth of centuries of mythic literary connections are within your student's grasp for the price of one dip. Encourage them to take a sip.

A Final Note on Genres

One thing I want to make clear before ending this lesson is that even though the Hero's Journey and archetypes seem to be an exclusive fantasy genre motif, they most definitely are not. The monomyth and archetypes can apply across any and all fiction genre borders. It's all in how the author interprets them.

For a fantasy story, the archetypes and monomyth may be taken quite literally—the hero is on a quest to retrieve the Elixir of Life, as in the Philosopher's Stone. Along the way he encounters very definite Threshold Guardians, as in Fluffy. Your students could use the same motif interpreted in a symbolic or psychological way in a comedy. When a boy gets a cool spaceman toy, the prior favored cowboy toy seeks to reclaim his position. But when the cowboy knocks the spaceman out a window, and then is pushed out himself, they cross a threshold into another world where they must work together to survive. (Thanks, *Toy Story*!)

The possibilities for playing and interpreting these mythic structures are only as limited as your student's imagination.

Lesson Seven

His Royal Snivellus
(Antiheroes and Ambiguity)

Severus Snape is the most discussed, dissected, disagreed upon, obsessed over character in the Harry Potter universe—even more so than Harry. Check out any online forum or companion book analyzing Harry Potter—they are sure to include a lengthy discussion of the Potions Master. Fan fiction is not complete if Snape doesn't make an appearance. And fan conferences are run over with Snape look-alikes.

There's one simple reason for this fascination. Harry, our hero, we know and understand. Snape, however, remained a mystery until the end. Many fans thought they understood Snape and identified with him, but to be honest, they weren't completely sure. He was a man of many themes, a man of mystery, a character of ambiguity.

All of which makes him a fascinating character study for your students.

This lesson, in a sense, will sum-up everything we've covered thus far in relation to characterization by performing an autopsy on one extremely compelling fictional man. We'll also push beyond characterization to analyze the themes your students may use to craft their stories and how to embody them in their characters.

Overview:

1) Snape's Progression Through the Series
2) An Example of Rowling's Deft Hand
3) A Man of Themes—Snape as a Vitriolic Antagonist
4) A Man of Mystery—Snape as a Symbol of Repentance and Redemption, but Whose?
5) A Man of Ambiguity—Snape's Gray Undies
6) How to Create Your Very Own Snape.

Please note: Our focus in this lesson is not to follow all the clues dropped about Snape in order to unravel his mystery plot, but rather to dissect how Rowling created his character and why it worked in order for your students to generate that same spark in their own creations. Let me acknowledge before we start, however, that this discussion will at times seem to sway further into fan analysis and even fanfic than a writing lesson. I hope you will bear with me until the end where I hope to tie it all together, because I believe when it comes to Snape, you must truly experience him as a fan before you can fully fathom how to create his aura as a writer.

Snape's Progression Through the Series

Snape, as the true Shapeshifter he is, changes and morphs from each book to the next, while maintaining his secrets and air of ambiguity:

- *Stone*—Hatred of Harry evident from beginning. Apparently the villain, but turns out to be protecting Harry from Quirrell.
- *Secrets*—Not much of a role one way or another (Rowling said she pulled out the Half-Blood thread from this book), but clearly dedicated to keeping the school open when its closing is threatened, while still bullying Harry and friends.
- *Azkaban*—Emphasis on his hatred for Sirius, Marauders in general. Extremely upset at Sirius' escape and his own denial of the Order of Merlin. No knowledge of Peter's treachery.
- *Fire*—First time we learn he was a Death Eater, and Dumbledore's vouching for him. Also, given secret assignment at the end for the Order of the Phoenix.
- *Phoenix*—He's in the Order, but not really trusted. Sirius doesn't think he's reformed. Tension while teaching Harry Occlumency. Claims to be spying on Death Eaters. Pensieve scene: we see him bullied horribly by James and insulting to Lily. Ministry of Magic scene: he saves Harry and others a second time by alerting the Order and giving Umbridge fake Veritaserum.
- *Half-Blood*—First time viewed outside Harry's POV in "Spinners End"—kind to Narcissa, disparaging of Wormtail and Bellatrix. Swears Unbreakable Vow to protect Draco, and then protects him throughout. Mysterious conversation Hagrid overhears between Snape and Dumbledore. Then at end, he kills Dumbledore and flees with the Death Eaters.
- *Hallows*—Except for his appearance at Malfoy Manor and then cursing the ear off George during Harry's escape from Privet Drive, Snape remains mostly in the background until the end. We are given the occasional reminder of him through news bulletins and Harry's angry thoughts. When during the final battle at Hogwarts Snape's mask is finally removed, the reader and Harry together see the truth that has hidden below the surface all along.

With his hook nose and greasy hair, from his loathing of Harry to his bullying of Gryffindor students, Snape gives Harry, and the reader, a nasty antihero to hate. But he gives the reader more. As his baggage (and undies) are revealed on page, the reader, along with Harry, develops a twinge of sympathy, a glimmer of compassion and understanding. Snape seems to only want to pursue the Dark Arts as a defense teacher, while supporting the Order as a double spy. Then he transforms again, turning into the coldest, bloodiest killer of the most beloved mentor. Or is he?

All of these contrasts and shifts contribute to what makes Snape a well-rounded character. For what truly makes Snape so obsessively compelling, above all the other endearing, eccentric, enjoyable characters Rowling created, we must delve deeper into the heart of Snape. To see him at his very worst and most complex.

An Example of Rowling's Deft Hand

Deft—that's a polite word for it. Other words include sly and sneaky. Or when a fan is dead-tired from following all the clues and still uncertain of where that sleight of hand leads, one might say misdirecting and downright misleading.

Let's break apart the flight scene following the killing of Dumbledore. Along with the immobilized Harry, the reader watches horrified as Snape casts the killing spell. We should be convinced of his Death Eater heart and hating him thoroughly. However, if you look deep into the words on the page, you'll see how subtly and yet openly Rowling works her twisting magic. (Also available on DeepRiver.press Writer's Resource page as a one-page handout.)

Harry tore past Hagrid and his opponent, took aim at Snape's back, and yelled, "*Stupefy!*"

He missed; the jet of red light soared past Snape's head; Snape shouted, "**Run, Draco!**" and turned. Twenty yards apart, he and Harry looked at each other before raising their wands simultaneously.

"*Cruc—*"

But **Snape parried the curse**, knocking Harry backward off his feet before he could complete it...

"*Cruc—*" yelled Harry for the second time, aiming for the figure ahead illuminated in the dancing firelight, but **Snape blocked the spell again**. Harry could see him sneering.

"No Unforgivable Curses from you, Potter!" he shouted over the rushing of the flames, Hagrid's yells, and the wild yelping of the trapped Fang. "You haven't got the nerve or the ability—"

"*Incarc*—" Harry roared, but **Snape deflected the spell with an almost lazy flick of his arm.**

"**Fight back!**" Harry screamed at him. "Fight back, **you cowardly**—"

Study the bolded sections. Even Harry can tell that Snape is not attacking but merely defending. Rowling deliberately chooses words that paint Snape not as a crazed murderer running for his life, but completely in control.

"**Coward, did you call me, Potter?**" shouted Snape. "Your father would never attack me unless it was four on one, what would you call him, I wonder?"

"*Stupe*—"

"**Blocked again and again and again until you learn to keep your mouth shut and your mind closed, Potter**!" sneered Snape, deflecting the curse once more. "**Now come!**" he **shouted at the huge Death Eater behind Harry.** "It is time to be gone, before the Ministry turns up—"

"*Impedi*—"

But before he could finish this jinx, excruciating pain hit Harry; he keeled over in the grass. Someone was screaming, he would surely die of this agony, Snape was going to torture him to death or madness—

"**No!**" roared Snape's voice and the pain stopped as suddenly as it had started; Harry lay curled on the dark grass, clutching his wand and panting; somewhere overhead Snape was shouting, "**Have you forgotten our orders? Potter belongs to the Dark Lord—we are to leave him! Go! Go!**"

(p. 602-603, *Half-Blood*)

It is only when Harry calls Snape "coward" that Rowling has him show a loss of control. However, through this scene, it's important to note the discrepancies from a man who just committed a grievous murder.

Notice first how Snape is shown as **protecting both Draco and Harry**:

1) "*Run Draco.*"—Snape turns at this point and engages Harry, protecting Draco by giving him time to escape.

2) "Now come!" *he shouted at the huge Death Eater behind Harry*—He's protecting, but who is he protecting, the Death Eater…or Harry *from* the huge Death Eater?

3) "*No!*" roared Snape's voice—and—"*Potter belongs to the Dark Lord—we are to leave him! Go! Go!*"—Snape stops the Death Eater from seriously harming Harry.

4) *Snape deflected the spell with an almost lazy flick of his arm*—and—"*Fight back!*"—It's obvious, even to Harry, that Snape is merely on the defensive, not the offensive. Only when Harry calls him a coward does Snape get angry and lashes out.

The second inconsistency becomes apparent in this line of dialogue—"*Blocked again and again and again until you learn to keep your mouth shut and your mind closed, Potter*!" *He's teaching!* Even as Snape runs for his life, after having murdered right in front of Harry's eyes, he's still acting as Harry's professor, teaching him once again the need to protect his mind from outside influence and to not let emotions rule his logic.

An astute reader must wonder: is this man who just murdered Dumbledore a Death Eater or not?

To keep the reader questioning and guessing, JK Rowling plants both sets of clues. Snape may be acting fully under Voldemort's orders and his Unbreakable Vow—protecting Draco and killing Dumbledore—sparing Harry because the Dark Lord ordered it. Or, he could be acting completely as a result of Dumbledore's prearranged plan and final plea—helping Dumbledore to sacrifice himself in order to save three lives (Draco, Harry, and Snape) —while protecting and teaching Harry even as he runs for his life.

The reader truly can find the clues to support either side. Snape remained a mystery. Yet, the baited and leaded line was cast for the discerning reader to bite.

What I guess happens in an example like the above is that Rowling plots out in detail both "Snape as loyal to Dumbledore" and "Snape as true Death Eater." She analyzes fully what he would say and how he would act in both situations, then she writes details from both into the story. At the end, she goes back and throws in the key clues that weigh the evidence in the direction she intends. Perhaps she also erases any actions that would firmly convince the reader of Snape as loyal Death Eater, anything that could truly not happen in any way, shape, or form if Snape were loyal to Dumbledore.

Thus, the clues are present for both interpretations, but the evidence is weighted toward one side. She did her job so well, that until the release of *Hallows*, many fans were fiercely divided as to where Snape's loyalties belonged. As always with JK Rowling, she wrote overt actions for Snape that hid subtextual meaning. However, the final interpretation is based on one of Rowling's predominant themes through the series—appearance can often be deceptive, and we must seek truth below the surface.

A Man of Themes—Snape as a Vitriolic Antagonist

Snape embodies many archetypes and plays several crucial roles in the series. Besides being an antihero and shapeshifter as we have already discussed, one of his primary roles is to serve as an immediate antagonist to Harry. If it weren't for Snape's daily pressure within the hallowed halls of Hogwarts, Harry would face almost no adult opposition. Snape is thus the adult counterpoint to Draco's more youthful bullying.

Pressure is necessary for the refinement of any base material. If you want your wood the smoothest, your sculpture the finest, your metal the purest, you must apply the pressure of abrasion or heat. Snape definitely rubs Harry the wrong way and strikes a torch to his anger. Voldemort is just too far away to apply the constant, never ceasing, daily pressure which Snape delights in.

One aspect of Snape which has not yet been explored in his role of antagonist is the analogy with Alchemy. Remember how we discussed the combination of Sirius Black, Albus Dumbledore (white), and Rubeus Hagrid (red) having alchemical symbolism? There's one more component to that formula for transformation which describes Snape perfectly—vitriol.

Vitriol, the most important liquid in alchemy, is distilled from an oily green substance and forms a highly corrosive acid. In the words of Paracelsus in *The Aurora of the Philosophers*, vitriol contained "viscous imperfections...take care above all that the matter [purified vitriol] shall not be exposed to the sun, for this turns its greenness pale."

Vitriol was often referred to as the Green Lion, and sometimes as the Green Dragon. Green in alchemy signifies possessing life, but not fully mature. The fully mature Philosopher's Stone is red. The Green Lion, or Green Dragon, are both symbols of power, intense and deadly. The Green Lion is sometimes seen as a symbol of corrosive rage and fury.

Snape anyone?

Vitriol's corrosiveness was an absolutely necessary component for the alchemical process of making gold out of lead. The prime matter had to be broken down before it could be reborn into a new, more refined, material. Most writers agree that a protagonist does not grow and develop without significant conflict being applied to his life. Without a doubt, Snape provided significant daily conflict to break Harry down and thus aid in his renewal.

Snape forces Harry to learn skills he otherwise would not, to open his mind to another way of being, to broaden his understanding of people and their outward appearance versus their inner truth. Snape saved Harry's life, even while hating him, forcing Harry to question deeper people's motives and actions. Dumbledore, the man Harry trusts above all others, trusts Snape, forcing Harry to at least partially consider that a man he finds vile has some merit in others' eyes. And Snape, quite painfully, forces Harry to view himself and his parents through a lens not quite as rosy as the one Harry favors.

Snape drives Harry to consider that one does not have to be perfect to be worthy...does not have to be loving to have loved.

A Man of Mystery—Snape as a Symbol of Repentance and Redemption, but Whose?

"I don't need help from filthy little Mudbloods like her!"

Lily blinked. "Fine," she said coolly. I won't bother in future..."

(p. 648, *Phoenix*)

In a fit of rage, Snape hurt the person he cared most about in the world and lost her friendship. Then, when he could have acted to save her whole family, he only sought to protect *her* life, and thus lost her forever. He spent the rest of his life in repentance, seeking redemption, while still angry at those he believed had stripped Lily from him.

Now, at the end of *Half-Blood*, consider where we left off with Harry in regards to Snape:

Harry uttered an inarticulate yell of rage: in that instant, he cared not whether he lived or died; pushing himself to his feet again, he staggered blindly towards Snape, **the man he now hated as much as he hated Voldemort himself—**

(p. 563, *Half-Blood*, Bloomsbury)

Harry is on a mission, not only to vanquish Voldemort, but perhaps even more personally, to kill Snape. And he has strong reason. He watched Snape murder Dumbledore and was unable to stop him. Harry is filled with rage and hatred. The hatred Harry feels here is a shadow of Voldemort. But the rage…the rage links him to Snape.

And Snape deserves it, right?

As we delve deeper, consider that one of the primary themes within the series is that appearances do not always reflect the inner truth. What you see with your own eyes can deceive you. We've had numerous examples, from the transfigured Animagi to the Polyjuiced pretenders. Within each book, there has been at least one major deception:

1. **Quirrell**—hiding behind a mask of ineptitude and fear.
2. **Lockhart**—appearing as a famous author while taking credit for other people's success; **Tom Riddle**—vicious killer hiding under his mask of Head Boy while framing innocent Hagrid.
3. **Wormtail**—masquerading twelve long years as Scabbers; **Sirius Black**—believed to be a betraying murderer.
4. **Barty Crouch, Jr.,**—loyal servant to Voldemort, posing as Mad-Eye, famous Auror.
5. **Umbridge**'s insincere mask of concern and righteousness.
6. *Half-Blood*—This one delves the deepest into Rowling's well of pretensions by appearing to unmask the traitor **Snape**.
7. Finally, in *Hallows*, **Snape**'s most intimate inner memories are given to Harry, along with the truth about his loyalties and desires throughout.

Rowling has twisted a character within each book. Without a doubt, Snape was the greatest twist up her wand. She did not introduce a new character for deception in the last book, but rather revealed the *major pretender* all along. By stripping off Snape's murderous mask from the end of *Half-Blood*, she played her trump card on her key themes: that you cannot always believe what you see, that a person's inner truth is not always reflected by their outward appearance, that the world is not divided between good people and Death Eaters, and that, to be redeemed, Harry needed to open his heart to more of Dumbledore's love and trust.

Think of how powerful it was for Harry to recognize that people of the shady gray of Snape also had a place in opposing the forces of pure evil. At Dumbledore's insistence, Harry had spent a year exploring Tom Riddle's background to the point that he almost felt compassion for a man who truly was the face of evil within the series, a man who killed time and time again to achieve immortality for himself.

Finally, Harry was forced to look deep enough into Snape's past to garner some sympathy for the man who had caused him constant, ceaseless trauma. He discovered the evidence that Snape truly was acting upon Dumbledore's plea and opened his mind to the realization that he had once again misconstrued the testimony of his own eyes.

At the end of *Half-Blood*, as you read of Harry flying after Snape, murderous rage in his heart, could you have imagined him naming his son after him one day? That's a powerful change.

Challenge your students: *Have your protagonist do what he previously considered impossible, and you've shown enormous character development and transformation.*

A shapeshifter such as Snape, a man of such ambiguity, exists for primarily one storyline purpose—to teach the hero and the reader a powerful lesson, a main theme of the story. For Rowling, this theme was that life is not always as we perceive it to be. Harry's final transformation, was to accept the inner reality of Snape and to claim Snape's redemption as his own.

In other words, when Harry could:

1. allow himself to grasp what many readers had already discerned
2. remember that he had been deceived many times before because outward appearances do not always reflect inner truth
3. accept that the wisest man whom he trusted more than anyone else in this world trusted Snape for good

reason, and

4. understand the core of what Dumbledore taught him—the terrible, awesome power of love above all other powers

Then, and only then, was Harry ready to unleash the ultimate power he possessed, the power of love for peoples of all types, of all Houses, and defeat a man who knew not love.

Harry and Snape didn't get a chance to apologize to each other, to offer each other back rubs or hugs, but through Harry acting upon Snape's dying gift of memories, they effectively joined their mighty forces and knowledge, combining the power of brave Gryffindor and cunning Slytherin, to wipe out the true face of evil, Voldemort. To claim their own personal redemption.

Was the death of vitriol necessary to the perfection of the Philosopher's Stone? With the themes Rowling played with, if you accept that Snape personified repentance and redemption, and if you believe that in Harry's final transformation he must see and understand Snape with new eyes, through the Dumbledore lens of trust, then it was inevitable that Snape act one more time to save Harry's life and died in the process—his ultimate act of repentance.

A man of opposition and antagonism, a man of mystery, a symbol of redemption. Still, Snape's appeal went even deeper, beyond the mystery and themes, to his very ambiguity.

A Man of Ambiguity—Snape's Gray Undies

It was one of JK Rowling's most memorable scenes from *Order of the Phoenix*, one that fans could not wait to see come to life on the big screen, and not just because they were eager to view the four marauders together, alive as teenagers. No, everyone wanted to see Snape and James go at each other. Many were dying to laugh at Snape's graying underpants.

> Behind [James], the Impediment Jinx was wearing off. Snape was beginning to inch toward his fallen wand, spitting out soapsuds as he crawled.
>
> "I wouldn't go out with you if it was a choice between you and the giant squid," said Lily.
>
> "Bad luck, Prongs," said Sirius briskly, turning back to Snape. "OY!"
>
> But too late; Snape had directed his wand straight at James; there was a flash of light and a **gash appeared on the side of James's face, spattering his robes with blood**. James whirled about; a second flash of light later, Snape was hanging upside down in the air, his robes falling over his head **to reveal skinny, pallid legs and a pair of graying underpants**.
>
> (p. 647, *Phoenix*)

I don't think those gray undies are thrown in casually for a bit of nasty flavor. Indeed, Rowling *possibly* crafted this whole scene around them.

This view through the Pensieve opens Harry's eyes to the fact that he'd placed his father on a pedestal that was both unhealthy and unrealistic. The world is not filled with good people and Death Eaters, but ultimately most of us live in various shades of gray. That's where Snape's exposed undies come in. Snape, like his undies, is one of the grayest.

Ambiguity, at its essence, is the lack of being defined in absolute terms. Snape was deliberately constructed by his creator to be a man of uncertain allegiance, trusted by few, doubted by many, living in a world of shadows, existing on both sides of the Dumbledore/Voldemort divide. A man who intentionally concealed secrets and motivations.

It takes a special character to serve this role. It cannot be the Hero, the Mentor, the Shadow—not in this type of commercial fiction, at least not for long. When a mythic world has been created where the ultimate fight between good and evil must battle to the death, it's left to the antihero to possess and embody the vast grayness in-between.

The role of a Snape character would probably not be as discernable or strong in a work where right and wrong are not as clearly polarized as in Harry Potter. In other words, in a work of literary fiction, where most characters exist in their own world of shadows, Snape would hardly stand out. However, in a world where the villain is deeply evil and the Hero must achieve a higher level of heroism than most of us would ever encounter in our lives, then the strong middle ground needs to be actively portrayed by a character who is a bit of both and yet neither one or the other.

Snape's shapeshifting directly relates to his ambiguity. His never-ending morphing keeps the reader off-guard, on the alert, and constantly wondering. Readers latch onto Snape because the uncertainty of his character commands it. His mysterious nature demands the reader's questions and inward exploration. What do *I* think about loyalty, appearances, the power of trust? Do *I* believe a person can be nasty and mean and still serve a higher good? Do *I* agree that a Slytherin and a Gryffindor have anything in common and can work together to defeat true evil? And who am I inside? Would I defend Snape, or bully him upside down?

Who you are inside will determine how you interpret Snape. Snape will be understood, in your mind, in direct accordance with your world view. That's why readers were so polarized. Snape draws the reader's involvement because that is his purpose.

Snape exists to keep the reader guessing, probing his mysteries, guessing at his allegiance...exploring our own...until the very end.

One last thing to note regarding Rowling's craft in the scene snippet above. See that other bolded section, the curse Snape threw at James that caused a gash on his head and made him bleed? What does that remind you of? We see here Snape casting the curse that Harry used on Draco in the next book, earning the wrath of the Prince himself.

Handy little bit of foreshadowing there. (This above section is also available on DeepRiver.press as a handout.)

Personal Note: This section on Snape has been a part of my workshop since I first developed it in 2006 and was part of the first edition of my writer's guide published in 2011. Imagine my delight, then, to see this November 2015 Tweet from Rowling:

Take Away: How to Create Your Very Own Snape

How does all this analysis apply to helping your students craft their own characters?

There are several ways. First, as educators, we should encourage our students to think deeply and broadly about their characters. Utilize the vast resources of themes and archetypes to flesh them out fully. Explore all questions and possibilities; determine to give their reader more. Ask them:

- How many twists can you provide your reader?
- How much backstory can you withhold until absolutely necessary?
- How many secrets and mysteries can you weave into the text?

To challenge them even more, use the following **Creating Your Own Snape: Student Handout** and **Mini Activity** to encourage them to create their own antihero or ambiguous character for their own story.

Creating Your Own Snape: Student Handout

As writers, we can challenge ourselves to make sure the real world in all its texture and complexity is reflected within our story. The creation of an ambiguous character helps in this goal. Once you have constructed your hero and antagonist and defined the themes that differentiate them, ask yourself:

- Have you created a character to embody the vast space of grayness that lies between?
- Have you got a Snape, ambiguous in nature, who could be viewed as friend and foe by both sides? A character, who like most of us is not totally good or evil but somewhere in between, who challenges the subtle nuances of your theme.
- Can you craft this character with a hint of mystery, to keep both your hero and your reader guessing, as they did with Snape, until the very end?

First, though, you must understand the theme you're working with. I was going to say **define** your theme, and for some of you that may work. You may be able to pick and choose between the themes you feel compelled to write. But for many of us, the wand chooses the wizard, the themes choose us, and it may even take some time for you to recognize the theme which has gripped you.

But grapple with it, question and understand your theme. Contemplate how far right and how far left you can explore the full range of your theme's meaning. How nasty will your villain be? Will he be someone completely unredeemable, or a person who will eventually accept change and redemption? Will your heroine start out strong and honorable, or only through growth and transformation drift closer to that side? Can you have a character in-between who helps your reader see the world and its diverse people through a wider lens? A character who helps the reader see herself?

The mystery of Snape lies in his ability to bring readers into the heart of the central questions of the series…where they are forced to explore more fully the power of your theme.

Because ultimately that's what Snape does, and that's why readers find him so enthralling. He makes us look at the idea of loyalty and courage in all its vast, multifaceted, diverse representations. He forces us to widen our lens, not narrow it, to question consistently through an open mind. By questioning, we involve ourselves, we deepen our self-awareness as to who we are, Slytherin or Gryffindor, Death Eater or Dumbledore's man through and through. Ultimately the way we see Snape directly reflects the way we see the world.

If you define an ambiguous character in your work, you pull your reader in deeper. To successfully draw out this character will require a lot of planning, fleshing out, and endless revision. Here are some tasks you need to consider:

1. Define your central theme and explore its wide range of meaning.
2. Define how one character can embody alternate sides of your theme.
3. Fully plot this character to show this diversity.
4. Decide on which side that character will ultimately live.
5. Then go back and plot how to weigh the character in the direction you want him to go, but without the reader guessing.
6. Make sure you keep your hero guessing and misunderstanding Mr. Ambiguity as well.
7. How does your hero's understanding of this character grow and change? How does this reflect your theme?
8. Last, but not least, never ever let your reader guess until the nitty gritty end.

You are probably working with different themes in your work than Rowling did in hers, but you too can cast a character who invokes reader involvement to this extreme if you will draw him ambiguously, torn between two worlds, embodying both, but committed to neither (at least on the surface) forcing the reader to analyze their own deep-seated positions and beliefs.

And don't forget the gray undies!

Creating Your Snape: Mini Activity

Use the workspace below to flesh out your character who most embodies the antihero or character of ambiguity:

Define your central theme and explore its wide range of meaning.
Which one of your characters can represent alternate sides of your theme?
Develop some characteristics and plot some actions to show the ambiguity of this character.
On which side of your theme will this character ultimately live?
What clues can you give to show the true nature of this character without tipping off your reader?
How does your hero's understanding of this character grow and change? How does this reflect your theme?
How does this character affect your protagonist's growth?

Lesson Eight

Of Grindelwald and Hitler
(Real World Relevance)

Many young writers care passionately about the world they live in and are seeking through their writing to make a difference. Many of them may also be going through some traumatizing personal experiences of their own. Writing is, and has always been, an excellent form of therapy. Helping your students tell their stories more effectively can be a very empowering experience, and not only for themselves. As the Hero's Journey shows, an ancient, intrinsic part of storytelling is to bring a healing elixir to our community.

Harry Potter not only changed how young people read, it also changed their lives. From fights with best friends to the trauma of dating, Harry's young readers found their every-day lives mirrored within his. But beyond their own personal issues, they found their Muggle world's larger concerns meaningfully portrayed by Rowling's magical characters. You have to initially read between the lines to find allusions to Hitler and Nazism, ethnic cleansing, and AIDS, but as the series matures, references to oppression, governmental fanaticism, and the media's towing of the line worked their way to the surface.

The best known examples of social commentary within *HP* are the allusions to Nazism and World War II. Here's just a hint from the first book:

> Considered by many the greatest wizard of modern times, Dumbledore is particularly famous for **his defeat of the dark wizard Grindelwald in 1945**, for the discovery of the twelve uses of dragon's blood, and his work on alchemy with his partner, Nicolas Flamel.

(p. 102-103, Sorcerer's Stone)

Many readers take Grindelwald for Hitler, the Death Eaters as an example of the Secret Service, and Mudblood hatred and killing as an allusion for racial cleansing. After all, just like the young Grindelwald and Dumbledore, Hitler and his forces ardently strove for "the greater good" of the true German race. The *HP* novels could thus be interpreted as a warning to not let intolerance lead us into another World War II scenario.

Another example Rowling uses is a bit more personal. Lupin, a tormented man with an illness which drives him out of a society that both fears and misunderstands him, seems a perfect example, for the time in which Rowling was writing, of the maligned AIDS patient.

And then there's Dolores Umbridge, who with her increasing totalitarian control of the students and administration, all under the righteous guise of doing what's best for their welfare in a world at war, seems a deliberate criticism of some educational systems, or political heads, during the years Rowling was writing. Likewise, the servitude of the house-elves could represent the invisible oppressed of almost any country on earth.

My purpose here is not to analyze or debate Rowling's social references in and of themselves, but to discuss how your students can work their own personal experiences and real-world relevance into their stories even if they're writing science fiction that occurs on a planet two-hundred light years away. *If they so choose.*

What subjects your students wish to portray in their stories and how they portray them will depend entirely on their voice (and thus their own personal concerns and lived experience), their genre, and their particular story. As their mentor, you can guide them through these choices so that they weave meaningful references into their story while engaging their reader and empowering themselves.

Overview:

In working in real-world references, have your students consider:
1) Their lived experience
2) Their genre, and
3) Their particular story.

Lived Experience

Within your classroom, you probably have students from diverse backgrounds, belief systems, economic situations, and experience. The power of Story is the power to explore any point of view the writer chooses, to get deeply into the head of another…or of ourselves.

Guide your students through some initial questions as they are choosing they type of story they will create:
1) Whose POV do you choose to represent in your story? Yourself, or someone else?
2) If yourself—What aspects of your life do you wish to examine deeper? Who do you think will benefit from your sharing it?
3) If someone else—What type of character do you find most fascinating? Especially consider the main conflict they would face and how this reflects on the world that you know. How can you push yourself through this character to learn more about a real-life situation that intrigues you?
4) Not every story your students write needs to be a deeply personal exploration, but, as writers, we always bring something of our lives into everything we write. Help your students channel this from the outset, as they are setting up their characters, plot, and conflict.

Their Genre

What experiences your students wish to explore may shape the choice of their genre. Some genres will be more open to obvious references than others. This is not totally determined by length, though in general, you will have more space to work with such references in a longer story. However, science fiction and fantasy, while quite often longer in word count, and while definitely open to real world relevance, will frequently need those references disguised in futuristic or fantasy-type garb. How Rowling worked her WWII references is a perfect example. She never mentions the words WWII, Nazism, Hitler, or ethnic cleansing, but they're all there wearing wizard robes and Mudblood clues.

The same is true for historical stories. Any contemporary commentary would need to wear an historical mask. Instead of discussing steroid use in sports, your student's Aztec Tlachtli player could get hyped up on cacao before the game.

Help your students consider and choose the genre of their story by the nature of the themes and experiences they wish to explore within.

Their Particular Story

The nature of your assignment may dictate the types of real-world relevance that your students may be able to choose from. On the other hand, writers approach stories from a variety of angles. For some, an intriguing character will draw them in, and they will wrap the story around her. For others, it's all about the plot, and their characters are shaped to meet its needs. And others may be gripped by a concept they wish to explore deeper.

With any of these approaches, the student can still choose to weave in personal or societal experiences if it will enhance the story they already have in mind. Not every experience they wish to share will fit within a particular story.

Assure your students they will write more. Perhaps if their experience of losing a loved one doesn't fit within this currently assigned lighthearted story, they should save it for the next assignment. Because, in the end, while stories may reflect real life, they cannot reflect *all* of it. Focus and insight are key to creating a story of deeper meaning.

Take Away

Whether subtly woven in or a direct reference, any personal or real-life issue your students choose to weave into their stories truly needs to fit the theme and style of that story, without preaching, otherwise it will stick out like Seamus' singed eyebrows. But encourage your students to reflect on this crucial aspect of writing with each story they craft. Because, for many, there is no more powerful tool to understand one's own inner personal or outer world than the power of crafting a story exploring both.

Real World Integration: Activity

DURATION:
One (1) hour class period (or there about). Later continuation during free-write time.

SYNOPSIS:
In this activity students will choose a real-world event with vast impact on their personal life or society with which their readers can identify. They will write a scene where the characters are exposed to a similar event that parallels with the real-world influence. Students should have the choice of selecting a personal experience that has shaped or molded their view of the world or a global event that resonates with readers directly.

CONTEXT:
Students should have completed activities to help them with plot development and feel comfortable developing characters.

STANDARDS:
A pillar of education hinges on reflection—this activity is well-rooted in external and possible internal reflection. Depending on the event students decide to use in their scene development, they will reflect in one of two ways. If they choose a global event from current topics or in history, they will explore how the even shaped the world and thus affected them personally—whether positively or negatively. If they choose a sincere account from their personal lives, they will reflect internally—*how have these events shaped my way of thinking?* Either option draws inspiration from reflection. Take it a step farther and have them reflect on their writing at the conclusion of this activity.

BEGIN WITH AN EVENT:
After choosing your real-world event consider what makes it significant to the reader. Think of ways to craft your scene to make it provocative and impacting. Consider the characters involved, who will be impacted the most from this experience? How can you cater your scene to show it's long-lasting effect on these characters?

SCENE DEVELOPMENT:
With the larger picture in mind, begin writing. Make use of good characterization, world-building, and plot development—don't short-change the reader just because you are practicing a new technique. Be sure to relate your story to the event you chose. If it's a world-event, make strong connections that, while maybe not blatantly obvious, can be identified with a short analysis.

Teachers: this may take some time; thus the recommendation is to assign the scene as homework.

ONCE THE SCENE HAS COOLED:
After the scenes are written, perhaps the next class period after it has been assigned for homework, have students investigate each other's work. Have students trade scenes. As they read, students should consider what event the text references or create questions of inquiry that help uncover the personal inspiration of the author—What questions should I ask the author to confirm an experience I suspect inspired this chapter?

REFLECT AND REPEAT:
Student should periodically reflect on their writing. Reflection serves two main goals—to help improve clarity for the sake of the reader, but also to recognize the great improvements students have made over the process of revision and deployment of practical writing techniques. Review. Reflect. Revise. Repeat.

Lesson Nine

Tossing Snowballs at Quirrell
(Writing with Humor)

Perhaps one of JK Rowling's craft secrets that endeared her to fans the most was her use of humor. From Peeves to Fred and George to Dumbledore, most of Rowling's characters knew how to toss a good one out there at just the right time. As humor is so hard to write, my guess would be that it's one of the most direct reflections of the author herself. So I imagine Rowling is quite the snarky lady.

Considering, however, that successfully conveying humor *is* so hard, plus personally subjective, how can you help your student incorporate it into their own writing? I've searched forums and memes and lists for some of Rowling's best loved funnies and have compiled them here to figure out exactly how she used humor in a way that appealed to her reader. Perhaps these examples will inspire your students to tickle their own literary funny bone.

Overview:

Here are the top eleven tricks for when, where, and how Rowling used humor successfully:
1. To introduce a character
2. To build character
3. When departing from character or showing a changing situation
4. To hint at romance
5. Short-term clues
6. Long-term foresight
7. To show the ridiculous
8. To lighten a serious situation
9. What goes around comes around
10. Style: Witty repartee
11. Style: One liners.

To Introduce a Character

"Fred you next," the plump woman said.

"I'm not Fred, I'm George," said the boy. "Honestly, woman, you call yourself our mother! Can't you *tell* I'm George?"

"Sorry, George, dear."

"Only joking, I am Fred," said the boy, and off he went.

(p. 92, *Stone*)

Right off the bat, the reader not only knew that Fred was a comic but that Mrs. Weasley was a harried mother. We also got the sense of a lighthearted, loving family who didn't take themselves too seriously.

To Build Character

Often, Rowling will use humor to show a different side to an already established character, such as she does in this example with Professor McGonagall:

"You look in excellent health to me, Potter, so you will excuse me if I don't let you off homework today. *I assure you that if you die, you need not hand it in.*"

(p. 109, *Azkaban*)

She also uses humor to contrast two characters:

"Well, you'd better hurry up, mate, or all the good ones will be gone," said Fred.

"Who're you going with, then?" said Ron.

"Angelina," said Fred promptly, without a trace of embarrassment.

"What?" said Ron, taken aback. "You've already asked her?"

"Good point," said Fred. He turned his head and called across the common room, "Oi, Angelina!"

Angelina, who had been chatting to Alicia Spinnet near the fire, looked over at him.

"What?" she called back.

"Want to come to the ball with me?"

(p. 394, *Goblet*)

We've had three books to get to know Fred, but here we are introduced to a slightly new aspect of him...a very cocky, self-assured male, so sure that the girl he wishes to take to the dance will go with him that he hasn't even asked. Fred serves as a foil to Ron, who can't bring himself to ask anyone.

When Departing from Character

A week after Fred and George's departure, Harry witnessed Professor McGonagall walking right past Peeves, who was determinedly loosening a crystal chandelier, and could have sworn he heard her tell the poltergeist out of the corner of her mouth, *"It unscrews the other way.*"

(p. 678, *Phoenix*)

While we've seen McGonagall make jokes upon occasion, as in the example earlier, we've never seen her advocate destruction of school property. Her assistance to Peeves would never have occurred in an earlier book. However, now the situation is dire, and McGonagall is facing a woman who is evil and undermining all Hogwarts stands for.

To Hint at Romance

But Ron was staring at Hermione as though suddenly seeing her in a whole new light.

"Hermione, Neville's right—*you are a girl*..."

"Oh well spotted," she said acidly.

(p. 400, *Fire*)

Although Hermione does not reply jokingly, she's rather angry, the situation is funny with Ron seeming to only now realize that his friend of four years is female. *Ahh*...already in *Goblet* the hormones are heating up, and readers are getting a hint at which ships will finally set sail in *Deathly Hallows*.

Short-Term Clues

As discussed in the Revealing Wormtail chapter, one of Rowling's simplest techniques for hiding a clue is to place it in a line of dialogue that appears nonsensical or a joke, which focuses the reader on the humor rather than the clue, and to make whatever that character says seem unimportant.

George and Fred are always good for a joke...and thus are prime candidates for hiding a few crucial clues. Through the twins' clowning, Rowling hit the reader with a clue to pay attention to Quirrell's turban...especially the back of it:

One morning in mid-December, Hogwarts woke to find itself covered in several feet of snow. The lake froze solid and the Weasley twins were punished for *bewitching several snowballs so that they followed Quirrell around, bouncing off the back of his turban.*

(p. 194, *Stone*)

She uses the twins again in *Secrets* to point the finger at the hidden villain:

"Oh, get out of the way, Percy," said Fred. "Harry's in a hurry."

"Yeah, he's off to the Chamber of Secrets for a cup of tea with his ***fanged servant***," said George, chortling.

Ginny didn't find it amusing either.

"Oh, don't," she wailed every time Fred asked Harry loudly who he was planning to attack next, or when George pretended to ward Harry off with a large clove of garlic when they met.

(p. 210, *Secrets*)

Fred and George jokingly toss the reader not one, but two clues. Not only does Rowling hint at the Basilisk through them, she also shows Ginny with a stronger than normal emotional reaction—clearly because of her guilty conscience! Finally, notice the juxtaposition of Ginny to the fanged servant—another favored clue technique we discussed earlier.

"Don't be prat, Neville, that's illegal," said George. "They wouldn't use the Cruciatus Curse on the champions. I thought it sounded a bit like Percy singing...***maybe you have to attack him while he's in the shower,*** Harry."

(p. 366, *Goblet*)

Here, too, Rowling inserts a very real clue in one of George's jokes. After all, Harry needs water to hear the merpeople sing. So, for future reference, whenever Rowling tosses out a joke, look for a hidden clue!

Long-Term Foresight

Rowling is even good at using the twins' comic antics to hint at important things to come a whole book (or four) in advance:

"Yeah, Montague tried to do us during break," said George.

"What do you mean, 'tried'?" said Ron quickly.

"He never managed to get all the words out," said Fred, "due to the fact that we forced him headfirst into that ***Vanishing Cabinet on the first floor.***"

Hermione looked very shocked.

"But you'll get into terrible trouble!"

"Not until Montague reappears, and ***that could take weeks, I dunno where we sent him,***" said Fred coolly.

(p. 627, *Phoenix*)

LOL! Those crazy twins!

But...wait...You mean there's a Vanishing Cabinet inside Hogwarts? And the twins don't know where it leads? And...didn't Harry hide in a mysterious large, black cabinet in Borgin and Burkes way back *in Chamber of Secrets*? (In case you didn't catch it—those Vanishing Cabinets are the means by which Draco lets the Death Eaters into Hogwarts in *Half-Blood Prince*).

Yes, here, through jokes, Rowling teases her reader to pay attention to these cabinets. They just might be important in a story to come!

"Right, you've got a ***crooked sort of cross***..." [Harry] consulted *Unfogging the Future.* "That means you're going to have '***trials and suffering***'—sorry about that—but there's a thing that could be ***a sun...hang on...that means 'great happiness'***...so you're going to suffer but be very happy..."

"You need your Inner Eye tested, if you ask me"...

(p. 105, *Azkaban*)

Ron and Harry are once again wasting time in Divination, but are their jokes totally wasted? Think for a moment...where did we hear about a cross during a scene of great suffering followed by a sun bringing great happiness? The ending of the whole series, the final chapters of *Deathly Hallows*. It is at King's Cross that Harry's self-sacrifice is fully realized, where Voldemort's soul is judged lacking. This is followed by the rising of the sun in the Great Hall at his greatest triumph, when peace is restored to the wizarding world. Perhaps as early as book 3, Rowling had envisioned the series' ending and planted a clue here…as a joke.

Note, a couple of paragraphs later in this scene above, Ron predicts Harry going to work for the Ministry of Magic (he later becomes an Auror) and a windfall of gold (that he got for winning the Triwizard Tournament).

Perhaps Ron should have gotten higher than a *poor* in Divination.

"Ah, think of the possibilities," said Ron dreamily. "It would've been so easy to push Malfoy off a glacier and make it look like an accident… ***Shame his mother likes him…***"

(p. 167, *Goblet*)

Ron shows great insight and premonition again as Mrs. Malfoy's love for her son figures prominently into those final scenes of *Deathly Hallows*.

To Show the Ridiculous

The twins are quite skilled at highlighting the ridiculous in everything, from Percy's rather pompous greeting of Harry:

"Harry!" said Fred, elbowing Percy out of the way and bowing deeply. "Simply *splendid* to see you, old boy—"

"Marvelous," said George, pushing Fred aside and seizing Harry's hand in turn. "Absolutely spiffing."

Percy scowled.

"That's enough, now," said Mrs. Weasley.

"Mum!" said Fred as though he'd only just spotted her and seizing her hand too. "How really corking to see you—"

(p. 62, *Azkaban*)

To more serious situations where Harry is being ostracized:

Fred and George, however, found all this very funny. They went out of their way to march ahead of Harry down the corridors, shouting, "Make way for the Heir of Slytherin, seriously evil wizard coming through…"

(p. 210, *Secrets*)

Fred and George are the perfect anarchists. They can always find the ridiculous in a situation and make you question the status quo. Rowling very effectively uses jokes to convey serious messages with the twins.

Let us not forget their subversive jingle to combat He Who Should Not Be Named, the most fearsome dark wizard of all time:

Why Are You Worrying about You-Know-Who?

You SHOULD Be Worrying About

U-NO-POO—

the Constipation Sensation That's Gripping the Nation!

(p. 113, *Half-Blood*, Bloomsbury)

Mrs. Weasley may have feared for her sons' lives, but they were the living embodiment of the Riddikulus spell.

To Lighten a Serious Mood

For Rowling, there seems to be no inappropriate time for a joke. She uses them quite effectively to cut through high tension scenes:

…when he straightened up again, there were six Harry Potters gasping and panting in front of him.

Fred and George turned to each other and said together, 'Wow—we're identical!'

(p. 48-49, *Hallows*, Bloomsbury)

All of the Harry Potter impersonators and their escorts are about to risk their lives. As we know, Mad-Eye will die. Even in these dark times, Rowling brings out the humor.

Somewhere in the distance they could hear Peeves zooming through the corridors singing a victory song of his own composition:

We did it, we bashed them, wee Potter's the One,
And Voldy's gone moldy, so now let's have fun!

"Really gives a feeling for the scope and tragedy of the thing, doesn't it?" said Ron...

(p. 597-598, *Hallows*, Bloomsbury)

Voldemort may be dead, but the Weasleys and the reader are still hurting from Fred's death and many others (Lupin, Tonks, *sob*). Yet Rowling does not hold back in fear of throwing a little humor in, even at this somber moment. Of course, she uses an insensitive Poltergeist to do so. This technique helps return the reader to equilibrium as the book draws to a close.

What Goes Around Comes Around

Rowling, like many writers, loves to return to certain aspects of her story and show how the situation has changed...often through the use of humor:

"So light a fire!" Harry choked.

"Yes—of course—but there's no wood!" Hermione cried, wringing her hands.

"HAVE YOU GONE MAD!" Ron bellowed. "***ARE YOU A WITCH OR NOT?***"

(p. 278, *Stone*)

'How—how're we going to get in?' panted Ron. 'I can—see the place—if only we just had—Crookshanks again—'

'Crookshanks?' wheezed Hermione, bent double, clutching her chest. '***Are you a wizard, or what?***'

(p. 523, *Hallows*, Bloomsbury)

From the first book to the last, a joke is revisited and the reader is able to reflect on the change of situation, characterization, and relationships that have occurred.

'How do you feel Georgie?' whispered Mrs Weasley.

George's fingers groped for the side of his head.

'Saint-like,' he murmured.

'What's wrong with him?' croaked Fred, looking terrified. 'Is his mind affected?'

'Saint-like,' repeated George, opening his eyes and looking up at his brother. 'You see...I'm holy. *Holey*, Fred, geddit?'

Mrs Weasley sobbed harder than ever. Colour flooded Fred's pale face.

'Pathetic,' he told George. 'Pathetic! With the whole world of ear-related humor before you, you go for *holey*?'

'Ah well,' said George, grinning at his tear-soaked mother. '***You'll be able to tell us apart now, anyway, Mum.***'

(p. 67, *Hallows*, Bloomsbury)

Remember the original boarding of the Hogwarts Express in *Stone*? Fred pretended to be George? We've circled back around to the beginning with a very different outcome.

Style: Witty Repartee

I love how Rowling uses the short, punchy, back and forth style of Lupin and Harry talking at cross purposes to great, and funny, effect:

"Excellent." said Lupin, looking up as Tonks and Harry entered. "We've got about a minute, I think. We should get out into the garden so we're ready. Harry, I've left a letter telling your aunt and uncle not to worry——"

"They won't," said Harry.

"That you're safe—"

"That'll just depress them."

"—and you'll see them next summer."

"Do I have to?"

(p. 54, *Phoenix*)

Style: One Liners

To finish off, here a few one-liners that left us chuckling:

"Do you think we've got nothing better to do in Potions than listen to Snape?"

(Ron, p. 159, *Secrets*)

"Lockhart'll sign anything if it stands still long enough."

(Ron, p. 174, *Secrets*)

"We tried to shut him in a pyramid, but Mum spotted us."

(George speaking of Percy, p. 63, *Azkaban*)

"His life's ambition is to have his head cut off and stuck up on a plaque like his mother," said Ron. "Is that normal, Hermione?"

(speaking of Kreacher, p. 76, *Phoenix*)

"No, I was merely reading the Muggle magazines," said Dumbledore. "I do love knitting patterns..."

(Emerging from Slughorn's bathroom, p. 73, *Half-Blood*)

"There's no need to call me 'sir,' Professor."

(Harry to Snape, p. 180, *Half-Blood*)

(This chapter is also available at DeepRiver.press on Writer's Resource page for use as a handout.)

Take Away

Kids love to write something that will make their friends laugh. However, there are so many ways humor can be incorporated into a story; it's as specific as it is personal.

Humor is best when it flows organically from the characters and situations already established. Therefore, the best advice for your students is to have them put themselves into the mindset of listening to their characters and letting them have a bit of fun. Even a serious story doesn't *always* have to be so serious.

Or, as Joss Whedon, another great storyteller, says:

"Make it dark, make it grim, make it tough, but then, for the love of *God*, tell a *joke*."

Writing with Humor: Activity

DURATION:

Approximately one (1) hour.

One (1) lecture period of about 15 minutes followed with practice in writing of approximately 30 minutes. This skill once learned will be used conjointly with other activities and as your students develop their own written works. Once they finish the initial writing practice, they will spend 15 minutes sharing with their classmates.

SYNOPSIS:

This activity is a hybrid between **think-pair-share** and **peer review**, through which they are introduced to the world of humor. Using examples from J.K. Rowling, students will create their own humorous situations and share with their classmates through the process of peer revision.

COMMON-SENSE APPROACHES TO TEACHING:

Interdisciplinary Creativity

Collaboration and Reflection

STANDARDS:

Collaboration is an essential part of teaching students to **be respectful of others**' ideas and learning the power of group progress. The humor activity also prompts students to **communicate effectively** by prompting them with the right questions to ask and providing the structure to give their **constructive feedback** to their peers.

BEFORE YOU BEGIN:

Students should read again their written works from either the Fan Fiction activity or a short story they have been writing in class. While reading, have students jot down the characters that appear in the story from most vocal to the ones who appear the least. Answer the following questions with regards to each character:

1. Do you use humorous dialogue or description in the scenes you have read?
2. Do you view any of your characters to be funny?
3. What is the mood of the selected chapter?

DISCUSSION AND LECTURE:

Lecture is never a fun word to use, but after the students are finished answering the three (3) questions, we want them to consider some examples from Rowling's work. Read for them select examples that you prefer, but be sure to include the example explaining the grim calm after the battle at Hogwarts after the death of Fred, Lupin, and Tonks. The death of endeared characters is never taken lightly by readers. Many would say it in not a time to be funny, but they'd be wrong. Or at least grim sentiments do not hinder the use of humor. Share these examples with your students, have them read some out loud and discuss the role humor plays in Harry Potter.

WRITING WITH HUMOR IN PRACTICE:

Now let us pepper in some humor. Have students work individually with their writing for 30 minutes.

Adding Humor to Your Story: Student Handout

After discussing the examples of where Rowling used humor in Harry Potter, think about your own story and brainstorm similar situations where you could use a similar technique. Plot out a few lines that you find amusing.

Rowling uses humor to:	Where in your story could use it:
To introduce a character	
To build character	
When departing from character or showing a changing situation	
To hint at romance	
Short-term clues	
Long-term foresight	
To show the ridiculous	
To lighten a serious situation	
What goes around comes around	
Style: Witty repartee	
Style: One liners	

Adding Humor to Your Story: Student Handout (continued)

Now that you have a few examples, choose your favorite and develop a short scene using that humor techniques. Make it good!

Did your message come across? Ask your peers! Trade stories and see if their humor was presented, well, humorously.

Have your partner answer the following questions about your scene:

1. Is the humor at the expense of a character in the story?

2. Is the humor transmitted through action, dialogue, or narration?

3. Do the jokes imply a need for culturally related knowledge?

    a. What do you have to know beforehand to understand it?

4. Did the humor come across clearly at first reading?

5. Which technique was used? (to introduce a character, to build character, to hint at romance, etc)

With all this considered, how can the humor be improved to achieve either (1) a clearly developed message to set the mood, (2) rapport between characters or reader and character, and/or (3) an aide to developing plot.

Use your classmates' critique to improve your use of humor and continue using these techniques throughout your writing as you move forward with other activities.

Lesson Ten

Catch Your Snitch!
(Writing with Pleasure)

Writing should be fun. If your students don't enjoy the story they're creating, how will their reader enjoy reading it?

By fun, I don't mean a limited understanding as laughter or lighthearted amusement. I mean a broader definition which involves total absorption into a world and characters that takes control of your mind until you realize it's two a.m., you have a busy day tomorrow, and you just couldn't stop writing until the very end. Wouldn't we all love to get this experience from grading our students' papers?

Above all, the readers of Harry Potter have fun. They get fully immersed in Rowling's magical world and don't want to leave. They enjoy the fantasy, the spells, the characters, and even the dark side, the emotional catharsis they experience from the triumph at the climax.

In writing the series, I think Rowling fully enjoyed herself as well. I imagine her chuckling as she hid another clue and then wickedly plotted its distraction, getting so immersed in her research that she didn't realize it was almost dawn, and thoroughly overcome with tears when she'd killed off Sirius and then Dumbledore.

In other words, I imagine her, just like her reader, fully engaged. Fully engaged, whether through curiosity, laughter, tears, or any other emotion (excepting hating the book) is what you want to encourage from your students as both reader and writer. Fully engaged is what I mean by fun.

Overview:

To explore how to ensure your student is having fun with their writing while considering their reader, we'll look at how to:

1. Meet reader emotional expectations.
2. Write like an Olympian.
3. Write what gives you fulfillment.

Meet Reader Emotional Expectations

Jennifer Enderlin, Executive V.P. and Publisher at St. Martin's, calls "fully engaged" the "really, really" factor. For a novel to work for her, to spark her interest to buy, it needs to meet the "really, really" criteria. If it's a thriller, then it needs to be really, really scary. If it's a comedy, then it needs to be really, really funny. Or, if it's a romance, then it needs to be really, really emotional. Because the Harry Potter series is so long and complex, it's able to strike all these chords.

For each writing assignment, encourage your students to consider both their own and their reader's emotional expectations. Again, this comes down to genre. Even though a reader may read across the board, they expect a different mood from a different read. While a reader may enjoy mysteries, science fiction, literary fiction, as well as romances, they pick what to read at a particular time based on the mood they're in and the emotions they wish to experience. Encourage your students to consider the mood they seek to strike and then strike it hard.

Write Like an Olympian

Make it fun also means make it look effortless. A good analogy for this is ice-skating. When you watch Olympic ice-skating, at least if you're like me, you thrill to the pleasurable merging of the artist and athlete into a seamless dance of emotion and beauty. Then someone falls. I want to turn away.

I hate seeing anyone hurt, dreams dashed—the soul-wrenching pain fractures the effortless illusion. I'm no longer watching a pleasurable fantasy, but am forced to listen to and acknowledge all the hours, days, months, years of sweat, blood, and tears that go into training these world-class athletes. The trials of the stiff competition, the time spent away from home and family, the fact that loss happens much more often than gold. All of which, while a valuable lesson to learn and understand in life, from a pleasure standpoint, is just not as much fun.

Our writing students will often rush through their assignments, eager to finish or, if committed to their story, to get to the end. In both cases, they are often oblivious to any errors in their writing. Perhaps this skating analogy above can teach them one of the most valuable lessons in writing: ***Try not to fall in front of your reader***. Readers don't want a shift in tone, a misused word or image, a piece of poor research to throw them out of the story. At that point, their illusion is broken. Their sense of living inside your student's world comes to a screeching halt, at least for a few minutes. If it happens often enough, or badly enough, the story will be set down not to be picked back up.

What your student is striving for as a writer is to make their story appear as effortless and beautiful as the gold medal Olympian skater, without the pain of any falls, without the interruption of having to analyze the work that they put into creating that illusion. Teach them to glide across the page like a graceful dance. Whether they like it or not, that takes endless hours of not-so-fun revision!

Within the Potter series, Rowling had a couple of technical falls. Because of her stature, she was able to fix one of them for future reprints (the famous wand-order effect in the graveyard scene of *Goblet* where James came out of the wand before Lily when the reverse should have happened). There have been other small glitches as well that fans have caught (and the Mark Evans[8] one caused quite a hoopla). Even with falls, she quickly picked herself up and skated magically to the end, with a passionate, loyal following.

Readers can be very forgiving, as long as the writer has captured their attention. Help your students understand that they don't have to do everything perfectly, but they must do many things very, very well. Revise, revise, revise. Make their work appear effortless so the reader will have the thrill of immersing themselves in a fully envisaged, engaging experience.

Write What Gives You Fulfillment

One other aspect of fun lives totally inside the writer. We've talked about this a bit before in the voice lesson, but it should be emphasized here. As much as possible with your writing assignments, encourage your students to write what gives them pleasure and meaning.

Notice I don't say "write what they enjoy reading" because I don't believe that to be completely true. I've heard this said many times before, but I disagree. Or at least I disagree in part. Writing takes a lot more time than reading. It's a much more intensive investment. While I may enjoy spending a few hours of my life reading a novel of physical comedy and witty banter, I may not have it within myself to think in a humorous manner day in and day out for months. Or the reverse may be true, I might enjoy a tormented tragedy upon occasion, but do I want to go to that darkness of emotion on a daily basis?

What I want to read for a few hours can reflect various moods, changing emotions, shifting situations in my day. What I choose to write for weeks or months reflects more deeply the meaning I give to my life, that inner person I am, my voice.

So I say, encourage your students to write to their voice. Write to who they are as a person. Encouraging your students to probe and meet their inner selves through the medium of writing may be one of the greatest gifts you leave with them.

Take Away

In the end, writing is about passion. Your students' passion. Their character's passion. Their story's passion. And finally, their reader's, even if, especially if, that reader is only you. Encourage them to pour their passion on the page each and every time they create. Don't revise it out. Revise it higher. Thus, they allow their reader to catch fire with their passion, to become fully engaged in their work.

To have fun!

---

[8] She named a boy whom Dudley beat up Mark Evans and had everyone speculating on his relationship to Lily. He wasn't. (http://harrypotter.wikia.com/wiki/Mark_Evans)

Lesson Eleven

Draco Loves Hermione! At Least in Fan Fiction
(Fan Fiction as a Tool for Creative Writing)

With the growing demands of local, state, and national standards, we teachers are often restricted in the amount of time we allow for our students to develop their creative writing. When done properly, character development and worldbuilding could take an entire semester before students feel comfortable moving forward with plot development. Lessons on designing these complex stories are ideal for specialty electives, but how can we honor a packed curriculum of a core English class while giving students adequate time to develop the interdisciplinary skills of creative writing? A perfect source of inspiration where most of the development has already been provided is fan fiction.

Fan fiction is fiction written by fans for fans, most often without commercial intent. It is an original story crafted from characters and worldbuilding of an established story not the author's own, usually unlicensed. Fanfic covers most genres, age groups, and mediums (book, TV, movies, cartoons, comics, Anime/Manga), but is generally more popular in the science fiction/fantasy realm (though definitely not limited there). Indeed, the modern version of fan fiction got its start with *Star Trek* the TV show, grew in popularity with *Star Wars* and the *Star Trek* movies, and then had an explosion with the onset of the Internet. Today, you'll find active fandoms online not only with Harry Potter, but with such diversity as:

- novels—the Hunger Games series and *Lord of the Rings*
- cartoons—*South Park* and anything anime
- TV—*Game of Thrones* and *Doctor Who*
- movies—*Star Wars* and anything from Marvel Comics

One theory of literary criticism sees fanfic as the modern day myth or folk story. If you've ever studied ancient myth from various cultures, you'll see (generally speaking) that most myths exist in more than one form. Depending on region and time period, the details, settings, characters, and plot of a given myth can vary quite dramatically, and yet still be recognizable as the same story. Who made these alterations? Ancient fanfic writers!

We all want our favorite stories to reflect our personal reality. With most modern-day epic myths being owned, copyrighted, and licensed by major motion picture studios, corporate publishing houses, or big-league authors, modern myth revisionists must rely on fan fiction in its Internet form to put their own imprint on the stories that have claimed meaning for their lives and their cultures.

Not only do fanfic authors put their own personalities into their favorite stories, they also give them a decidedly creative spin. In Harry Potter fan fiction, Harry can go back in time and be trained by Merlin; a married Ron and Hermione can raise Voldemort and Bellatrix's baby[9]; and Draco can have a romantic relationship with Hermione. Anything is possible, and considering the number of stories written, everything is likely to occur. Many writers have learned their craft through writing fanfic. It is a popular medium with a built-in network of feedback and support.

What this means for you as a teacher is that fanfic offers your students both loads of possibilities and dangers you

---

[9] Note: this was written in the first edition of this book, pre *Cursed Child.*

145

and their parents will want to avoid. Sexual fanfic is extremely popular. So, while you may very well want to guide your most enthusiastic writing students to partake of this opportunity, you should also help guide them carefully.

Overview:

We'll discuss the following issues that you'll want to familiarize yourself with concerning fanfic:

1. Encouraging your enthusiastic young writers through fanfic.
2. How to avoid the online dangers.
3. Get your students in contact with authors.

Writing Fan Fiction

For the beginning writer, crafting their own fanfic is a proven method for learning the craft, experimenting with various formats and creative possibilities, and even garnering a few fans. There are so many resources online that will give unbiased feedback that a student can learn quickly what works and what doesn't. By working with established characters (plus those they introduce), they will be free to devote their attention to learning writing techniques and strengthening their plotting skills, as well as experimenting with how creative they can become within an already defined universe.

Because fanfic writers of contemporary fandoms are generally not pursuing a homework assignment or publishing with their stories, it is also incredibly freeing. Students can follow their Muse wherever she leads without worrying whether it meets a particular rubric. It's also an excellent alternate route toward creating a student's own originated fiction.

I'm not suggesting that you encourage all your creative writing students to try fanfic if they have no such interest. The average student can learn quite well through the traditional route of crafting characters from scratch and submitting to critique groups and contests. I'm merely suggesting that if you have a student who identifies as a writer and is eager to create outside the classroom, then fanfic is an excellent route to learn the craft and get immediate, fabulous feedback from online sources. With the quick response time available to the fanfic writer, if they work hard at it, they can shorten their learning curve tremendously.

Here are a few sites that have very active boards:

http://www.fanfiction.net/ for hundreds of thousands of fanfic stories

http://archiveofourown.org/

http://harrypotterfanfiction.com/

If your students have any interest in fan fiction, try it out. Give it a wave. You may be pleasantly surprised by how freeing it is for them to work within an already defined world.

Avoiding Online Dangers

However, you must be aware that when you encourage your eager young writers to seek out and participate in online fanfic that they *will* come across sexual content. For teachers of upper-level high school, this may not be a concern. But if you're teaching middle grade or younger, you may want to tread carefully. Most authors self-regulate their stories for age-appropriate content by labeling them with a rating (PG, PG 13, R, etc.), by submitting to appropriate sites, and may even carry explicit warning about the content. But not all authors or fansites do.

Rowling gave her first ever fansite award to *Immeritus* (www.immeritus.org), a Sirius Black fansite which promotes and publishes fanfic, but is careful to moderate their submissions and classifies those of more adult content into a restricted section. Rowling favored sites which respected her desire to keep X-rated material apart from her younger fans. As her fansite award was highly coveted during the time she was giving it, the bigger websites online did whatever they could to meet her expectations.

I highly recommend that you scout out any of the fanfic sites you wish to use in your lessons or refer your young writers to. You may also want to involve the parents in this discussion in a manner you deem appropriate. With proper controls and awareness, online fanfic communities can be a rich resource for your developing and eager young writers.

Author Interaction

Never has it been easier for readers to be in contact with their favorite authors. In recent years, even Rowling has become more proactive in connecting with her readers, especially through Pottermore (discussed in the next section) and Twitter. She's become known for reaching out to fans struggling with difficulties, often sending personal letters of encouragement, other times donating items to auction for large causes. You may want to consider having a student or your class reach out to Rowling on social media. While the chances of getting Rowling to personally reply may seem smaller than winning the lottery, I believe it's a good thing to help students realize that most writers are completely human and within reach. It makes their own dreams of becoming an author seem more realistic.

Rowling, while not a recluse, is known for maintaining a certain amount of privacy. However, many other authors are even more open and proactive in supporting and meeting their fans. Many will reply to their fanfic writers, offering advice and encouragement, and some attend fan conferences or release parties.

Many authors are now available for school talks through Skype. Authors can talk with your class on techniques of writing or discuss their novel and how they wrote it. The possibilities are as full as the numbers of authors out there willing to speak virtually for free or cheaper than an in-house visit. If you've not tried this option yet, here are a few resource for hooking up your class:

- DeepRiver.press Writer's Resource page where I list options for Skype visits or on-site workshops
- http://skypeanauthor.wikifoundry.com/
- http://www.katemessner.com/authors-who-skype-with-classes-book-clubs-for-free/

Have your class come up with creative ways they could best learn from an author through a Skype visit. The more time they spend preparing for such a visit will benefit them when the author can share insight beyond the normal questions they get asked frequently and that are easily found anywhere.

Pottermore: Continuing the Engagement Post Potter

Rowling opened Pottermore, an online fan portal, in 2011 to serve as both an independent publisher for her electronic Potter series as well as to continue the connection with her rabid Potter fan base even as she moved on to writing the Cormoran Strike series. By continually supplying them with new insights and backstories not previously mentioned in the books along with enchanting interactive story art, Rowling kept her readers actively engaged in her completed series while enticing the always emerging new readers into her market.

Initially, the website consisted of a guided tour through all seven books, which included games to play, duels to fight, houses to be sorted into, and cups to win. In 2014, Rowling switched the site administration from Sony to Apple and changed its focus. The site now not only publishes and sales enhanced, illustrated and animated e-books, but is also a news hub for the ever-expanding wizarding world, including publishing the electronic editions of the script books for *Harry Potter and the Cursed Child* and *Fantastic Beasts and Where to Find Them.*

I would encourage you to explore Pottermore as another possible resource for your young writers. Through these online pages, Rowling has released backstories for her characters, worldbuilding tidbits that didn't make it into the series, and even more importantly, her thoughts on crafting the series. It's a gold mine for getting into the thought processes of a very successful storyteller. I'd highly recommend it to any writer wanting to learn from a bestselling mentor.

Take Away

In writing a book that so encouraged reader involvement to explore deeper layers, Rowling encouraged all the fan interaction, whether online or off, that has occurred in the nearly twenty years since the publication of *Philosopher's Stone.* Without that fan involvement, there would not have been the hype, the massive release parties, the hit movies. Or the theme parks…but let's not even go there. Fan involvement is what made the bestseller a phenomenon.

Many of your students may begin your class already as Harry Potter fans. Others may grow to appreciate this engaging story and exceptional storyteller through the course of your work together. All students though, may appreciate the opportunity to learn more about the author and the opportunity to engage with other writers. Through fan fiction, you can engage your students' interests and deploy these writing techniques without the lengthy exploration often required when starting from scratch. In many cases, students will choose to place themselves in a well-established world with diverse characters where they may utilize creative techniques to continue developing the author's world while allowing their own imagination free reign. (To engage your students through fan fiction try the activity below.)

While you may not have experienced fanfic as part of your own writing journey, I encourage you to explore this possibility for your students. But scout it out ahead of time and be sure of the sites you recommend, especially if your students are young. I warn you, though, many eager young writers who begin sharing fanfic works find it quite compelling and can't stop writing. Let's hope so!

Note—If you'd like to learn more about the fandom side of the Harry Potter phenomenon, I highly recommend from the webmistress of *The Leaky Cauldron*, Melissa Anelli's book, *Harry, A History.*

Fan Fiction: Activity

DURATION:

Four (4) independent writing periods of approximately 45 minutes each. Ideal for breaking up other activities and to keep students engaged.

SYNOPSIS:

In this activity, students will deploy the writing techniques of worldbuilding, characterization, and backstory while trying their hand at fan involvement through fan fiction.

CONTEXT:

Before beginning this activity, students should read the chapters on worldbuilding and characterization as well as the activities that accompany them. They should choose a series of books or other fictional franchise that they enjoy and know well—Star Wars, Harry Potter, Marvel Comics, etc.

COMMON-SENSE APPROACH TO TEACHING: Interdisciplinary Creativity, Collaboration & Reflection

STANDARDS:

Most state and national standards require students to produce clear and coherent writing with strong development, organization, and style. Their writing should be appropriate for the task at hand and should consider the purpose and audience. Students will plan, revise, edit, rewrite, and try new approaches as a way of focusing on a specific purpose and audience. Students will use the Internet to research, produce, publish, and update their writing products.

BEFORE YOU BEGIN:

Students will first decide on which fictitious world they will base their fan fiction around. Next, have students choose two (2) characters who typically don't interact in the selected series. For example, they could choose Molly Weasley and Luna Lovegood. Finally, they should choose a setting. Have students think about a place they often visit in real life—a restaurant, doctor's office, public park, etc. Once these three items are selected students are ready to begin.

DELIVERY & GROUP ELEMENT (OPTIONAL):

You should scaffold each section on the student handout in timed blocks. Give students just enough time to complete each section in the activity, but not enough to get off task. Have students discuss their work throughout the activity at the end of each timed block. Challenge them to ask their classmates for ways to improve a character's backstory or develop their plot with more depth. Once students have a product they are pleased with, ask for volunteers to share a section from their fan fiction. Use the following questions of orientation to help the participants discuss which skills were used effectively and which can be improved upon.

1. What elements of the student's work are most memorable? What stands out for you?
   - The use of powerful adjectives? A unique character profile? The plot of the scene?
2. Where does the story begin to become unclear or uninteresting?
3. What elements from question 1 can be used to improve the weaker areas of the student's work?

ADAPTION FOR A YOUNGER AUDIENCE

Demanding writing activities such as fan fiction can be difficult if they are not properly scaffolded. We recommend you begin with a comic strip activity. Minimalize the writing to include pertinent dialogue and let the pictures help develop the character and setting. Then have students write what they have drawn, describing to the best of their ability the images in their comic. In pairs they can trade description and attempt drawing what they read. If the original images match closely to the images the reader creates, then the description is effectively expressing the author's intention.

Fan Fiction: Student Handout

Today you are going to write a short scene based on a story you love. You will give your own spin to a preexisting world and characters. Welcome to the exiting world of fan fiction.

1. Choose a fandom world—something from a TV series, collection of books, or movies.
2. Select two (2) characters from this fandom who share no prior interaction—make sure they are interesting characters.
3. Choose a real place from your own life to inspire the setting—where will the two characters interact?

Consider the real-world setting you have selected. Do you recall a similar location within your fandom world? The Muggle world of Harry Potter has commercial banks whereas the wizarding world has Gringotts. If there is a similar real-world setting to a location you seek to create, you may base your descriptions off it, but be sure to give it a twist to fit your fandom world. Alternatively, if there is not a clear equivalent, try to combine similar settings to create a new one within that fandom.

Also, take ordinary objects that would typically appear in the real world and describe them using new words based on the fandom world you chose. Use the following chart to help fill your world.

Real-world Object	Story-world Counterpart	Adjectives and Description
Flashlight...	Wand—*lumos*...	with a flip of the switch—with a flick of her wand....

CHARACTERIZATION:

With a setting well underway, we turn our gaze to characterization. e will further develop our selected characters while considering their descriptions and interactions in canon. The goal is not to change the personalities of these existing characters, but rather to use what we know about their personalities to expose them to new situations and capture their responses given their character in canon. There is plenty of fan fiction that sets out to change the course of canon and offer a more preferable outcome to disagreeable events, but this requires more plot development and more time. This activity is intended to continue a story or create a new chapter that could happen independently and not change the plot of the original series.

DEVELOP A PLOT:

Choose an excursion that your two characters could participate in where they are exposed to an uncomfortable or challenging experience. Try choosing an experience in which each character would respond differently. It doesn't have to be a life-changing episode, but one where you can further develop the world and its characters.

SPRINKLE IN SOME BACKSTORY:

A great way to engage your audience in the lives of your characters is with backstory. While writing your fan fiction, consider a moment where you hint at the character's previous experiences. Backstory is a good way to justify a character's reaction to current events. Be careful, however, you don't want to lose all the mystery in your characters. Make sure you are only releasing small details—just enough to keep the reader curious.

PULLING THE PIECES TOGEHER:

After developing your fan fiction, consider posting it on a fanfic website for others to read and comment. The dialog that your interpretation inspires can lead to additional fanfic and ultimately more practice developing plot, settings, and characters.

POPULAR FANFIC SITES:

https://www.fanfiction.net/
http://archiveofourown.org/
http://harrypotterfanfiction.com/

Lesson Twelve

Fantastic Beasts and Where to Find Them
(Hatching Artistic and Marketing Vision)

Theater-goers in London can now experience what is being called the eighth Harry Potter story—*Harry Potter and the Cursed Child*—while readers from around the world can share virtually in that experience. In November, a new era of the wizarding world was brought to screen through the magic of *Fantastic Beasts and Where to Find Them*. JK Rowling's Pottermore, in association with its print partners, is bringing both of these script books to a wider audience.

As Rowling's artistic and marketing vision continues to expand, we are left to wonder—where does such powerful magic come from? Did she perhaps nip back into Dumbledore's tomb and steal the Elder Wand?

I've watched Rowling's career ascend for years. While I've always admired that one writer could combine so strong a sense of business as well as creativity, I admit to having also felt a sense of disconnect. I mean, seriously, just because JK Rowling can do what she does, doesn't mean the more mortal writers among us could do the same. She's got millions to spend, connections across continents, and leaders in industries dying to work with her. She's JK Rowling!

But the thing is, she wasn't when she started. You know the story. We all know the story. The rags to riches inspiration of a single mother on British welfare scribbling away at her story in a cafe while baby Jessica slept. How that book, which was initially turned down by twelve British publishers, went on to sell to a small house, and by way of word of mouth, playground to playground, finally made it big.

Rowling left many Easter eggs hidden within her novels. Throughout this book we've analyzed those she left for her readers. But I see other types hiding as well...eggs hinting at her success as a writer, waiting to be hatched by other writers, especially the young storytellers she has inspired so well. If you are mentoring young writers who wish to make any field of storytelling a career, these clues tell of the personal tools they will need if they are to unite artistic and marketing vision to make it in the highly competitive publishing or media world.

As this final chapter is meant to be personal encouragement directly to young writers based on the words of JK Rowling, it's my intention that you copy it and pass it out to them individually. As such, it is written directly to them. For more detailed information on the publishing process, you may want to encourage your students to check out more resources on my blog at HarryPotterforWriters.com or the Writer's Resource page on my publisher's site at DeepRiver.press.

Overview:

So, what would JK Rowling say to young writers who, like her younger self, don't have the best resources or connections and are yet determined to get their stories out to readers while staying true to their own artistic vision?

In my opinion, she's already given some of her best advice, nestled within the lines of her characters:

1) "Anything's possible if you've got enough nerve."
2) "…mend that broken vanishing cabinet…"
3) "You've got strengths if I say you've got them."
4) "If you are holding out for universal popularity…you will be in this cabin for a very long time."
5) "Maybe you don't have to do this all by yourself…"

Channel Your Inner Ginny

"The thing about growing up with Fred and George," said Ginny thoughtfully, "is that you sort of start thinking anything's possible if you've got enough nerve."

(p. 655, *Phoenix*)

I am not so naive as to believe that nerve is all you need to succeed at storytelling. Resources and connections *do* make a difference. Some writers will have a leg-up on their journey to publication and bestseller lists. Some will have many more obstructions set in their path. However, determination, developing your talent, and hard work matter even more.

With the difficulties you'll face, if you don't have nerve, you'll get left behind. Publishing is brutal, not because of the people in it. They're lovely. But because of the extremely stiff competition. The only way to succeed is to believe in yourself and keep going no matter how much disappointment you face. Or how many rejections you get.

Rowling faced a lot of rejection when she first started out. The difficulties she lived through while writing *Philosopher's Stone* have become part of her author legend. It definitely takes nerve to write a novel while caring for an infant as a single mother.

To be honest, though, the failure she would have faced then, when only family and friends knew her name, would be nothing compared to what she faces now. As she ventures into new territory by publishing two script books while transforming herself into both a playwright and script writer, surely she shares in Fred and George's nerves. Half the world is waiting for her to stumble so they can sneer and say how Harry Potter was just a one-off thing.

There is no harm in analyzing the risks and rewards of publishing and deciding that you are better suited to another profession. However, if you are certain that you *must* tell your stories and have them reach readers, then you must dig deep and find your Fred and George-inspired nerve. For navigating the many paths of publishing is like walking over a bed of coals, and nerve is what you must have to strengthen your soles. Nerve, and an ability to see beyond the Vanishing Cabinet.

Mend Your Vanishing Cabinet

What magical item from Hogwarts would you claim if you could get your hands on it?

While the Marauder's Map would surely come in handy for many writers, especially those trying to stalk the beta reader or agent currently reading their manuscript, the reality is we have Twitter and Snapchat for that.

No, the magical item within the series I feel is most appropriate for writers is one used by Death Eaters to breach the walls of Hogwarts. I'm talking of the Vanishing Cabinet. That set of magical boxes which Draco spent a year repairing to permit the Death Eaters entry into Hogwarts, and the path to killing Dumbledore.

"I had to mend that broken Vanishing Cabinet that no one's used for years."...

"Montague told me that when he was stuck in the Hogwarts one, he was trapped in limbo but sometimes he could hear what was going on at school, and sometimes what was going on in the shop, as if the cabinet was traveling between them, but he couldn't make anyone hear him..."

(p. 586-587, *Half-Blood*)

What fascinates me about the Vanishing Cabinets is both their location and their function. Hearing voices at both ends while stuck in limbo, traveling between two different worlds. Where no one can hear you scream. Feeling as if you can't communicate with either side and can't do anything about it.

That's just like many young writers starting out. Unable to get an agent, unable to sell a book or script, unable to do anything really. Yet, thanks to the claustrophobic nature of social media, we hear all that's going on around us from other writers passing us by, almost like a high school hallway. And when you're stuck, hearing the good news happening just beyond your cabinet kind of sucks. Even when you're truly happy for your friends.

So how do you get unstuck?

Montague did it by Apparating...into a toilet. Draco experimented for months, killing who knows how many birds in the process, before he was able to perform the proper spell and open the passageway.

Like Draco, we must learn not to be wishy washy. Make up your mind about what you're going to do and do it. It helps to have Death Eaters breathing down your neck.

Like Montague, sometimes we need to think outside the Vanishing Cabinet. Don't wait around for someone to save you. Take a strong action, even if it lands you in the toilet.

If you take the plunge and pursue writing as a career, you'll get a lot of advice along the way. Sometimes you'll be subjected to standard advice that is perfectly good for most writers most of the time. That does not mean it's good for you at this moment. Rowling was told very early in her career not to quit her day job. Ha!

Publishing is never easy. If you're going to succeed, you must be decisive. Make your own choices as to what's best for you. You'll make mistakes, that's for sure. But it's better to proceed firmly on what you think is the right path now than hesitate and get shoved into a Vanishing Cabinet.

Play to Your Strengths

"--play to your strengths."

"I haven't got any," said Harry, before he could stop himself.

"Excuse me," growled Moody, "you've got strengths if I say you've got them. Think now. What are you best at?"

(p. 344, *Goblet*)

There is a reason why Rowling went from writing fantasy to writing mysteries (with a detour via adult social satire). She kept playing to her strength. While the Harry Potter series may have been set in a fantasy world, it was very much a whodunit, as she has said herself[10]. She sharpened her teeth on the clues she trailed through each book and across the whole seven-book series. It was only natural that she'd play to her strengths in choosing her next series and go with a detective story.

And now she's back to the fantasy world that she created so vividly. With *Cursed Child* and *Fantastic Beasts* coming out in the same year, surely Rowling is flying high on her talent.

Sometimes as writers, we have to write a lot before we know what we write well. Finding our talent is a bit like finding our author voice…it comes through the practice. Often, we'll only know by seeing how our readers react.

How often have you heard an author say that the book they loved the most tanked with readers, while one they were embarrassed about soared? Sometimes, like Harry, we have a hard time recognizing what we're good it.

Perhaps you need a pseudo-Moody to give you an objective opinion. Take the time to talk with people who've read your work and will give you honest feedback. Your creative writing teacher is your best first beta reader. Get *them* to tell *you* where your strengths lie. Then evaluate your strategies and techniques to ensure you're playing to your strengths. While we always want to improve in our weak areas, it definitely pays, in these competitive times, to know how to call forth your broomstick.

Don't Hide Away, Waiting for Universal Popularity

"Really Hagrid, if you are holding out for universal popularity, I'm afraid you will be in this cabin for a very long time."

(p. 454, *Goblet*)

Rita Skeeter has written one of her acidic articles revealing the giant heritage of our favorite gameskeeper. Already owls have started pelting Dumbledore, calling for him to fire Hagrid. But will Dumbledore and Harry, Hermione, and Ron let Hagrid hide his face? No way.

Putting your story out into the world is a scary process. If you've spent time on Goodreads or read any other online reviews, you know that the reception may not be what you hoped for. No one achieves universal popularity. Not even Rowling.

Goblet of Fire was one of her toughest books to write. She had written about half of it when she realized she had a huge plothole and had to tear it apart and rewrite. Coupled with the writing difficulties, she faced her first lawsuit for copyright infringement plus increasing scrutiny in the media. I imagine this quote was born of her very real experience.

While most people associate Rowling with world-wide adoration, she's also received more than her fair share of attacks. She has faced lawsuits for plagiarism, attacks on the quality of her work, and, as her online voice has grown stronger, hostility from people whose position she opposes.

The bigger the target you are, the more numerous the trolls. Rowling keeps putting herself out there, because she

---

[10] https://www.pastemagazine.com/articles/2014/07/jk-rowlings-new-crime-series-to-run-longer-than-ha.html

believes in her stories and her views. As a writer, there is no chance you will face universal popularity. In reading feedback from beta readers or online reviewers, keep in mind that the more passionate they are the better. If people either love or hate your story, that's a good thing. You've aroused their emotions. What you don't want is indifference.

The business surrounding storytelling is subjective. As artists, we invest heavily in evaluations of our work while being exposed to constant and often opposing opinions from agents, editors, readers, and reviewers. But dealing with this is part of our job.

Trolls aren't just in the dungeon. In publishing, trolls live everywhere. You can't hide out in your cabin waiting for their army to pass. You must face them and keep on writing.

Form Your Own Dumbledore's Army

> "Maybe you don't have to do this all by yourself, mate."
> (Ron to Harry, *Order of the Phoenix* film)

This point may seem to contradict the *be decisive* message of the Vanishing Cabinets above. But being decisive does not mean ignoring good counsel or not partnering with strong people.

While writing may be a solitary sport, publishing is not. You've got to have a team.

One thing I've noticed in the number of writers that I have critiqued or edited over the years—there seems to be a direct correlation between the writers who ask for help to those who succeed. Going it alone in this industry is a potion for disaster.

Find the people who will support you, not tear you down. That doesn't mean seek out someone who will blindly love everything you do. Mothers are never a good source of an objective opinion. Pull together a team who will respect you and share their honest opinions in a way that is not destructive. While pursuing a career which many consider a waste of time, that is sometimes hard to find.

When in 2011 Rowling left her first agent, she received flack in the media, labeled as disloyal. An agent/editor relationship is one of business, not a marriage as it is so often compared to.

It was shortly before this break that Rowling began her new venture, establishing her team at Pottermore and self-publishing her electronic books. Soon after she branched out into the theater production that would eventually become *Cursed Child*. She's built a solid team of support and is obviously accomplishing great things with them.

Whether through local writer groups or online social media, today's writers have many resources at hand to learn their craft and connect with other writers. Professional writer associations such as Society of Children's Book Writers and Illustrators, Romance Writers of America, Science Fiction and Fantasy Writers of America, and Mystery Writers of America provide professional resources to their members and often host writing workshops. Your school may host a creative writing club. If not, why not start one yourself? You can also find writing friends online, from all parts of the world, to share your writers' journey. The fanfic resources mentioned earlier provide excellent support. Utilize these resources to connect with new people who may also become your critique partners or beta readers or good friends.

In this aspect of your own quest into the publishing world, don't imitate Harry. Do not try to go it alone. You may write in all the solitude you need to, but when it comes time to navigate the trials and tribulations of the writer's career, build up your Dumbledore's Army and always have a good base of support around you.

Take Away

JK Rowling found and freed her own fantastic beast when she successfully united her artistic vision with her marketing prowess. She used this power to build a vast publishing empire that spread her vision into every corner of the world. Today, she continues to challenge both her imagination and the businesses of publishing, filmmaking, and theater as she crosses into new formats and expands her wizarding world. Therefore, let us end on some lessons she taught us within her stories on how to free the fantastic beast hiding within us all:

- Get your nerve,
- Take decisive action,
- According to your strengths,
- Don't hide away when things get tough,
- Find your support team. And never go it completely alone.

Hermione's Bookbag

(S.P. Sipal's Publications)

Soon to be Released:
Fantastic Secrets Behind Fantastic Beasts and Where to Find Them

Previously Published:

- *A Writer's Guide to Harry Potter*, second edition—July 2016
- *Southern Fried Wiccan*—March 2015
- "Lighting the Sacred Way" in *Journeys of Wonder 2*—October 2012
- "Running Raw" in *Sweeter Than Tea*—June 2012
- *Egyptian Myths in Harry Potter*, an editorial in three parts; Mugglenet.com—July 2007
- "Grandma's Cupboards" in *On Grandma's Porch*—June 2007
- *One Last Memory*; a Featured Editorial on Mugglenet—Feb. 2007
- "From Online to Paperback: The Making of The Plot Thickens" and "Geomancy and Alchemy in Harry Potter" in *Proceedings of Accio UK 2005*—July 2006
- *Ultimate Unofficial Guide to the Mysteries of Harry Potter: Analysis of Book 5*; by Galadriel Waters; Wizarding World Press—June 2005. (editor and contributor.)
- "A Family Treasure" in *More Sweet Tea*—April 2005
- "Chamber of Thoth" and "Geomancy and Alchemy Gems in Harry Potter" in *The Plot Thickens…Harry Potter Investigated by Fans for Fans*; Wizarding World Press—November 2004

Check out Susan's blog at HarryPotterforWriters.blogspot.com and Twitter feed @HP4Writers for continued discussion of how to improve your writing with Harry Potter as your text.

The Professors
(About the Authors)

S.P. Sipal is a writer, editor, and international speaker who has presented the material in this guide since the Harry Potter phenomenon gripped the nation. Susan celebrated the release of the last Harry Potter book, *Deathly Hallows*, as a presenter at a fan conference in London. Her writing workshops, school and college lessons, and numerous fan conference presentations have been met with enthusiasm and repeat requests.

Susan lives in North Carolina with her husband and two children. You can find her on Twitter @HP4Writers, her website at SPSipal.com, and her blog at HarryPotterforWriters.blogspot.com.

Dalton Perkinson is a language acquisition teacher in North Carolina currently dedicated to developing globally inspired language curriculum with real-world approaches. His passions are rooted in a strong linguistic background that is focused on the analysis of English influence on the language production of immigrant Spanish-speaking natives. Through a linguistic study of Indo-European, Altaic, and Sino-Tibetan languages, and practical language accommodation techniques, Perkinson has constructed authentic language resources for independent learners and language academies.

To book Susan or Dalton for speaking engagements, interviews, and other Harry Potter or educational events, please contact publicity@DeepRiverPressInc.com.

Acknowledgements

We wish to thank the following people for their help and support:

- First, to all the writers and Harry Potter fans who've attended workshops throughout the past twelve years. All of you have helped shape this text.
- To Kayla Laine Perkinson for beautifully drawn and fan-inspired illustrations that liven up all these words.
- To Martina Boone for her constant support.
- To Greg Schultz for his exquisite cover.
- To Lisa London for her extreme patience.

Finally, none of this analysis would be possible without JK Rowling and her incredible imagination. She has inspired millions in so many ways, not the least of whom are the next generation of writers seeking their own golden storytelling snitch.

Thank you for reading. If you liked the material in this guide, please consider leaving a review at your favorite review site.

Appendix

Here are a few resources we hope may be helpful to you and your students.

DeepRiver.press

On our Writer's Resource page, we provide:

Electronic downloads of the charts in this guide.

Expandable, electronic file of all the handouts to use for live documents.

Information on workshops we provide, both via Skype and in-person.

Handouts of certain sections of the book as mentioned within.

Extra activities geared to younger students.

We will also be continuously updating with affordable handouts and activities for a variety of classroom needs.

Other books in the series:

A Writer's Guide to Harry Potter by S.P. Sipal

Fan Fiction Sites Online:

FanFiction.net (http://www.fanfiction.net/) -- for hundreds of thousands of fanfic stories

Archive of Your Own (http://archiveofourown.org/) – fanfic, fan art, fan videos, and podfic

Harry Potter Fan Fiction (http://harrypotterfanfiction.com/) – all Harry Potter fanfic

Resources for Young Writers:

NaNoWriMo's Young Writers Program (https://ywp.nanowrimo.org/) – The very popular National Novel Writing Month has started a site specifically geared to young writers. Consider encouraging your more avid students to participate in the November month-long writing challenge.

New Pages Young Authors Guide (http://www.newpages.com/writers-resources/young-authors-guide) – Resource to find literary magazines and contests for young writers.

TeenInk (http://www.teenink.com/) – Magazine, books, and website all written by teens.

Wattpad – While this site is not limited to teens, it is a very popular site for sharing stories and receiving feedback.

YALSA – Young Adult Library Services Association (http://www.ala.org/yalsa/) – Great resource for discovering library resources for teen readers and writers. Sponsors several literary awards.

Professional Associations of Writers:

These organizations may be a good resource for your students seriously interested in pursuing writing as a career. As a teacher, they may also be able to connect you with local writing chapters and authors.

Society of Children's Book Writers and Illustrators (http://www.scbwi.org/)

Romance Writers of America (https://www.rwa.org/)

Science Fiction and Fantasy Writers of America (https://www.sfwa.org/)

Mystery Writers of America (http://mysterywriters.org/)

Recommended Books:

The Hero with a Thousand Faces by Joseph Campbell

The Writers Journey by Christopher Vogler

Writing the Breakout Novel by Donald Maass

Goal, Motivation and Conflict by Debra Dixon

Save the Cat by Blake Snyder

The Complete Writer's Guide to Heroes and Heroines by Tami Cowden and Caro LaFever

The Emotion Thesaurus: A Writer's Guide to Character Expression by Angela Ackerman and Becca Puglisi

Harry, A History by Melissa Anelli

Other Educational Publications from Deep River Press

A Complete Teacher's Manual for Darker The Night by Sabrina Beasley—World War II fiction from the perspective of German Civilians; for use as comparison/contrast with Holocaust stories.

Index